Beginning Scala

Second Edition

Vishal Layka
David Pollak

Apress®

Beginning Scala, Second Edition

ISBN-13 (pbk): 978-1-4842-0233-3

ISBN-13 (electronic): 978-1-4842-0232-6

Managing Director: Welmoed Spahr
Lead Editor: Steve Anglin
Development Editor: Rosemarie Graham
Technical Reviewer: Rohan Walia
Editorial Board: Steve Anglin, Louise Corrigan, Jonathan Gennick, Robert Hutchinson, Michelle Lowman, James Markham, Susan McDermott, Matthew Moodie, Jeffrey Pepper, Douglas Pundick, Ben Renow-Clarke, Gwenan Spearing, Steve Weiss
Coordinating Editor: Mark Powers
Copy Editor: Linda Seifert
Compositor: SPi Global
Indexer: SPi Global
Artist: SPi Global
Cover Designer: Anna Ishchenko

Distributed to the book trade worldwide by Springer Science+Business Media New York, 233 Spring Street, 6th Floor, New York, NY 10013. Phone 1-800-SPRINGER, fax (201) 348-4505, e-mail orders-ny@springer-sbm.com, or visit www.springeronline.com. Apress Media, LLC is a California LLC and the sole member (owner) is Springer Science + Business Media Finance Inc (SSBM Finance Inc). SSBM Finance Inc is a Delaware corporation.

For information on translations, please e-mail rights@apress.com, or visit www.apress.com.

Apress and friends of ED books may be purchased in bulk for academic, corporate, or promotional use. eBook versions and licenses are also available for most titles. For more information, reference our Special Bulk Sales–eBook Licensing web page at www.apress.com/bulk-sales.

Any source code or other supplementary material referenced by the author in this text is available to readers at www.apress.com/9781484202333. For detailed information about how to locate your book's source code, go to www.apress.com/source-code/.

Contents at a Glance

Contents

About the Authors

 **Vishal Layka** is the chief technology officer of Star Protocol and has over a decade experience in JVM languages. Vishal is actively involved in machine learning, inferential statistics, and pattern recognition using R, Python, Mahout, and Spark. When he needs a break from technology, Vishal reads eclectically from calculus to star formation.

David Pollak has been writing commercial software since 1977. He wrote the award-winning Mesa spreadsheet, which in 1992 was the first real-time spreadsheet. Wall Street companies traded billions of dollars a day through Mesa. In 1996, David sold his company to CMP Media and became CTO of CMP Media's NetGuide Live and was one of the first large-scale users of Java and WebLogic to power an Internet site. In 1998, David released Integer, the world's first browser-accessible, multiuser spreadsheet. Since 2000, David has been consulting for companies that include Hewlett-Packard, Pretzel Logic/WebGain, BankServ, Twitter, and SAP. David has been using Scala since 2006 and is the lead developer of the Lift Web framework. David blogs Scala at `http://scala-blogs.org` and rants about things on his personal blog at `http://blog.lostlake.org`. But David can most often be found on the Lift user group, `http://groups.google.com/group/liftweb/`.

About the Technical Reviewer

Rohan Walia is a Senior Software Consultant with extensive experience in client-server, web-based, and enterprise application development. He is an Oracle Certified ADF Implementation Specialist and a Sun Certified Java Programmer. Rohan is responsible for designing and developing end-to-end applications consisting of various cutting-edge frameworks and utilities. His areas of expertise are Oracle ADF, Oracle WebCenter, Fusion, Spring, Hibernate, and Java/J2EE. When not working, Rohan loves to play tennis, hike, and travel. Rohan would like to thank his wife, Deepika Walia, for using all her experience and expertise to review this book.

Introduction

Ouch! That hurts my brain! Stop making me think differently. Oh, wait . . . it hurts less now. I get it. This different way of solving the problem has some benefits. I felt that way after my first year of law school. I felt that way for a while when I began coding Scala. What's this Option thingy? Give me back my null! How do you get the fifth element from a Seq? On and on it went. Day after day of head-splitting paradigm changing and breaking 30 years of coding habits, I am somewhat at peace with the Scala way of coding. Yes, my coding habits were borne out of 6800 machine code coding. Talk about imperative coding. That's all you've got when you've got an accumulator, a program counter, and an index register. I grew up through BASIC, Pascal, C, C++, Objective-C, and Java. And along comes this Scala stuff, this functional-objective way of thinking, these compositional design patterns. Who thought up this wacky stuff?

After more than two years of coding Scala, I've come to understand that the Scala idioms are really better. My brain has finally stopped hurting. I've finally stopped fighting for flow of control statements. I see that it's more important for me to take small elements and compose them together into complex systems. I understand that if a method always returns the same output given the same input, I can safely glue that function together with other functions into a very complex structure. I understand that explicit looping in my code is a distraction from the business logic that is buried in the code. My path was hard, and I hope yours will be easier.

The first step in writing Scala is not being afraid of the fact that Scala's going to warp your brain. The next step in writing Scala is accepting that your code is going to look like Java, Ruby, Python, whatever code for a while. It will take you time and effort and more time to code Scala using the idioms in this book. It will take you time to design code that fits into Scala paradigms and to discover and devise paradigms of your own. It will take time but hopefully less time than it took me.

This book is for you. It's my attempt to show you a different way of thinking about and writing code. I hope that you'll enjoy our journey through Scala together. I hope that by the end of this book you'll have a new perspective on coding. I hope that you'll be writing better code and fewer lines of code yet are happier about the code that you're writing. So, come along. Stick that little toe in the Scala waters and see if they feel as good for you as they have for me.

Who This Book Is For

This book is for folks with some programming background who want to dip their little toe into Scala, check the temperature, and perhaps wade in some more.

How This Book Is Structured

Chapters 1 through 3 are meant to give you a basic grounding in Scala syntax and Scala idioms. Chapters 4 through 7 tour key Scala features, including functions, pattern matching, Scala Collections and traits. Chapter 8 is a deep dive into Scala's type system. Chapter 9 discusses Scala and Java interoperability. Chapter 10 rolls the pieces together with an exploration of DSLs and Scala's parser combinator library. Chapter 11 discusses the standard build tool SBT. Chapter 12 shows how to develop web applications using Scala web framework. Chapter 13 discusses some best practices for Scala.

Prerequisites

You should have the Java JDK 1.6 or higher installed on your machine as well as Scala 2.10 or higher.

Downloading the Code

The source code for this book is available to readers under the **Source Code/Downloads** tab of this book's home page, which is located at www.apress.com/9781484202333.

CHAPTER 1

Getting Started with Scala

Scala is a contraction of the words "scalable" and "language." The scalability of a language is different from the scalability of a program or application. The scalability of a program is defined in terms of its performance, while the scalability of a language has a broad ranging definition, in that the high scalability of Scala is a consequence of the fusion of object-oriented and functional programming. Scala's functional programming constructs let you compose complex functions from simple functions. Scala's object-oriented constructs let you structure highly adaptable objects through innovations in object-oriented constructs of Java. While Java has undoubtedly ushered in a wave of new era in software development, this initial chapter discusses why Scala supplants Java as a worthy successor and gets you started on a wonderful journey of great distances.

Why Scala?

Scala is a language that addresses the major needs of many Java developers. It is a statically typed, mixed-paradigm, JVM language with a terse and flexible syntax, a superior type system bestowing the developer with the ability to be more efficient with less code and minimum ceremony. Now let's explore some idioms that make Scala such a promising and a state-of-art language.

A Concise Language

Scala is a programming language designed to make your program, well, concise. Let's take a quick look at how your code can be concise using Scala. Listing 1-1 shows a simple Java class that you would write to encapsulate a book object.

Listing 1-1. A Book Class in Java

```
class Book{
private String title;
private int numberOfPages;

public Book(String title, int numberOfPages) {
this.title = title;
this.numberOfPages = numberOfPages;
}
}
```

There is nothing special about Listing 1-1. It is a simple Book class that encapsulates the title of the book and number of pages in what amounts to eight lines, not to mention loads of parentheses, braces, and semicolons floating around. Now compare Listing 1-1 with Listing 1-2, which is the same Book class written using Scala.

1

Listing 1-2. A Book Class in Scala

```scala
class Book(title: String, numberOfPages: Int)
```

You don't have to be a Scala expert to appreciate how succinct and terse Listing 1-2 is compared to Listing 1-1, although if you have a keen eye, you would immediately notice in Listing 1-2, omitted extraneous semicolons, to say the least.

Lightweight Syntax

Scala does not include the useless, even troublesome, features of Java such as static members, primitive types, `break` and `continue` statements, enums, or wildcards just to name a few. Scala has a lightweight syntax that is a result of two design decisions:

- Not taking a "one size fits all" philosophy but aiming at allowing the users to structure their programs to suit their needs

- Including features such as type inference and extensible APIs

We will explain type inference in the subsequent sections; meanwhile here is an example of `Case` classes, so you can appreciate the lightweight syntax of Scala. `Case` classes are the Scala equivalent of Java POJOs and will be explained in Chapter 3. The essence of `Case` classes is that they don't have all the boilerplate code that goes with Java POJOs such as `getter` and `setter` methods, `equals` and `hashCode` methods, `toString` method to name a few. There are several other handy methods that are also generated from `Case` classes. These and several other features will be explained in this book in detail; meanwhile, just to get a feel of light-weightiness of Scala syntax, breeze through the code that we present in this section starting with Listing 1-3.

Listing 1-3. Lightweight Book POJOin Scala

```scala
case class Book(var title: String, var numberOfPages: Int)
```

Even though we have not shown you how to install Scala and execute Scala programs, we'll compile Listing 1-3 for you so that we can show you its equivalent in Java. We've put the code in Listing 1-3 in a file named `Book.scala`.

Then we compile the file using this command:

```
>scalac Book.scala
```

This creates two class files, `Book.class` and `Book$.class`.
We then disassemble `Book.class` with this command:

```
> javap Book
```

Listing 1-4 illustrates the Java equivalent for Listing 1-3 generated by `javap` command. This is how your Java Book class would have looked if you had written code for all the features power-packed in a single line of Scala code in Listing 1-3.

Listing 1-4. Java Equivalent of Book POJO in Listing 1-3

```java
public class Book implements scala.Product,scala.Serializable {
  public static scala.Option<scala.Tuple2<java.lang.String, java.lang.Object>>unapply(Book);
  public static Book apply(java.lang.String, int);
  public static scala.Function1<scala.Tuple2<java.lang.String, java.lang.Object>, Book> tupled();
  public static scala.Function1<java.lang.String, scala.Function1<java.lang.Object,
Book>>curried();
  public java.lang.String title();
  public void title_$eq(java.lang.String);
  public int numberOfPages();
  public void numberOfPages_$eq(int);
  public Book copy(java.lang.String, int);
  public java.lang.String copy$default$1();
  public int copy$default$2();
  public java.lang.String productPrefix();
  public int productArity();
  public java.lang.Object productElement(int);
  public scala.collection.Iterator<java.lang.Object> productIterator();
  public boolean canEqual(java.lang.Object);
  public int hashCode();
  public java.lang.String toString();
  public boolean equals(java.lang.Object);
  public Book(java.lang.String, int);
}
```

Consider Listing 1-4 and then count how many lines of code the Java equivalent Book class has.

Multiparadigm Language

Scala is a programming language that provides a best-of-two-worlds experience for developers. Dynamic-language users will find Scala's concise syntax and type inferencing a way to reduce the boilerplate needed when writing programs in Java. Functional programmers will find Scala's powerful type system a great way to reason about code. Scala also has many functional programming facilities, including features found in pure functional languages such as Haskell.[1]

Object-Oriented Language

Scala is a pure object-oriented language that does not include primitive types and in that sense everything is an object. Thus, an operation between two objects is viewed as an invocation of a method on the first operand to send a message to the second operand. Because numbers are objects in Scala, they also have methods. And in fact, an arithmetic expression such as the following:

```
1 + 2 * 3 / x
```

is equivalent to the following expression:

```
(1).+(((2).*(3)).∕(x))
```

---

[1]http://www.haskell.org/haskellwiki/Haskell

Scala supports not only pure object-oriented programming, unlike Java, but Scala also improves upon Java's support for OOP with the addition of traits. Scala traits are akin to Java interfaces with an important difference. The Java interface defines a set of methods that must be implemented on all classes that implement the interface. Scala traits can do everything that Java interfaces can do, but they can also include method implementations. This comes in very handy because you don't have to create complex class hierarchies to avoid duplicating code. Other than traits, Scala does not support static members like Java does, because static members are not associated with an actual instance. Instead a Scala class can provide a singleton object. A singleton object is declared using the object keyword, as shown in Listing 1-5.

Listing 1-5. Singleton Object in Scala

```
object HelloWorld {
    def greet() {
        println("Hello World!")
    }
}
```

Listing 1-5 defines a singleton object called HelloWorld. You can call the method greet in the following manner:

```
HelloWorld.greet()
```

This is like calling a static method in Java, except you are calling the method on a singleton object instead. We look at singleton objects in greater detail in Chapter 3.

Functional Language

Scala is a functional language, which means that you can pass functions to methods and functions, and return them from methods and functions, as well as assign them to variables. A function is a block of code that takes parameters and returns a value. As we mentioned earlier, everything is an object in Scala, so functions too must be objects. We will illustrate this through an example. Listing 1-6 defines a function that returns square of a number.

Listing 1-6. A Simple square Function

```
(i: Int) => { i * i }
```

With a little bit of imagination or if you have a mathematical bent it is not very difficult to understand Listing 1-6. It defines a function that takes an Int parameter and returns a value that is square of the provided Int.

Now we will show you functions are objects, in this case we intend to show that the square function defined in Listing 1-6 is an object in Scala. You can assign the function to a variable as shown in Listing 1-7 as you would assign any object to a variable and you can pass the function as an argument to a method, just as you would pass any other object as an argument to a method.

Listing 1-7. Assigning the Function to a Variable

```
val square = (i: Int) => { i * i }
```

The variable square in Listing 1-7 is an instance of a function. You can now invoke square just as you would call a method as shown in Listing 1-8.

Listing 1-8. Invoking the square Function

```
square(3)
```

We've just scratched the surface of functional programming. Functional programming is one of the aspects that makes Scala difficult to learn or atleast it makes it appear difficult. We will explain functional programming in detail in Chapter 4.

Interoperability and Seamless Integration with Java

Scala can be used in tandem with Java programs. Scala can call any Java code, subclass any Java class, and implement any Java interface. Java code can call into Scala code if the Scala code subclasses a Java class or implements a Java interface. Scala code, under the hood, reuses Java libraries and Java types. Scala allows you to add value to existing Java code because Scala was designed for seamless interoperability with Java and because ultimately Scala programs compile to JVM bytecode.

There are features of Scala, however, that cannot be accessed from Java, including traits with defined methods, classes and methods that have names, which are illegal in Java, and Scala's advanced types. We will show how to access these from Java in Chapter 10.

Language for the Java Virtual Machine

The JVM is the runtime environment that provides you with the ability to use different programming languages. With the latest version, Java 8, Java is no longer a *privileged* JVM language and is now simply one of the many languages that run on the JVM (for a long time it's been common to run other languages on the JVM, it's just that Java is now no longer privileged). The JVM languages can be largely classified into two types:

- Languages designed for the JVM, such as Clojure, Groovy, Java, and Scala.
- Existing languages ported to theJVM, such as JRuby, Jython, and Rhino.

Scala source code is intended to be compiled to Java bytecode, so that the resulting executable code runs on a Java virtual machine. Java libraries may be used directly in Scala code and vice versa.

We introduced a few idioms that make Scala so powerful. However, there are many other features that we did not mention. We will discuss them in detail throughout this book. Next we will start writing some Scala. To that end, you need to install Scala first.

Installing Scala

As a JVM language, Scala requires the use of a Java runtime. Scala 2.11, the latest version as of writing this book, needs at least Java 6, but we recommend installing at least Java 7 for improved performance. You can download the latest JDK from Oracle, which is available for most platforms. Once installed, verify you have at least Java 6 by running `java -version` from the command line as shown:

```
>java -version
```

```
java version "1.8.0-ea"
Java(TM) SE Runtime Environment (build 1.8.0-ea-b73)
Java HotSpot(TM) Client VM (build 25.0-b14, mixed mode)
```

Once Java is installed, download the Scala 2.11 distribution from http://www.scala-lang.org/download/. Installing Scala is relatively simple and should only take a few minutes. On UNIX systems (including Mac OS X), download the software from the Scala download page to a directory on your computer such as $HOME/scala, and then add these lines to your $HOME/.bash_profile file:

```
export SCALA_HOME=/Users/Al/scala
PATH=$PATH:/Users/Al/scala/bin
```

Once you've done this you should have access to the scala and scalac commands at your command line. You can follow a similar process if you're using Microsoft Windows, or you can use an MSI installer from the download page at the link provided earlier. Once installed run the scala command from the command line as shown:

```
>scala
```

```
Welcome to Scala version 2.11.1 (Java HotSpot(TM) Client VM, Java 1.8.0-ea).
Type in expressions to have them evaluated.
Type :help for more information.
```

```
scala>
```

When you see the Welcome to Scala version 2.11.1 message and the scala> prompt you are in the Scala interpreter, also called REPL(read-eval-print loop), and you are ready to start coding. In the section that follows, you will learn what REPL is and how to use it.

Scala at the Command Line and Scala Scripts

Scala offers different ways to run programs:

- Interactively at a REPL command line.

- Single-file Scala scripts.

- Compile your Scala programs into class files that can be combined into JAR files, as in Java.

We will now look at each of these ways to run programs.

Interactive Scala

You'll find the Scala REPL familiar if you have already used other REPL shells such as those in Python, Ruby, or Groovy. The REPL is an excellent tool to learn the Scala language quickly. Let's get started using the REPL by implementing the ubiquitous "Hello World" application. To start Scala's REPL, open a command prompt and type scala. You should see the following:

```
>scala
```

Using the interactive interpreter you can run your first Hello World by using the println method:

```
scala> println("Hello World!");
```

You can enter single lines of code and multiline code on REPL to evaluate and compile. First we will look at how to use single lines of code on REPL, later we will see how to enter multiline code on REPL.

You can start typing as shown here and see how the single-line code is evaluated in Scala:

```
scala> 1 + 1
```

```
res0: Int = 2
```

The output is a result variable res0 and the type of the value Int. As you can see, Scala interpreter infers the value type as Int for you. Any variables you created are available for the lifetime of your session, that is, you can use res0 from the previous output like so:

```
scala> res0 * 8
```

```
res1: Int = 16
```

Now you can go on to use res1 and so on.

You saw that Scala interpreter infers the value type for you. Let's now create a String variable:

```
scala> val x = "Hello World"
```

```
x: String = Hello World
```

As you can see Scala interpreter infers the String type for you. Now test the interpreter a little bit. We will use the result variable from the previous output, x, which is a String type such that it returns an Int:

```
scala> var xl = x.length
```

```
xl: Int = 11
```

As you can see Scala interpreter returns an Int value.

Now we will access Java library:

```
scala> import java.util._
```

```
import java.util._
```

Now that we have java.util library in session we can use it, like so:

```
scala> val d = new Date
```

```
d: java.util.Date = Sat Jun 14 21:12:00 CEST 2014
```

A help system is available and can be started by entering the :help command. You can see there are several commands available. For example, until now we have been entering single-line code on REPL. A multiline paste mode supports entering multiple lines of code to be compiled together, and external source code and libraries can be loaded at any time.

Enter the :paste command on REPL. You see this output:

```
scala> :paste
```

```
// Entering paste mode (ctrl-D to finish)
```

Now enter multiline code as shown:

```
scala> :paste
```

```
// Entering paste mode (ctrl-D to finish)
```

```
val v = 5
if (v==5)
print("true ")
else
print("false ")
```

```
// Exiting paste mode, now interpreting.
true v: Int = 5
```

```
scala>
```

To quit the interpreter, type :quit or :q

```
scala> :quit
```

Scala Scripts

Another way to execute Scala code is to type it into a text file and save it with an extension .scala. You can then execute that code by typing filename.scala. Open up your favorite text editor: Emacs, vi, TextMate, whatever. Create a new file called HelloWorld.scala and place the following line in it:

```
println("Hello World!")
```

Save the file. In Scala, it's short, simple, and to the point.

Open a terminal window or command prompt, change to the directory where the file is, and type:

```
scala HelloWorld.scala
```

You should see:

```
Hello World!
```

In Scala, you can write simple programs that look and feel like scripts that you would write in Ruby or Python. In this case, you're calling the println method with the string constant Hello World! It's a thin layer on top of System.out.println(). This is like the java.lang package that is automatically imported in every Java program.

Scala scripts do not have an explicit main method. In fact, when you run your script, Scala wraps the entire file into the main method of a class, compiles the code, and calls the generated main method. All you have to do is put valid Scala code in a file.

You can access the command-line arguments in your script with the argv variable, which is an Array[String].

Compiling Scala Programs

You have already seen how to compile Scala programs using the scalac command line tool. You can compile Scala programs just as you compile Java programs, and the results are JVM class files that can be packaged into JAR files. The Scala compiler requires that source files contain one or more class, trait, or object definitions. To compile Scala source files into class files, type the following:

```
> scalac File1.scala File2.scala
```

However, startup time for the compiler is non-trivial. You can also compile using the fast Scala compiler, fsc available as REPL command. You can see this when you type :help on REPL:

```
> fsc File1.scala File2.scala
```

fsc is a separate compiler process that continues to run, waiting for new compilation jobs, even after the compilation process is finished. This results in much faster compilation times, but if you're on a machine with limited RAM, you might not want to keep the compilation process alive.

■ **Note**   fsc is very useful for smaller projects. For larger projects, there are some better options, two of which follow.

If you are working on medium-sized to large projects, you probably use some sort of build tool such as Ant or Maven. There are Scala plug-ins for both Ant[2] and Maven,[3] so you can integrate Scala code into existing Java projects with very little effort and no requirement of using new build tools. Finally, similar to Maven or Ant, SBT[4] is an open source build tool for Scala and Java projects, which provides native support for compiling Scala code and integrating with many Scala test frameworks and dependency management, continuous compilation, testing, and deployment.

■ **Note**   Java requires you to put a public class in a file named after the class. For example, you should put class HelloWorld in file HelloWorld.java. In Scala, however, you can name .scala files anything you want, no matter what Scala classes or code you put in them. However, it is recommended to name files after the classes they contain as is done in Java, so as to easily locate classes from file names.

---

[2]http://ant.apache.org/
[3]http://maven.apache.org/
[4]http://www.scala-sbt.org/

Your First Scala Programs

In this section, we're going to write a couple of basic Scala programs. These programs will give you a sense of Scala's flavor and get you acquainted with running Scala programs.

Hello World

Yep, it's the ubiquitous "Hello World" program again. But this time you will execute the Hello world program in the context of an application. As you know, you can execute Scala code by first compiling it using the scalac command line tool. Then the code will need to be executed in the context of an application so you will need to add an object with a main method (see Listing 1-9).

Listing 1-9. HelloWorld

```
object HelloWorld {
def main(args: Array[String]) {
println("Hello,World!")
}
}
```

░ **Note**   A semicolon at the end of a statement is usually optional.

You learned earlier that Scala does not support static members like Java does, because static members are not associated with an actual instance. We showed you that instead of static members, Scala provides an object construct with which you can declare a singleton object. You will learn more about singleton objects in Chapter 3.

In Listing 1-9, the main method is defined in an object, not in a class. Scala program processing starts from the main method, which is a mandatory part of every Scala program. The main method is not marked as static. The main method is an instance method on a singleton object that is automatically instantiated. There is no return type. Actually there is Unit, which is similar to void, but it is inferred by the compiler.

You can explicitly specify the return type by putting a colon and the type after the parameters:

```
def main(args: Array[String]) : Unit = {
                }
```

Scala uses the def keyword to tell the compiler that this is a method. There is no access level modifier in Scala. You have public modifier in Java in this context. Scala does not specify the public modifier because the default access level is public.

Printing Some Numbers

Let's write a program that will print the numbers from 1 to 10 in the Print1.scala file:

```
for {i <- 1 to10}
println(i)
```

You can run the code by typing scala Print1.scala in the terminal. The program assigns the numbers 1 to 10 to the variable and then executes println(i), which prints the numbers 1 to 10. for means much more in Scala than in Java. You can nest expressions in a for comprehension (the fancy Scala name for the for statement). In the Print2.scala file, put

```
for {i <- 1 to10
j <- 1 to10}
println(i* j)
```

In this program, we are iterating over 1 to 10 in an outer loop and assigning each number to i. In the inner loop, we are also iterating from 1 to 10 and assigning each number to j. The product of i * j is printed, so you'll see 10 lines output. There are many more uses of the for comprehension that we'll cover later in the book.

Summary

In this chapter, you got a glimpse of what Scala is, and why it should be learned. You looked at how to build and run Scala programs. You saw how Scala interpreter (REPL) provides a learning environment. We walked through some Scala programs that demonstrated various aspects of Scala. In the next chapter, we'll dive deeper in the basics of Scala.

CHAPTER 2

■ ■ ■

Basics of Scala

Scala is a multi-paradigm language. This chapter introduces functional programming concepts in tandem with nonfunctional programming concepts. This chapter is aimed at making you comfortable with the building blocks of the Scala language. Before embarking on an in-depth journey of Scala, this chapter introduces the basic concepts of Scala that should give you enough understanding to enable you to write useful programs. To that end, we had to leave out some details. We do cover the detailed explanation in the subsequent chapters.

In Chapter 1 you learned to interact with the REPL by typing in expressions. Essentially, everything in Scala is an expression. Expressions and statements in Scala are the same as in Java. The difference between statements and expressions is that a statement does not return a value, while an expression does. However, you might come across situations where an expression does not return any value. This may sound like we are contradicting ourselves, but let's clear this up by means of an example. If you type the following expression on REPL, you will clearly see that it returns a value:

```
val x = 2
```

The value returned by this expression looks like this, as you can see on the REPL:

```
x: Int = 2
```

Here, Int is the data type of the value returned. Now enter the following expression:

```
val x = println(2)
```

The output on the REPL looks like this:

```
2x: Unit = ()
```

The expression val x = println(2) does not return any value. Nevertheless, the Scala compiler discerns the type of x as a special type in Scala for expressions that do not return value, called Unit. This mechanism of inferring the type of the value from its assignment is called type inference. So everything in Scala is an expression. Understanding this is crucial in understanding how, in functional languages, variables are bound to expressions and keep a single value during their entire lifetime due to the requirements of referential transparency. We will explain this in detail in Chapter 4. We begin this chapter by exploring variables and type hierarchy in Scala. All the other concepts introduced in this chapter such as functions, collections, built-in control structures, and pattern matching leverage on the power of expressions. Functions, collections, and pattern matching are introduced briefly in this chapter. We will describe functions, collections, and pattern matching in detail in the subsequent chapters aimed at each of these concepts.

Variables

In Scala, there are three ways you can define variables: val, var, and lazy val. Scala allows you to decide whether or not a variable is immutable (read-only) when you declare it.

An immutable variable is declared with the keyword val. This means that it is a variable that cannot be changed.We will create a value with the name x and assigned with a literal number 10.

```
val x= 10
```

Now when you press Enter, the REPL(R) reads the value definition you entered, (E) evaluates it, and (P) prints it as affirmation. The new value, named x, is now defined and available for use as shown in the following code:

```
scala> val x = 10
x: Int = 10
```

The value x is now available for use. Remember that we are using it, not changing it. We use it like so:

```
x*x
```

```
scala> x*x
res0: Int = 100
```

You can choose to make use of res0 (result) value just like any value you explicitly define:

```
scala> res0 + 1
res1: Int = 101
```

You can make use of res1 too, like so:

```
res0 + res1
```

```
scala> res0 +res1
res2: Int = 201
```

Here the values res0 and res1 are added, resulting in the value 201 being returned and stored in the new value named res2.

Now let's try to reassign a new value to x like so:

```
x= 202
```

```
scala> x=202
<console>:8: error: reassignment to val
       x=202
         ^
```

x is declared as val and is an immutable variable so you cannot reassign a new value to x. Now let us declare a mutable variable. A mutable variable is declared with keyword var like:

```
var y  = 10
```

```
scala> var y = 10
y: Int = 10
```

Now let's reassign a new value to y, like so:

```
y = 11
```

```
scala> var y = 10
y: Int = 10
```

You can reassign a new value to y as y is mutable, but you cannot reassign the variable to a different type. In the previous expression, y is assigned an Int type. Let us now assign it to a Double:

```
y = 10.5
```

```
scala> y = 10.5
<console>:8: error: type mismatch;
found    : Double(10.5)
 required: Int
       y = 10.5
         ^
```

However, defining a variable of type Double and assigning it an Int value will work because Int numbers can be converted to Double numbers automatically:

```
scala> var z =10.5
z: Double = 10.5
scala> z = 11
z: Double = 11.0
```

Lazy val variables are calculated once, the first time the variable is accessed. Only vals can be lazy variables. You would use a lazy val if the variable may not be used and the cost of calculating it is very long.

```
scala> val x = 10e20
x: Double = 1.0E21
scala> val y= 10e30
y: Double = 1.0E31
scala> lazy val z = x*y
z: Double = <lazy>
scala> var x = 10
x: Int = 10
```

Scala Type Hierarchy

Unlike Java, there are no primitive types in Scala. All data types in Scala are objects that have methods to operate on their data. All Scala's types, from numbers to collections, exist as part of a type hierarchy. Every class that you define in Scala will also belong to this hierarchy automatically. Figure 2-1 shows the hierarchy of Scala's core types.

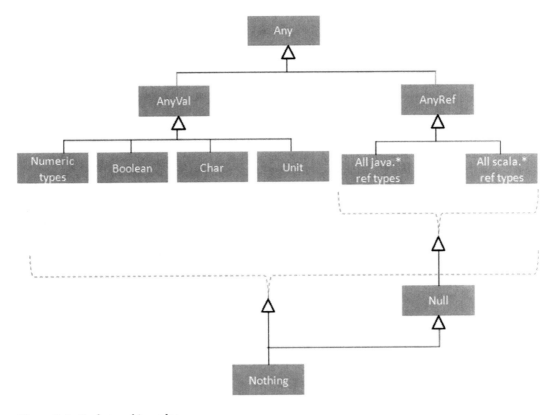

Figure 2-1. *Scala type hierarchy*

We will cover each of these core types shown in Figure 2-1 in this section, except `Scala.*` ref types. There are several ref types in `Scala.*`, such as Collection and several others and we will cover these in the subsequent chapters. In this section we will begin our discussion with Any, AnyVal, and AnyRef types, followed by Numeric types, Boolean, Char, Unit, and finally we will explain Nothing and Null.

Any, AnyVal and AnyRef Types

Class Any is the root of the Scala class hierarchy and is an abstract class. Every class in a Scala execution environment inherits directly or indirectly from this class. AnyVal and AnyRef extend Any type. The Any, AnyVal, and AnyRef types are the root of Scala's type hierarchy. All other types descend from AnyVal and AnyRef. The types that extend AnyVal are known as value types. For example, as you will see in numeric types in this section, Double is an abstract final class that extends AnyVal and the types that extend AnyRef are known as reference types (i.e., nonvalue Scala classes and user-defined) classes.

Numeric Types

The numeric data types in Scala constitute Float and Double types along with Integral data types such as Byte, Short, Int, Long, and Char.

Table 2-1 displays Scala's numeric data types.

Table 2-1. *Scala's Numeric Data Types*

Data type	Description
Byte	Integers in the range from –128 to 127
Short	Integers in the range from –32768 to 32767
Int	Integers in the range from –2147483648 to 2147483647
Long	Integers in the range from –9223372036854775808 to 9223372036854775807
Float	The largest positive finite float is 3.4028235×10^{38} and thesmallest positive finite nonzero float is 1.40×10^{-45}
Double	The largest positive finite double is $1.7976931348623157 \times 10^{308}$ and the smallest positive finite nonzero double is 4.9×10^{-324}

Scala supports the ability to automatically convert numbers from one type to another in the order Byte ➤ Short ➤ Int ➤ Long ➤ Float ➤ Double.

where the Byte type is the lowest and can be converted to any other type as illustrated in the following example:

```
scala> val x: Byte = 30
x: Byte = 30
```

You can assign x to a Short type as illustrated in the following example:

```
scala> val y: Short = x
y: Short = 30
```

Likewise you can assign x to an Int, Long, Float, Double, and Scala will automatically convert the numbers for you as illustrated in the following example:

```
scala> val z: Double = y
z: Double = 10.0
```

Scala does not allow automatic conversion in the order reverse from mentioned earlier. For example Scala will automatically convert a Long to a Float and Double but not from Long to an Int as illustrated in the following example:

```
scala> val x: Long = 10
x: Long = 10
scala> val y: Int = x
<console>:8: error: type mismatch;
 found    : Long
 required: Int
val y: Int = x
```

Boolean Type

The Boolean type is limited to the literal true or the literal false as illustrated in the following example on REPL:

```
scala> val x = !false
x: Boolean = true
```

As you can see, Scala discerns the type of x as Boolean.

Char Type

Char literals are written with single-quotes, distinguishing them from String literals, which are written with double quotes as you will see in the following section. The following example illustrates the Char type:

```
scala> val x = 'X'
x: Char =  X
```

Unit type

The Unit type is used to define a function that doesn't return data. It is similiar to the void keyword in Java. We have introduced Unit type in Chapter 1. We insert the code again here for quick reference in Listing 2-1.

Listing 2-1. Main Method with Unit Type

```
def main(args: Array[String]) : Unit = {
                            }
```

The Unit literal is an empty pair of parentheses, () as illustrated in the following example.

```
scala> val empty = ()
empty: Unit = ()
```

Nothing and Null Types

Nothing and Null types are at the bottom of the Scala type hierarchy shown in Figure 2-1 Null is a subtype of all reference types that is, it is a subtype of *all* AnyRef types that exist to provide a type for the keyword null. Scala does not have a null keyword. But why Scala even has Null type you ask. This will be explained later in this book as it involves few other concepts that cannot be introduced at this point. Because Null is not a subtype of value types, that is, subtype of AnyVal, null is not a member of any such type. For instance, it is not possible to assign null to a variable of type scala.Int.

Nothing is a subtype of every other type to provide a compatible return type for operations that affect a program's flow. One of the usages of Nothing is that it signals abnormal termination. Nothing is a trait that is guaranteed to have zero instances. It provides a return type for methods that never return normally (i.e., a method that always throws an exception). You will see one example of Nothing later in this book.

In best practiced Scala, you never use null values. If you're coming from a language like Java, any time you feel like using a null, use an Option instead. This will be explained in Chapter 6 and Chapter 13.

This concludes the core types in Scala hierarchy. If you have a keen eye, you must have noticed that String type was not discussed in this section. This is because String type in Scala is built on the String type of Java. Now we will briefly introduce how strings are used in Scala.

Strings

Scala's String is built on Java's String and adds additional features such as string interpolation to Java's String.

Following example illustrates a string literal using double quotes:

```
scala> val hello = "Hello"
hello: String = Hello
```

String Interpolation

String interpolation is a mechanism to combine your values inside a string with variables. The notation for interpolation in Scala is an s prefix added before the first double quote of the string. Then dollar sign operator $ can be used to reference the variable.

Listing 2-2 illustrates the usageof string interpolation.

Listing 2-2. String Interpolation

```
val bookTitle = "Beginning Scala" // creating a String
s"Book Title is ${ bookTitle}" // String interpolation
```

You can try this code on REPL as shown:

```
scala> val bookTitle = "Beginning Scala"
bookTitle: String = Beginning Scala
scala> s"Book Title is ${ bookTitle}"
res0: String = Book Title is Beginning Scala
```

Functions

Scala has both functions and methods. A Scala method is a part of a class that has a name and a signature, whereas a function in Scala is a complete object that can be assigned to a variable. A function definition can appear anywhere in a source file.

Function without Parameter

To define a function in Scala, use the def keyword followed by the method name and the method body as shown in Listing 2-3.

Listing 2-3. hello Function

```
def hello() = {"Hello World!"}
```

The equal sign = is used as a separator between the method signature and the method body.
Here is the output:

```
scala> def hello() = {"Hello World!"}
hello: ()String
```

You can invoke this function using either hello() or hello.
In the preceding method definition you can also include the optional return type as shown in Listing 2-4.

Listing 2-4. Optional Return Type in the Method Definition

```
def hello():String = {"Hello World!"}
```

```
scala> def hello():String = {"Hello World!"}
hello: ()String
```

You can invoke this function using either hello() or hello.
It is also possible to remove the parentheses from the method body altogether as shown in Listing 2-5.

Listing 2-5. Method Body Without the Parentheses

```
def hello() = "Hello World!"
```

```
scala> def hello() = "Hello World!"
hello: ()String
```

You can invoke this function using either hello() or hello.
You can also remove the parentheses from the method signature altogether as shown in Listing 2-6.

Listing 2-6. Method Signature Without Parentheses

```
def hello = "Hello World!"
```

```
scala> def hello = "Hello World!"
hello: String
```

Function with Parameters

Now you will look at the function involving parameters as shown in Listing 2-7.

Listing 2-7. Function with Parameter

```
def square (i:Int) = {i*i}
```

The body of the functions are expressions, where the final line becomes the return value of the function.

```
scala> def square (i:Int) = {i*i}
square: (i: Int)Int
```

You can invoke this function as square(2).
You can provide multiple parameters in a function. Multiple parameters are separated by commas as illustrated in Listing 2-8.

Listing 2-8. Function with Multiple Parameters

```
def add(x: Int, y: Int): Int = { x + y }
```

You can now invoke this function by passing actual parameters to the add function as shown in the following example on the REPL:

```
scala> def add(x: Int, y: Int): Int = { x + y }
add: (x: Int, y: Int)Int
scala> add(5, 5)
res0: Int = 10
```

This concludes the brief introduction to Scala functions. We will describe functions in detail in Chapter 4. Now we will introduce arrays, lists, ranges, and tuples.

Arrays, Lists, Ranges, and Tuples

Next we introduce arrays, lists, ranges and tuples so that you can use them for subsequent sections of this chapter. We will explain lists in detail in Chapter 6.

Arrays

The array is a common data structure consisting of a collection of elements of the same type. Elements are associated with an index, usually an integer, which is used to access or replace a particular element.

Basically, there are two ways to define an array: either you can specify the total number of elements and then assigns values to the elements, or you can specify all values at once.

For example books is declared as an array of Strings that may hold up to three elements as shown in Listing 2-9.

Listing 2-9. Array of Strings

```
var books:Array[String] = new Array[String](3)
Try Listing 2-9 on REPL as shown:
```

```
scala> var books:Array[String] = new Array[String](3)
books: Array[String] = Array(null, null, null)
scala>
```

Here books is declared as an array of Strings that may hold up to three elements. You can simplify the declaration as shown in Listing 2-10:

Listing 2-10. Simplifying Array Declarations

```
var books = new Array[String](3)
```

```
scala> var books = new Array[String](3)
books: Array[String] = Array(null, null, null)
scala>
```

You can also define the books array as shown in Listing 2-11.

Listing 2-11. Another Way of Array Declaration

```
var books = Array("Beginning Scala", "Beginning Java", "Beginning Groovy")
```

You can assign values to individual elements or get access to individual elements, using commands as illustrated in Listing 2-12:

Listing 2-12. Assigning Values or Accessing Individual Elements

```
books(0) = "Beginning Scala"; books(1) = "Beginning Java"; books(2) = "Beginning Groovy"
println(books(0))
```

The index of the first element of an array is the number 0 and the index of the last element is the total number of elements minus one.

Lists

In Scala Lists, all elements have the same type like arrays, but unlike arrays, elements of a list cannot by changed by assignment. The list that has elements of type T is written as List[T]. Types in Scala deserve a chapter of their own and will be discussed in detail in Chapter 8. There are two ways to create a list: either you can create the list in the similar manner you create arrays or you can use :: cons operator. We will show you both the ways of creating lists.

First we will show the more traditional approach. Listing 2-13 shows how you can create an empty list.

Listing 2-13. Creating an Empty List

```
val empty: List[Nothing] = List()
```

```
scala> val empty: List[Nothing] = List()
empty: List[Nothing] = List()
scala>
```

Note that the type of the list is Nothing.
You can create the list of books as shown in Listing 2-14:

Listing 2-14. Creating a List of Books

```
val books: List[String] = List("Beginning Scala", "Beginning Groovy", "Beginning Java")
```

Both these lists can be defined using a tail Nil and ::. Nil also represents the empty list. Differences between Nothing and Nil will be described in Chapter 13. An empty list can be defined using Nil as shown in Listing 2-15:

Listing 2-15. An Empty List Using Nil

```
val empty = Nil
```

Nil in Listing 2-15 is known as the tail of the list.

```
scala> val empty = Nil
empty: scala.collection.immutable.Nil.type = List()
```

The books list can be defined using a tail Nil and :: as illustrated in Listing 2-16.

Listing 2-16. Creating a List of Books Using a Tail Nill and ::

```
val books = " Beginning Scala" :: ("Beginning Groovy" :: ("Beginning Java" :: Nil))
```

```
scala> val books = " Beginning Scala" :: ("Beginning Groovy" :: ("Beginning Java" :: Nil))
books: List[String] = List(" Beginning Scala", Beginning Groovy, Beginning Java)
scala>
```

The operations on the lists can be expressed in terms of head and tail methods, where head returns the first element of a list and tail returns a list consisting of all elements except the first element.

```
scala> books.head
res0: String = " Beginning Scala"
scala> books.tail
res1: List[String] = List(Beginning Groovy, Beginning Java)
scala>
```

Ranges

Ranges can be defined by their start, their end, and the stepping value.

To create a range in Scala, use the predefined the method to as illustrated in the Listing 2-17:

Listing 2-17. Creating Range Using the Method to

```
1 to 5
Try Listing 2-17 on REPL as shown.
```

```
scala> 1 to 5
res0: scala.collection.immutable.Range.Inclusive = Range(1, 2, 3, 4, 5)
scala>
```

You can also create a range with the upper limit exclusive of its upper limit using the predefined method until as shown in the Listing 2-18.

Listing 2-18. Creating a Range Using the Until Method

```
1 until 5
```

Try Listing 2-18 on REPL as shown:

```
scala> 1 until 5
res1: scala.collection.immutable.Range = Range(1, 2, 3, 4)
scala>
```

Note that for 1 to 5, a Range(1,2,3,4,5) is created, but for 1 until 5 a Range with upper limit exclusive Range(1,2,3,4) is created.

You can also create a Range with stepping values using the predefined method by as shown in Listing 2-19.

Listing 2-19. Creating a Range Using the Method By

```
1 to 20 by 4
```

```
scala> 1 to 20 by 4
res2: scala.collection.immutable.Range = Range(1, 5, 9, 13, 17)
scala>
```

Tuples

A tuple is an ordered container of two or more values of same or different types. Unlike lists and arrays, however, there is no way to iterate through elements in a tuple. Its purpose is only as a container for more than one value. Tuples are useful when you need to group discrete elements and provide a generic means to structure data. You can create a tuple in two ways:

- By writing your values separated by a comma and surrounded by a pair of parentheses

- By using a relation operator (->)

Listing 2-20 shows a tuple containing an Int, a Boolean, and a String using the former method.

Listing 2-20. Tuple Using Values Separated by a Comma and Surrounded by a Pair of Parentheses

```
val tuple = (1, false, "Scala")
```

If you try Listing 2-20 on REPL, you will see the diverse types of elements contained in the tuple:

```
scala> val tuple = (1, false, "Scala")
tuple: (Int, Boolean, String) = (1,false,Scala)
```

Listing 2-21 shows a tuple created using a relation operator:

Listing 2-21. Tuple Using Relation Operator

```
val tuple2 ="title" -> "Beginning Scala"
```

```
scala> val tuple2 ="title" -> "Beginning Scala"
tuple2: (String, String) = (title,Beginning Scala)
```

Individual elements of a tuple can be accessed by its index, where the first element has an index 1. Listing 2-22 shows accessing the third element of the tuple.

Listing 2-22. Accessing an Element of the Tuple Using Index

```
val third = tuple._3
```

```
scala> val third = tuple._3
third: String = Scala
```

Built-in Control Structures

The Scala built-in control structures are if, while, for, try, and match expressions. Scala's built-in control structures are sufficient to provide features that their imperative equivalents provide, but because all of Scala's control structures (except while loops) result in some value, these control structures support functional approach as well. We will explain this in detail in Chapter 4.

If Expressions

The result of if expressions in Scala is always Unit. The result of if/else is based on the type of each part of the expression. Listing 2-23 illustrates if expressions in Scala.

Listing 2-23. If Expression in Scala

```
if (exp) println("yes")
```

Listing 2-23 prints "yes" if exp is true. Like Java, an if expression may have a multiline code block as illustrated in Listing 2-24.

Listing 2-24. Multiline If Expression

```
if (exp) {
println("Line one")
println("Line two")
}
```

The if/else in Scala behaves like the ternary operator in Java:

```
val i: Int = if (exp) 1 else 3
```

and either (or both) parts of the expression may have multiline code blocks as illustrated in Listing 2-25.

Listing 2-25. Multiline Else

```
val i: Int = if (exp) 1
else {
val j = System.currentTimeMillis
(j % 100L).toInt
}
```

While Loops

The while and dowhile constructs are called loops, not expressions, because they don't result in any values. The type of the result is Unit. while is used very rarely in Scala code. It turns out that a value (and in fact, only one value) exists whose type is Unit.

while executes its code block as long as its expression evaluates to true, just like Java. In practice, using recursion (a method calling itself) provides more readable code and enforces the concept of transforming input to output rather than changing, mutating, variables. Listing 2-26 shows the while loop construct.

Listing 2-26. While Loop

```
while (exp) println("Working...")
while (exp) {
println("Working...")
}
```

For Comprehension

A For Comprehension is a very powerful control structure of Scala language. Not only does it offer the ability to iterate over a collection, but also provides filtering options and the ability to generate new collections.

Basic for Expression

This is a very basic feature of the for expression. First we need a collection over which the for expression will iterate. We create a list of books as shown in Listing 2-27:

Listing 2-27. A Book Ccollection

```
 val books = List("Beginning Scala", "Beginning Groovy", "Beginning Java", "Scala in easy
steps", "Scala in 24 hours")
```

As you can see on REPL, the type of the books list is List[String].

```
scala> val books = List("Beginning Scala", "Beginning Groovy", "Beginning Java", "Scala in
easy steps", "Scala in 24 hours")
books: List[String] = List(Beginning Scala, Beginning Groovy, Beginning Java, Scala in
easy steps, Scala in 24 hours)
```

Now we can write a very basic for expression to iterate over the books list as shown in Listing 2-28.

Listing 2-28. Basic for Expression

```
for (book<-books)
println(book)
```

In Line 1 of Listing 2-28, the for expression creates a temporary variable called book for each element in the list books with the corresponding value of that element. The left-arrow operator is called a generator because it generates corresponding values from a collection to be used in an expression.

Here is the output:

```
scala> for (book<-books)
     | println(book)
Beginning Scala
Beginning Groovy
Beginning Java
Scala in easy steps
Scala in 24 hours
```

Filters

A filter is an if clause inside the for expression that is used to filter the collection when you do not want to iterate through the entire collection.

So you can find all Scala books in our list of books as illustrated in Listing 2-29.

Listing 2-29. Using Filter

```
for(book<-books
 if book.contains("Scala")
 ) println(book)
```

Here is the output:

```
scala> for(book<-books
     | if book.contains("Scala")
     | ) println(book)
Beginning Scala
Scala in easy steps
Scala in 24 hours
```

Variable Binding

You can define variables inside for expressions. You can then re-use these variables within the body of your for expression as illustrated in Listing 2-30.

Listing 2-30. Variable Binding in For Comprehension

```
 for {book <- books
 bookVal = book.toUpperCase()
} println(bookVal)
```

Note that bookVal is not declared as a val, but you can still reuse it. This proves to be very useful in situations where you want to transform the elements in your collection while looping through them such as when we transform each book in the books list to uppercase.

Yielding

In Scala's for expression you can use the `yield` keyword to generate new collections.

The type of the collection generated from the for expression is inferred from the type of the collection being iterated over. We show the example of yielding a collection in Listing 2-31.

Listing 2-31. Using Yield in for Comprehension

```
var scalabooks = for{
book <-books
if  book.contains("Scala")
}yield book
```

```
scala> var scalabooks = for{
     | book <-books
     | if  book.contains("Scala")
     | }yield book
scalabooks: List[String] = List(Beginning Scala, Scala in easy steps, Scala in 24 hours)
```

The filtered result is yielded as a value named book. This result is accumulated with every run inside the for loop, and thus accumulated collection is assigned to the value scalabooks.

The scalabooks is of type List[String], because it is a subset of the books list, which is also of type List[String].

try expressions

Exception handling in Scala is implemented differently, but it behaves exactly like Java and works seamlessly with existing Java libraries. All exceptions in Scala are unchecked; there is no concept of checked exception. Scala facilitates a great deal of flexibility in terms of the ability to choose whether to catch an exception.

Throwing exceptions is the same in Scala and Java as shown in Listing 2-32.

Listing 2-32. Throwing Exception

```
throw new Exception("some exception...")
```

The `try/finally` construct is also the same in Scala and Java as shown in Listing 2-33.

Listing 2-33. try/finally in Scala

```
try {
throw newException("some exception...")
} finally{
println("This will always be printed")
}
```

The `try/catch` construct is different in Scala than in Java, in that, try/catch in Scala is an expression that results in a value and that the exception in Scala can be pattern matched in the catch block instead of providing a separate catch clause for each different exception. Because try/catch in Scala is an expression, it becomes possible to wrap a call in a `try/catch` and assign default value if the call fails. Listing 2-34 shows a basic `try/catch` expression with pattern matched catch block.

Listing 2-34. try/catch in Scala

```
try {
file.write(stuff)
} catch{
case e:java.io.IOException => // handle IO Exception
case n:NullPointerException => // handle null pointer
}
```

Listing 2-35 shows an example of wrapping a call in try/catch by calling `Integer.parseInt` and assigning a default if the call fails.

Listing 2-35. Wrapping a Call in try/catch and Assigning a Default if the Call Fails

```
scala> try{Integer.parseInt("dog")}catch{case_ => 0}
```

```
res16:Int = 0
```

You can see in Listing 2-35, calling Integer.parseInt and defaulting to 0 if an exception is thrown. You can see the output in Listing 2-36 when the call `Integer.parseInt` does not fail.

Listing 2-36. When the Call Does not Fail

```
scala> try{Integer.parseInt("44")} catch{case _ => 0}
```

```
res17:Int = 44
```

Match Expressions

Scala's match expressions are used for pattern matching by allowing you to construct complex tests in very little code and are extremely flexible constructs that enable matching arbitrary items, such as types, content of the data structure, regular expressions, and even ranges of numeric types. Pattern matching is like Java's switch statement, but you can test against almost anything, and you can even assign pieces of the matched value to variables. Like everything in Scala, pattern matching is an expression, so it results in a value that may be assigned or returned. The most basic pattern matching is like Java's switch, except there is no break in each case as the cases do not fall through to each other. Listing 2-37 matches the number against a constant, but with a default.

Listing 2-37. Using Match Expression

```
44 match {
case 44 => true// if wematch 44,theresult is true
case _ => false// otherwisetheresult isfalse
}
```

Like C#, you can match against a String as shown in Listing 2-38.

Listing 2-38. Matching Against a String

```
"David"match {
case "David"=> 45 // the result is 45 if we match "David"
case "Elwood" => 77
case _ => 0
}
```

We will explain pattern matching in detail in Chapter 5.

Comments

Scala comments are much like Java and C++ comments. Multiline comments start with /* and ended with */.

```
/*
This is a multiline comment:
*/
```

A single-line comment is started with // and continues to the end of the line:

```
// This is a single line comment
```

In Scala, you can nest multiline comments:

```
/*
This is an outer comment
/* And this comment
is nested
*/
Outer comment
*/
```

Summary

We've covered a lot of ground in this chapter. We did an overview of Scala's syntax and basic constructs. Some of the concepts in this chapter, such as pattern matching and for comprehensions, are functional programming concepts. But because Scala is a multi-paradigm language, we included them with the rest of the nonfunctional programming concepts and will be described in detail in later chapters. In the next chapter, we're going to explore object orientated programming in Scala.

CHAPTER 3

■ ■ ■

Object Orientation in Scala

The essence of OOP is modelling abstractions for handling complexities in software development, by means of classes and objects. Finding the right abstractions, however, remains an arduous quest. An object in software is an abstraction of a real-world object, comprising essential properties and behaviors that set it apart from other objects. OOP is successful because object-oriented languages implement a number of principles such as encapsulation, inheritance, and polymorphism that make the software design and construction process much simpler and elegant when compared to other antiquated approaches. To illustrate these principles we concoct an abstraction with the aid of a classic example of shapes:

```scala
class Shape {
def area:Double = 0.0
}
```

We defined a supertype called Shape that has a method area that computes the area of the shape. We are not interested in every aspect of Shape. Instead, we center our attention on area of the shape. As far as one can tell, our choice, driven by the task we are trying to accomplish, is subjective. Based on your mathematical bent, you could choose other geometrical characteristics of shape involving circumference, major or minor axes, and so on. Affording this subjectivity is the corollary of the abstraction, so to speak. Now that we have abstraction in place, let's discuss the three principles of OOP—encapsulation, inheritance, and polymorphism. We could have a myriad of shapes to subtype the Shape type we pick such as Rectangle and Circle as illustrated in Listing 3-1.

Listing 3-1. Concrete shapes

```scala
class Rectangle(val width:Double,val height:Double) extends Shape {
override def area:Double = width*height
}
class Circle(val radius:Double) extends Shape {
override def area:Double = math.Pi*radius*radius
}
```

Each of these classes takes some arguments and extends Shape, then overrides the method of Shape. A subtype is guaranteed to have all the members of the supertype. This is the mainstay of Inheritance. Although, you might not always want the members of subtype thus inherited to do the same things that members of supertype do and you can choose to change the implementation of the methods of the supertype. Changing the implementation of a method of the supertype is called *overriding*. One thing to note is that we cannot alter the width and the height of a Rectangle and the radius of the Circle objects because if the field is a val, as the fields width, height, and radius in our code are, Scala generates only a getter method for it. This is a trivial example of encapsulation. In encapsulation, the fields of an object are accessible only through its methods. In other words, one can either mutate or access the state of an object only by invoking its specific methods. This property is known as encapsulation. We can now write code that takes an instance of Shape and then pass to it an instance of either Rectangle or Circle:

```
def draw(s:Shape)
```

Now, consider two calls made to this function, like so:

```
val circle = draw(new Circle(3))
val rectangle = draw(new Rectangle(2,3))
```

The reason this works is that inheritance guarantees that any method we could call on an instance of Shape will be defined in the subtypes, that is, code that can work with multiple types. This is the heart of polymorphism. Because of polymorphism, we could create a new subtype of Shape at any point in the future and it would work with this code. Now that you've got the gist of the three principles of OOP let's examine the parts that make the machine function.

Classes and Objects

A class is a blueprint for creating objects that are the concrete instances of a class. A class definition consists of field declarations and method definitions. Fields are used to store the state of an object and methods may provide access to fields, and alter the state of an object. Let's start with a simple example of a blueprint for creating Book objects:

```
class Book
```

You can type this code on REPL to get the following output:

```
scala> class Book
defined class Book
```

The preceding Scala declaration that defined the Book class corresponds to this Java declaration:

```
public class Book {
}
```

You can confirm this by decompiling the class with the following javap command

```
scala> :javap -c Book
Compiled from "Book.scala"
public class Book {
  public Book();
    Code:
       0: aload_0
       1: invokespecial #12                 // Method java/lang/Object."<init>":()V
       4: return
}
scala>
```

Once you've defined a class, you can create objects from the class with the keyword new. To create an instance of Book, you can type the following:

```
new Book
```

But, this works just as well:

```
new Book()
```

```
scala> new Book
res0: Book = Book@181ba0
scala> new Book()
res1: Book = Book@d19e59
scala>
```

Constructors

A class consists of class members such as fields and methods. Fields hold the state of an object and are defined with either val or var. Methods complete the computational tasks of the object and are defined with keyword def. In Scala, the entire body of the class is the constructor. If the constructor takes zero parameters, you can omit the parameter list. In this section you will learn some different configurations of constructors with parameters.

Constructors with Parameters

Scala differentiates between a constructor declared with val fields, var fields, private val, or private var and fields without var or val.

Parameter Declared as a val

If the constructor parameter is declared as a val, Scala generates only a getter method for it. Note that only a getter method is generated, a setter method is not generated. Let's declare a field as val as shown here:

```
class Book( val title:String)
```

You can now decompile this code. As you can see, Scala generates a title method. You can use this method to access the field.

```
scala> :javap -c Book
Compiled from "Book.scala"
public class Book {
  public java.lang.String title();
//.....
  public Book(java.lang.String);
//....
}
```

Because the constructor field is defined as a val, the value of the field is immutable by definition. Therefore, Scala generates only the getter method and no setter method.

```
scala> val book = new Book("Beginning Scala")
book: Book = Book@c6dd25
scala> book.title
res0: String = Beginning Scala
scala> book.title = "new title"
<console>:8: error: reassignment to val
       book.title = "new title"
              ^
```

Note In Scala, if the constructor or method takes zero parameters, you can omit the parameter list.

Parameter Declared as a var

As you might have guessed, if the constructor parameter is declared as a var, Scala generates both accessor and mutator methods.

```
class Book( var title:String)
```

If you decompile this code, you can see the generated mutator method with an unusual name, title_$eq.

```
scala> :javap -c Book
Compiled from "Book.scala"
public class Book {
  public java.lang.String title();
//.......
  public void title_$eq(java.lang.String);
//.........
  public Book(java.lang.String);
//........
}
```

So when you set the field, like so

```
book.title("new title")
```

Scala converts it to the following:

```
Book.title_$eq("Beginning Scala")
```

As you can see, you can mutate the field of Book object because it was declared with keyword var.

```
scala> val book = new Book("Beginning Scala")
book: Book = Book@19cfd87
scala> book.title = "new title"
book.title: String = new title
scala> book.title
res0: String = new title
```

Parameter Declared as a private val or var

You can add the private keyword to a val or var field to prevent getter and setter methods from being generated. In this case the fields could only be accessed from within members of the class:

```
class Book(private var title: String) {
def printTitle {println(title)}
 }
```

```
scala> val book = new Book("Beginning Scala")
book: Book = Book@1352aed
scala> book.title
<console>:9: error: variable title in class Book cannot be accessed in Book
              book.title
                  ^
scala> book.printTitle
Beginning Scala
```

Parameter Declared without val or var

Scala does not generate getter or setter when neither val nor var are specified on constructor parameters. As you can see here, you cannot access the field title of the Book.

```
scala> class Book(title: String)
defined class Book
scala> val book = new Book("Beginning Scala")
book: Book = Book@125b4a4c
scala> book.title
<console>:12: error: value title is not a member of Book
book.title
^
```

At first sight, parameter declared without val or var and the parameter declared as private val or private var behaves in the same manner. To appreciate the difference between the two, look at Listing 3-2.

Listing 3-2. Parameter with val

```scala
class Book(private val title: String) {
  def printTitle(b: Book) {
    println(b.title)
  }
}
```

```scala
scala> val book = new Book("Beginning Scala")
book: Book = Book@ea05be
scala> book.printTitle(new Book("Beginning Erlang"))
Beginning Erlang
```

As you can see in this case, you can change the title of the Book because the title is a private field that is accessible to this object and the other objects of Book. Now, the parameter of the constructor is declared without val or var as shown in Listing 3-3:

Listing 3-3. Parameter without val/var

```scala
class Book(title: String) {
  def printTitle(b: Book) {
    println(b.title)
  }
}
```

The title field is accessible only to this object as you can see in the output below.

```
>scalac Book.scala
Book.scala:3: error: value title is not a member of Book
    println(b.title)
            ^
one error found
```

Now that you have learned the different configurations of the constructor, you can provide a default value for a constructor parameter that gives other classes the option of specifying that parameter when calling the constructor.

Here's a simple declaration of a Book class with one constructor parameter named title that has default value of "Beginning Scala":

```scala
class Book (val title: String = "Beginning Scala")
```

Because the parameter is defined with a default value, you can call the constructor without specifying a title value:

```scala
scala> val book = new Book
book: Book = Book@4123cd31
scala> book.title
res0: String = Beginning Scala
```

You can also specify the `title` value of your choice when creating a new Book:

```
scala> val book = new Book("new title")
book: Book = Book@4cg3407d
scala> book.title
res1: String = new title
```

You can also choose to provide named parameters as shown in the following code:

```
scala> val book = new Book(title="Beginning Scala")
book: Book = Book@46aaf1d2
scala> book.title
res0: String = Beginning Scala
```

Auxiliary Constructor

You can define one or more auxiliary constructors for a class to provide different ways to create objects. Auxiliary constructors are defined by creating methods named `this`. In this way you can define multiple auxiliary constructors, but they must have different signatures. Each auxiliary constructor must begin with a call to a previously defined constructor. Listing 3-4 illustrates a primary constructor and two auxiliary constructors.

Listing 3-4. Auxiliary constructor

```
class Book (var title :String, var ISBN: Int) {
def this(title: String) {
this(title, 2222)
}
def this() {
this("Beginning Erlang")
this.ISBN = 1111
}
override def toString = s"$title ISBN- $ISBN"
}
```

Given these constructors, the same Book can be created in the following ways:

```
val book1 = new Book
val book2 = new Book("Beginning Clojure")
val book3 = new Book("Beginning Scala", 3333)
```

```
scala> val book1 = new Book
book1: Book = Beginning Erlang ISBN- 1111
scala> val book2  = new Book("Beginning Clojure")
book2: Book = Beginning Clojure ISBN- 2222
scala> val book3 = new Book("Beginning Scala", 3333)
book3: Book = Beginning Scala ISBN- 3333
```

An auxiliary constructor just needs to call one of the previously defined constructors. For instance, the auxiliary constructor that takes the title parameter calls this(title, ISBN) and the no-arg constructor this() calls this(title).

Method Declaration

Scala method declarations have the def keyword, the method name, parameters, optional return type, the = keyword, and the method body.myMethod takes no parameters and returns a String:

```
def myMethod():String = "Moof"
```

myOtherMethod takes no parameters and returns a String, but the return type is not explicitly declared because the compiler infers the return type. It is recommended to use type inferencing judiciously; if it's not immediately obvious what the return type is, declare it explicitly.

```
def myOtherMethod() = "Moof"
```

You declare the parameters inside the method declaration's parentheses. The parameter name must be followed by the parameter's type:

```
def foo(a: Int):String = a.toString
```

You can declare multiple parameters:

```
def f2(a: Int, b:Boolean):String= if (b)a.toStringelse"false"
```

You can pass the type of a parameter or the return type as a parameter. The following code takes a parameter p and a type parameter T and returns a List of T. Thus, if you pass an Int, you'll get a List[Int], and if you pass a String, you'll get a List[String]. For the most part, the type inferencer calculates the type parameters so you don't have to explicitly pass them.

```
scala> deflist[T](p:T):List[T] = p :: Nil
list: [T](T)List[T]

scala> list(1)
```

```
res2:List[Int]= List(1)
```

```
scala> list("Hello")
```

```
res3:List[java.lang.String] = List(Hello)
```

And the last parameter in the list may be repeated—a variable-length argument. If the last parameter is a variable-length argument, it is a Seq of the type of the variable-length argument, so in this case the as parameter is a Seq[Int]:

```
def largest(as: Int*): Int = as.reduceLeft((a, b)=> a maxb)
```

A variable-length argument method may be called as follows:

```
largest(1)
largest(2,3,99)
largest(33, 22,33,22)
```

You can mix type parameters with variable-length arguments:

```
def mkString[T](as: T*):String = as.foldLeft("")(_ + _.toString)
```

And you can put bounds on the type parameters. In this case, the types that are passed in must be Number or a subclass of Number:

```
def sum[T <:Number](as:T*): Double = as.foldLeft(0d)(_ + _.doubleValue)
```

Methods can be declared within any code scope, except at the top level, where classes, traits, and objects are declared. Methods can reference any variables in their scope as seen in Listing 3-5.

Listing 3-5. Methods can reference any variables in their scope

```
def readLines(br: BufferedReader) = {
var ret: List[String] = Nil

defreadAll():Unit= br.readLinematch {
case null =>
case s => ret ::= s ; readAll()
}

readAll()
ret.reverse
}
```

In this example, the readAll method is defined inside the scope of the readLines method. Thus, the readAll method has access to the variables br and ret because these variables are within the scope of the readLines method. The readAll method calls a method on br, and it updates ret, even though these variables are not explicitly passed to readAll. As we go through more examples in subsequent chapters, we'll see how being able to use methods within methods and having access to all the variables in scope comes in handy.

Overriding methods in Scala is different than Java. Methods that override declared methods must include the override modifier. Methods that override abstract methods may include the override modifier as shown in Listing 3-6.

Listing 3-6. An abstract method without override

```
abstractclassBase {
defthing: String
}
classOneextends Base {
defthing= "Moof"
}
```

Methods that take no parameters and variables can be accessed the same way, and a `val` can override a `def` in a superclass as shown in Listing 3-7. This principle of uniform access turns out to be very useful.

Listing 3-7. Using override

```
classTwoextends One{
overridevalthing= (new java.util.Date).toString
}
classThree extends One{
overridelazy valthing= super.thing + (newjava.util.Date).toString
}
```

Code Blocks

Method and variable definitions can be single lines:

```
def meth9() = "Hello World"
```

Methods and variables also can be defined in code blocks that are denoted by curly braces:{ }. Code blocks may be nested. The result of a codeblock is the last line evaluated in the codeblock as shown in Listing 3-8.

Listing 3-8. The result of a codeblock

```
def meth3():String = {"Moof"}
def meth4():String = {
val d = new java.util.Date()
d.toString()
}
```

Variable definitions can be code blocks as well. This comes in handy when defining `val` variables, and the logic required to compute the value is non-trivial.

Listing 3-9. variable definition code block

```
val x3:String= {
val d = new java.util.Date()
d.toString()
}
```

Call-by-Name

In Java, all method invocations are call-by-reference or call-by-value (for primitive types). What this means is that the parameter's value, or reference in the case of an AnyRef, is placed on the stack and passed to the callee. Scala gives you an additional mechanism for passing parameters to methods (and functions): call-by-name, which passes a code block to the callee. Each time the callee accesses the parameter, the code block is executed and the value is calculated. Call-by-name allows you to pass parameters that might take a longtime to calculate but may not be used. Call-by-name also allows you to create flow of control structures such as while, doWhile, and so on.

We declare a nano method, which prints a message and returns the current time with nano-second resolution:

Listing 3-10. Call by name

```
def nano() = {
println("Gettingnano")
System.nanoTime
}
```

Next, we declare the delayed method, which takes a call-by-name parameter by putting the => symbol between the variable name and the type. delayed prints a message demonstrating that the method has been entered. Next, delayed method prints a message with t's value. Finally, delayed method returns t.

Listing 3-11. Call by name parameter

```
def delayed(t:=> Long) = {
println("Indelayed method")
println("Param:"+t)
t
}
```

Let's see what happens when we call delayed with nano as a parameter:

```
scala> delayed(nano())
```

```
Indelayed method
Gettingnano
Param: 4475258994017
Gettingnano
res3:Long = 4475259694720
```

This indicates that delayed is entered before the call to nano and that nano is called twice. Let's compare this to call-by-reference:

Listing 3-12. Call by reference

```
def notDelayed(t:Long) = {
println("Innotdelayed method")
println("Param:"+t)
t
}
```

Let's try calling notDelayed:

```
scala> notDelayed(nano())
```

```
Gettingnano
Innotdelayed method
Param: 4513758999378
res4:Long = 4513758999378
```

nano is called before `notDelayed` is called because the parameter to `notDelayed`, nano, is calculated before `notDelayed` is called. This is the way Java programmers expect code to work.

Method Invocation

Scala provides a number of syntactic variations for invoking methods. There's the standard Java dot notation:

```
instance.method()
```

But if a method does not take any parameters, the ending parentheses are optional:

```
instance.method
```

This allows methods without parameters methods to appear as properties or fields on the target instance. This results in more visually pleasing code.

Methods that take a single parameter can be invoked just as in Java:

```
instance.method(param)
```

But methods that take a single parameter can be invoked without dots or parentheses:

```
instance.method param
```

Because Scala allows method names to contain symbols such as +, -, *, and ?, Scala's dotless method notation creates a syntactically neutral way of invoking methods that are hard-coded operators in Java.

```
scala> 2.1.*(4.3)
```

```
res5:Double = 9.03
```

```
scala> 2.1* 4.3
```

```
res6:Double = 9.03
```

Finally, you invoke multiparameter methods in Scala just as in Java:

```
instance.method(p1, p2)
```

If a Scala method takes a type parameter, typically, the type parameter will be inferred by the compiler, but you can also explicitly pass the type parameter:

```
instance.method[TypeParam](p1,p2)
```

Objects

In Scala, you can use object to refer to an instance of a class as in Java and you can also use `object` as a keyword. In this section you will see how to use `object` as a keyword.

Singleton Objects

Scala does not have static members. Instead, Scala has singleton objects. A singleton object definition looks like a class definition, except instead of the keyword class you use the keyword object. A singleton is a class that can have only one instance. For instance, you might create a singleton object to represent a Car like so:

```
object Car {
def drive { println("drive car") }
}
```

With Car defined as an object, there can be only one instance of it, and you can call its methods just like static methods on a Java class:

```
object Main extends App {
Car.drive
}
```

Unlike classes, singleton objects cannot take parameter. You can use singleton objects for many purposes, including collecting related utility methods, or defining an entry point to a Scala application. In Chapter 1 you used the object keyword to launch your application. There are two ways to create a launching point for your application: define an object with a properly defined main method or define an object or that extends the App trait. The first approach was shown in Chapter 1. For the second approach, define an object that extends the App trait as shown here:

```
object Hello extends App {
println("Hello, world")
}
```

Scala provides a trait, scala. Application that your singleton object should extend for launching the application. Then you place the code you would have put in the main method directly in the singleton object. Now you can compile and run this application. Note that in both approaches, Scala applications are launched from an object, not a class. We will discuss trait in a later section of this chapter and then look into it in detail in the Chapter 4.

Companion Objects

In Scala, both a class and an object can share the same name. When an object shares a name with a class, it's called a companion object, and the class is called a companion class. A companion object is an object that shares the same name and source file with another class or trait. A trait could be seen as a Java interface. Using this approach lets you create static members on a class. The companion object is useful for implementing helper methods and factory. We want to implement a factory that creates different types of shapes. If we want to implement this shape factory in Scala, we will need only one source file. We use a companion class Shape and a companion object Shape, which acts as a factory.

Listing 3-13. Companion object

```
trait Shape {
  def area :Double
}
```

```
object Shape {
private class Circle(radius: Double) extends Shape{
    override val area = 3.14*radius*radius
  }

private class Rectangle (height: Double, length: Double)extends Shape{
    override val area = height * length
  }

  def apply(height :Double , length :Double ) : Shape = new Rectangle(height,length)
  def apply(radius :Double) : Shape = new Circle(radius)

}
```

```
scala> val circle = Shape(2)
circle: Shape = Shape$Circle@1675800
scala> circle.area
res0: Double = 12.56
scala> val rectangle = Shape(2,3)
rectangle: Shape = Shape$Rectangle@1276fd9
scala> rectangle.area
res2: Double = 6.0
```

A singleton object that does not share the same name with a companion class is called a standalone object.

Packaging and Imports

A *package* is a named module of code. Java and Scala convention dictates that package names are the reversed domain name of the code owner. For example, the packages in the Lift Web Framework (http://liftweb.net) begin with net.liftweb. Typically, the package also contains a descriptive name for the module. For example, the Lift utility package is net.liftweb.util. The package declaration is the first non-comment line in the source file:

```
package com.liftcode.stuff
```

Scala packages can be imported so that they can be referenced in the current compilation scope. The following statement imports the contents of the scala.xml package:

```
import scala.xml._
```

Import statements are made in the scope of prior imports. The following statement imports the scala.xml.transform package:

```
import transform._
```

You can import a single class and object (more on objects later in chapter), for example, HashMap from the scala.collection.mutable package:

```
import scala.collection.mutable.HashMap
```

You can import more than one class or object from a single package, for example, `TreeMap` and `TreeSet` from the `scala.collection.immutable` package:

```
import scala.collection.immutable.{TreeMap, TreeSet}
```

Finally, you can import a class or object and rename it. For example, you can import the `JSON` class/object from the `scala.util.parsing.json` package and rename it to `JsonParser`:

```
import scala.util.parsing.json.{JSON=> JsonParser}
```

`import` can be used inside any codeblock, and the `import` will be active only in the scope of that code block. For example, you can import something inside a class body as shown in Listing 3-14:

Listing 3-14. Using import inside class body

```
classFrog {
importscala.xml._
defn:NodeSeq= NodeSeq.Empty
}
```

Scala's `import` statement can also import the methods of an object so that those methods can be used without explicit reference to the object that owns them. This is much like Java's `static import`. Combining local scope import and importing objects allows you to fine-tune where the objects and their associated methods are imported as shown in Listing 3-15.

Listing 3-15. Combining local scope import andimporting objects

```
scala> objectMoose{
defbark = "woof"
}
definedmodule Moose

scala> importMoose._
import Moose._

scala> bark
```
```
res78:java.lang.String = woof
```

Inheritance

Scala supports single inheritance, not multiple inheritance. A child (or derived) class can have one and only one parent (or base) class. The sole exception is the root of the Scala class hierarchy, Any, which has no parent. You saw that classes in Scala are declared very much like Java classes, but can also have parameters. Let's define a simple class that will be used to describe some aspects of inheritance as illustrated in Listing 3-16.

Listing 3-16. Vehicle class

```scala
class Vehicle (speed : Int){
val mph :Int = speed
    def race() = println("Racing")
}
```

The Vehicle class takes one argument, which is the speed of the vehicle. This argument must be passed when creating an instance of class Vehicle, as follows: new Vehicle(100). The class contains one method, called race.

Extending Class

Extending from a base class in Scala is similar to extending in Java except for two restrictions: method overriding requires the override keyword, and only the primary constructor can pass parameters to the base constructor.

It is possible to override methods inherited from a super class in Scala as illustrated in Listing 3-17:

Listing 3-17. Overriding methods inherited from a super class

```scala
class Car (speed : Int) extends Vehicle(speed) {
override val mph: Int= speed
override  def race() = println("Racing Car")
}
```

The class Car extends Vehicle class using the keyword extends. The field mph and the method race needs to be overridden using the keyword override.

Listing 3-18 shows another class Bike that extends Vehicle.

Listing 3-18. Vehicle hierarchy

```scala
class Vehicle (speed : Int){
val mph :Int = speed
    def race() = println("Racing")
}
class Car (speed : Int) extends Vehicle(speed) {
override val mph: Int= speed
override  def race() = println("Racing Car")

}
class Bike(speed : Int) extends Vehicle(speed) {
override val mph: Int = speed
override  def race() = println("Racing Bike")

}
```

Save Listing 3-18 in a file vehicle.scala and compile using:

```
>scalac vehicle.scala
```

Now you can enter the REPL using the scala command and create the vehicle object as shown here:

```
scala> val vehicle1 = new Car(200)
```

With this command, Scala creates the vehicle1 object as shown here:

```
vehicle1: Car = Car@19a8942
```

Now you can use this vehicle1 object created by Scala to access the speed of the Car:

```
scala> vehicle1.mph
```

Scala REPL emits the speed of the Car as shown here:

```
res1: Int = 200
```

In the similar manner, you can execute the race method of vehicle1:

```
scala>vehicle1.race()
```

Scala interpreter emits the output as shown here:

```
Racing Car
```

Now you can create the Bike object and access its property and method:

```
scala> val vehicle2 = new Bike(100)
vehicle2: Bike = Bike@b7ad3
scala>vehicle2.mph
res4: Int = 100
scala> vehicle2.race()
Racing Bike
```

Traits

Suppose you want to add another class to your vehicle hierarchy. This time you want to add a Batmobile. A Batmobile can race, glide, and fly. But you cannot add glide and fly methods to the Vehicle class because in a nonfictional world, Car and Bike that extend Vehicle do not glide or fly—not yet at least. So, in this case if you want to add Batmobile to your vehicle hierarchy, you can use a trait. Traits are like interfaces in Java, which can also contain code. In Scala, when a class inherits from a trait, it implements the interface of the trait, and inherits all the code contained in the trait. Listing 3-19 shows flying and gliding traits.

Listing 3-19. flying and gliding traits

```
trait flying {
    def fly() = println("flying")
}

trait floating gliding {
def gliding() = println("gliding")
}
```

Now you can create the Batmobile class that extends Vehicle class along with the flying and gliding traits, as shown in Listing 3-20.

Listing 3-20. Using with

```
class Batmobile(speed : Int) extends Vehicle(speed)  with flying with gliding{
override val mph: Int = speed
override  def race() = println("Racing Batmobile")
override def fly() = println("Flying Batmobile")
override def float() = println("Gliding Batmobile")

}
```

In Scala, traits can inherit classes. The keyword extends is also used when a class inherits a trait as its parent. The keyword extends is also used even when the class mixes in other traits using the with keyword. Also, extends is used when one trait is the child of another trait or class.

You can now create a Batmobile in the REPL as illustrated here:

```
scala> val vehicle3 = new Batmobile(300)
vehicle3: Batmobile = Batmobile@374ed5
```

Now you can access the fly method of the Batmobile shown here:

```
scala> vehicle3.fly()
Flying Batmobile
```

Now create a list of vehicles, then you can use the maxBy method provided by Scala collections library to find the fastest vehicle in the list.

```
scala> val vehicleList = List(vehicle1, vehicle2, vehicle3)
vehicleList: List[Vehicle] = List(Car@562791, Bike@e80317, Batmobile@374ed5)
scala> val fastestVehicle = vehicleList.maxBy(_.mph)
fastestVehicle: Vehicle = Batmobile@374ed5
```

Case Classes

Scala has a mechanism for creating classes that have the common stuff filled in. Most of the time, when we define a class, we have to write the toString, hashCode, and equals methods. These methods are boilerplate. Scala provides the case class mechanism for filling in these blanks, as well as support for pattern matching. A case class provides the same facilities as a normal class, but the compiler generates toString, hashCode, and equals methods (which you can override). Case classes can be instantiated without the use of the new statement. By default, all the parameters in the case class's constructor become properties on the case class. Here's how to create a case class:

```
case classStuff(name:String, age: Int)
```

You can create an instance of Stuff without the keyword new (you can use new if you want):

```
scala> vals = Stuff("David", 45)
```

```
s: Stuff = Stuff(David,45)
```

The case class's to String method does the right thing:

```
scala> s.toString
```

```
res70:String = Stuff(David,45)
```

Stuff's equals method does a deep comparison:

```
scala> s == Stuff("David",45)
```

```
res72:Boolean = true
```

```
scala> s == Stuff("David",43)
```

```
res73:Boolean = false
```

And the instance has properties:

```
scala> s.name
```

```
res74:String = David
```

```
scala> s.age
```

```
res75:Int = 45
```

If you want to write your own class that does the same thing as a case class does, it would look like Listing 3-21:

Listing 3-21. Implementing case features in a class on its own

```
classStuff(val name: String,valage: Int) {
overridedeftoString = "Stuff("+name+","+age+")"
overridedefhashCode= name.hashCode+ age
overridedefequals(other: AnyRef)= othermatch {
case s: Stuff=> this.name== s.name &&this.age == s.age
case _ => false
}
}
```

```
objectStuff {
defapply(name: String, age: Int) = newStuff(name,age)
defunapply(s: Stuff)= Some((s.name, s.age))
}
```

Case classes also come in handy for pattern matching, a topic we'll explore in Chapter 6.

Value Classes

In Chapter 2, we described Scala type hierarchy where we showed Any class and its two children AnyRef and AnyVal. We explained that all user-defined classes written in Scala (or Java) extend AnyRef.

With value classes, Scala allows user-defined value classes that extend AnyVal, that is, value classes enable you to write classes on the AnyVal side of the Scala type hierarchy. Value classes are a new mechanism in Scala to avoid allocating runtime objects. Value classes allow you to add extension methods to a type without the runtime overhead of creating instances. This is accomplished through the definition of new AnyVal subclasses. The following illustrates a value class definition:

```
class SomeClass(val underlying: Int) extends AnyVal
```

The preceding SomeClass class has a single, public val parameter that is the underlying runtime representation. The type at compile time is SomeClass, but at runtime, the representation is an Int. A value class can define defs, but no vals, vars, or nested traits classes or objects. Listing 3-22 illustrates a def in the value class SomeClass.

■ **Note**   A value class can only extend a universal trait. We will explain this in Chapter 7.

Listing 3-22. Using def in the value class

```
    class SomeClass(val i: Int) extends AnyVal {
def twice() = i*2
}
```

Here SomeClass is a user-defined value class that wraps the Int parameter and encapsulates a twice method. To invoke the twice method, create the instance of the SomeClass class as follows:

```
scala> val v = new SomeClass(9)
v: SomeClass = SomeClass@9
scala> v.twice()
res5: Int = 18
```

At runtime the expression is optimized to the equivalent of a method class on a static object:

```
SomeClass.twice$extension(9)
You can check this by compiling SomeClass using scalac and then execute the following
command:
javap -v SomeClass
```

Behind the scenes the Scala compiler generates a companion object for the value class and makes the v.twice() calls to the twice$extension method in the companion object. "$extension" is the suffix added to all the methods extracted from the companion class.

One use case for value classes is to combine them with implicit classes. Using an implicit class provides a more convenient syntax for defining extension methods, while value classes remove the runtime overhead. Implicit classes will be described in detail in Chapter 8.

Scala versus Java versus Ruby

Scala, Java, and Ruby are all object-oriented languages. They share many similarities and some differences. In this section, we'll compare and contrast these popular languages.

Classes and Instances

Scala and Ruby are pure object-oriented languages. Everything in each language is an instance of a class. In Java, there are primitives and statics that are outside of the OO model. In Scala and Ruby, all operations on entities are via method calls. In Java, operators are treated differently and are not method calls. The uniformity of instances in Scala means that the developer does not have to perform special tests or to have different code paths to deal with primitive data types (int, char, long, and so on.) The following is legal in Scala:

```scala
scala> 1.hashCode
```

```
res0:Int = 1
```

```scala
scala> 2.toString
```

```
res1:java.lang.String = 2
```

You can define a method that takes a function that transforms an Int to an Int:

```scala
scala> defwith42(in: Int=> Int) = in(42)
```

and pass a function that is applying the +method to 33:

```scala
scala> with42(33+)
```

```
res4:Int = 75
```

At the language level, it's very convenient and easy on the brain and the design to have everything be uniform. Scala and Ruby's pure OO approach achieves this goal. As a side note, you may worry about performance. The Scala compiler optimizes operations on JVM primitives such that the performance of Scala code is nearly identical to the performance of Java code.

Traits, Interfaces, and Mixins

Every Java class, except Object, has a single superclass. Java classes may implement one or more interfaces. An interface is a contract that specifies the methods an implementing class must have. Java has interfaces. Interfaces define a contract for a given class. A class has zero or more interfaces. Interfaces define the methods that the class must implement. Parameters to a method call may be specifically defined as classes or interfaces. Interfaces provide a powerful mechanism for defining the contract that a given class must implement, requiring that a parameter to a method implement particular methods without specifying the concrete class of the parameter. This is the basis for dependency injection, using mocks in testing, and other abstraction patterns.

Scala has traits. Traits provide all the features of Java interfaces. However, Scala traits can contain method implementations and variables. Traits are a great way of implementing methods once and mixing those methods into all the classes that extend the trait.

Ruby has mixins, which are collections of methods that can be mixed into any class. Because Ruby does not have static typing and there is no way to declare the types of method parameters, there's no reasonable way to use mixins to define a contract like interfaces. Ruby mixins provide a mechanism for composing code into classes but not a mechanism for defining or enforcing parameter types.

Object, Static, and Singletons

In Java, a class can have static methods and data. In this way, there is a single point of access to the method, and there's no need to instantiate a class in order to access static methods. Static variables provide global access to the data across the JVM.

Scala provides a similar mechanism in the form of objects. Objects are implementations of the singleton pattern. There is one object instance per class loader. In this way, it's possible to have globally shared state. However, objects adhere to Scala's uniform OO model, and objects are instances of classes rather than some class-level constant. This allows objects to be passed as parameters.

Ruby has a singleton mixin that provides the singleton pattern in Ruby programs. In addition, Ruby also has class-level methods. In Ruby, you can add methods to the class. There is one instance of a class object per class in Ruby. You can add methods and properties to class objects, and those become globally available without instantiating an instance of the class. This provides another mechanism for sharing global state.

Functions, Anonymous Inner Classes, and Lambdas/Procs

The Java construct to pass units of computation as parameters to methods is anonymous inner classes. The use of anonymous inner classes was popularized with the Swing UI libraries. In Swing, most UI events are handled by interfaces that have one or two methods on them. The programmer passes the handlers by instantiating an anonymous inner class that has access to the private data of the enclosing class.

Scala's functions are anonymous inner classes. Scala functions implement a uniform API with the apply method being the thing that's invoked. The syntax for creating functions in Scala is much more economical than the three or four lines of boilerplate for creating anonymous inner classes in Java. Additionally, the rules for accessing variables in the local scope are more flexible in Scala. In Java, an anonymous inner class can only access final variables. In Scala, a function can access and mutate vars.

Ruby has a collection of overlapping features that allow passing blocks, procs, and lambdas as parameters to methods. These constructs have subtle differences in Ruby, but at their core they are chunks of code that reference variables in the scope in which they were created. Ruby also parses blocks such that blocks of code that are passed as parameters in method calls are syntactically identical to code blocks in while and if statements.

Scala has much in common with Ruby in terms of an object model and function passing. Scala has much in common with Java in terms of uniform access to the same code libraries and static typing. Scala has taken the best of both Java and Ruby and blended these things into a very cohesive whole.

Summary

This chapter took you through the OOP constructs of Scala. You learned how class and constructor definition in Scala differs from Java. You also learned several ways of configuring the constructor. You learned several new concepts such as traits and case classes. These concepts will be discussed in detail in subsequent chapters. In the next chapter you will learn the functional aspects of Scala.

CHAPTER 4

Functional Programming in Scala

In the non-fiction work *Old Times on the Mississippi*, Mark Twain wrote: "When I was a boy of 14, my father was so ignorant I could hardly stand to have the old man around. But when I was 21, I was astonished at how much the old man had learned in seven years". Functional programming is the old man that comes to the rescue when writing robust concurrent software. Functional programming treats computation as the evaluation of mathematical functions and avoids state and mutable data. It is a declarative programming paradigm, in which programming is done with expressions. The imperative style of programming emphasizes sequence of operations characterized by iteration with loops, mutating data in place, and methods with side effects where the order of side effects is critical toward the right effect. The basic constructs in an imperative language, such as Java, are imperative statements that change the state of a program, as illustrated here:

```
x = x + 1
```

The functional style of programming emphasizes the results; characterized by passing function values into looping methods, immutable data, and methods with no side effects where the order in which operations occur is of no importance. In a functional language such as Scala, the basic constructs are declarative, as seen here and there are no side effects:

```
f(int x){return x + 1}
```

In functional language, the computation proceeds primarily by evaluation expressions. As a language that supports functional programming, Scala encourages an expression-oriented programming (EOP) model.

Expression-Oriented Programming

In expression-oriented programming every statement is an expression. To understand EOP, you have to understand the difference between a statement and an expression. A statement executes code, but does not return any value, for example:

```
customer.computeDiscount()
```

An expression returns value. Expressions are blocks of code that evaluate to a value as seen here:

```
val discount = computeDiscount(customer)
```

> **Note** An expression-oriented programming language is a programming language where every construct is an expression, and thus evaluates to a value.

In Scala, the following expression returns a result:

```
scala> 2 + 2
res0: Int = 4
```

The strength of expression-oriented programming is more discernible from an if/else expression, which also returns a value in Scala:

```
val test = if (3 > 2) "true" else "false"
```

The preceding if clause checks a conditional expression and returns one expression or another, depending on the value of the conditional expression. An if block in Java does not evaluate to a value. The code as illustrated here is illegal in Java, in contrast to Scala, because the if clause in Java is a statement, not an expression.

```
boolean test = if (3 > 2) "true" else "false"
```

To accomplish the same effect shown in the Scala if clause, you have to use the ?: syntax in Java as illustrated here:

```
boolean test = 3 > 2 ? true : false ;
```

In Java, there is a difference between if and ?:—if is a statement while ?: is an expression. The if clause in Scala is much more like ?: in Java than the if clause in Java. Scala has unified the concept of ?: with its if blocks and so Scala has no ?: syntax.

> **Note** As mentioned earlier, every construct in Scala is an expression where the order in which operations occur is of no importance and therefore these expressions can be executed in any order. This simple concept has a deep implication in concurrency in multicore programming where you can execute expressions in parallel. We explore concurrency in Chapter 10.

A Pure Function

In mathematics, functions are nothing short of pure, in that they lack side effects. Consider the classic functions in(x):

```
y = sin(x).
```

Regardless of how many times sin(x) gets called, sin(x) does not modify the state. Such a function is called a pure function and is oblivious to the context. This obliviousness to the surrounding context is known as *referential transparency*.

Referential Transparency

An expression is referentially transparent if it can be substituted by its resulting value, without changing the behavior of the program, regardless of where the expression is used in the program. For instance, you can assign the expression of two immutable variables x and y to a third variable z, like this:

```
val z = x + y
```

Now, anywhere the expression x + y is used throughout the given scope of your program, you can substitute it by z within that scope, without affecting the result of the program. As stated before, functional programming gives you the right foundation to think about concurrency. The three keystones of this foundation are: referential transparency, higher-order function, and immutable value. Understanding these key elements is crucial to understanding functional programming. In functional programming, a pure function with one or more input parameters, does not mutate the input parameters and always returns the same value for the same input.

■ **Note**   A pure function is referentially transparent and has no side effects.

A pure function is free of side-effects, however, a function that never cause side effects would be useless. A language that does not sanction side effects would be useless, as input and output is essentially the ramification of side effects.

We have introduced sufficient theory for you to begin to explore Scala functions. In Chapter 2, you learned the basic syntax of Scala functions and how you can declare, define, and call functions. Before continuing with the sections that follow in this chapter, we recommend you skim through the Scala functions introduced in Chapter 2.

Now we will get started with a basic functional construct in Scala—the function literal.

Function Literal/Anonymous Function

A literal is the simplest form of expression. A literal is a notation for representing a fixed value in source code. Almost all programming languages have notations for atomic values such as integers, floating-point numbers, strings, and so on. Literals are often used to initialize variables. In the following, 1 is an integer literal:

```
int x = 1;
```

Scala, allows you to express functions as literals. Function literals allow you to have an expression of a function type that you can write in a short format without declaring a name for it. A function type could be one of the following:

- The type of a variable or parameter to which a function can be assigned

- An argument of a higher-order function taking a function parameter

- The result type of higher-order function returning a function

The syntax for a function literal starts with a parenthesized comma–separated list of arguments followed by an arrow and the body of the function. A function literal is also called an anonymous function, that is, a function without any name specified with function literal syntax. Consider an add function:

```
val add = (x: Int, y: Int) => x + y
```

Using the function literal you can define the add function as illustrated here:

```
(x: Int, y: Int) => x + y.
```

A function literal is instantiated into objects called *function values*. A function value is a function object and you can invoke the function object in the same manner as you invoke any other function. The function object extends one of the FunctionN traits, such as Function0, Function1, and so on up to Function22. Depending on the number of arguments in the function, the corresponding FunctionN trait is chosen by the compiler. For a function with two arguments, the compiler elects Function2 as the underlying type. For a function with 3 arguments compiler chooses Function3 , for a function with 4 arguments, Function4 and so on.

Because the function value is an object, it could be stored in a variable and it could be invoked using the parentheses function-call as illustrated here:

```
scala> val add = (a: Int, b: Int) => a + b
add: (Int, Int) => Int = <function2>
scala>add(1, 2)
res23: Int = 3
```

The invocation of this function is converted to a call to the apply method of the function class instance, which is assigned to the variable.

From these kind of function literals the Scala compiler generates a function object that mixes in one of the FunctionN traits—the left side of the → becomes the parameter list and the right side becomes the implementation of the apply method. Every function that you define in Scala becomes an instance of an implementation that features a certain FunctionN Trait ranging from Function1 up to Function22.

Now, to take a deeper look into Function traits we first write a function that calculates the area of a rectangle as illustrated here:

```
val areaOfRectangle:(Int, Int) => Int = (width:Int, height:Int) => {
width*height
}
```

When you run this function in REPL you will see that compiler elects and chooses the Function2 Trait for this function. Why? Simply because there are two arguments to this function.

```
scala> val areaOfRectangle:(Int, Int) => Int = (width:Int, height:Int) => {
     |   width*height
     | }
areaOfRectangle: (Int, Int) => Int = <function2>
```

You can invoke this function as seen here:

```
scala> areaOfRectangle(5,3)
res01: Int = 15
```

Now, let's take a look at Trait scala.Function2 in the Scala package:

```
trait Function2[-T1, -T2, +R] extends AnyRef {
    ...
abstract def apply( v1 :T1, v2 :T2 ) : R
    ...
}
```

This shows only the apply method. The two type parameters T1, T2 in the apply method take the type of the arguments, while type parameter R represents the function's return type.

For every function that you define in Scala, the compiler comes up with an instance of the appropriate Function Trait, where the type parameters are parameterized with the given types of the arguments and the return type of the function.

In the areaOfRectangle function we defined earlier, the type of areaOfRectangle function is

```
(Int, Int)  =>Int
```

This is same as illustrated here:

```
Function2[Int,Int,Int]
```

So we could have also defined our add function this way:

```
val areaOfRectangle:  Function2[Int,Int,Int]  = (width:Int, height:Int) => { width*height }
```

You can test this on REPL as seen here:

```
scala> val areaOfRectangle:  Function2[Int,Int,Int]  = (width:Int, height:Int) => { width*height }
areaOfRectangle: (Int, Int) => Int = <function2>
```

Now, you could explicitly call the method apply on a given function as illustrated:

```
areaOfRectangle.apply(5,3)
```

You can test this on REPL as illustrated here:

```
scala> val area = areaOfRectangle.apply(5,3)
area: Int = 15
```

You could go a step further and define a function by implementing an appropriate Function Trait and define its required apply method. Let's do this for the areaOfRectangle function:

```scala
val areaOfRectangle :(Int, Int) => Int = new Function2[Int, Int, Int]{
        def apply(width:Int, height:Int):Int = {
                width*height
        }
}
```

You can test this on REPL as seen here:

```scala
scala> areaOfRectangle(5,3)
res18: Int = 15
```

Now that you have learned function values and function types, you will see how you can use a function literal to pass it into a method that takes a function, or to assign it to a variable. Now we will discuss these in detail in the following section.

First Class Function and Higher Order Function

One of the key factors in Scala that beautifully blends functional paradigm into object-oriented paradigm is that functions are objects. In functional programming, functions are first-class citizens. A first-class function is a function that can be

1.   Assigned to variables,

2.   Passed as an argument to the *other function*, and

3.   Returned as values from the *other function*.

The *other function* emphasized in point 2 that takes a function as an argument and the *other function* emphasized in point 3 that returns a function, are called higher-order functions. In the sections that follow, you will learn about all three aspects of a first class function.

Note   In functional programming, functions are first-class citizens, meaning functions can be assigned to variables, functions can be passed to other functions, and functions can be returned as values from other functions. And such functions, which take functions as arguments or return a function, are called higher-order functions.

Function as Variable

Just as you pass String, Int, and other variables around in an OOP, you can pass a function around like a variable. You can define a function literal, and then assign that literal to a variable. The following code defines a function literal that takes an Int parameter and returns a value that is twice the amount of the Int that is passed in:

```
(i: Int) => { i * 2 }
```

You can now assign that function literal to a variable:

```
val doubler = (i: Int) => { i * 2 }
```

```
scala> val doubler = (i: Int) => { i * 2 }
doubler: Int => Int = <function1>
```

The variable doubler is an instance of a function, known as a function value. You can now invoke doubler as illustrated here:

```
doubler(2)
```

```
scala> doubler(2)
res25: Int = 4
```

Under the hood, doubler is an instance of the Function1 trait, which defines a function that takes one argument. In terms of implementation, doubler is a function created using the keyword val and assigned to a variable. To define the doubler as a method instead of as a function you have to define the doubler method in a class, and use the keyword def to define a method.

Beyond just invoking doubler, you can also pass it to any function (or method) that takes a function parameter. We will discuss this in the following section.

Function as Parameter

You can create a function or a method that takes a function as a parameter. For this, first define a method that takes a function as a parameter.

```
def operation(functionparam:(Int, Int) => Int) {
println(functionparam(4,4))
}
```

```
scala> def operation(functionparam:(Int, Int) => Int) {
     |  println(functionparam(4,4))
     | }
operation: (functionparam: (Int, Int) => Int)Unit
```

The operation method takes one parameter named functionparam, which is a function. The functionparam function takes two Int and returns an Int. The operation method returns a Unit that indicates that operation method returns nothing.

Next, define a function that matches the expected signature. The following add function matches that signature, because it takes two Int arguments and returns an Int:

```
val add = (x: Int, y:Int) => { x + y }
```

Now you can pass an add function into the operation method:

```
operation(add)
```

```
scala> operation(add)
8
```

Any function that matches this signature can be passed into the operation method. Let's define two new functions named subtract and multiply that take two Int and return an Int:

```
val subtract = (x: Int, y:Int) => { x - y }
val multiply = (x: Int, y:Int) => { x*y }
```

Now you can pass these functions into your operation method:

```
operation(subtract)
```

```
scala> operation(subtract)
0
```

```
operation(multiply)
```

```
scala> operation(multiply)
16
```

Returning a Function

You can return a function from a function or method. In order to do this, first define an anonymous function.
The following code declares an anonymous function that takes a String argument and returns a String:

```
(name: String) => { "hello" + " " + name }
```

Now we will define a method that returns the anonymous function that we just defined.

```
def greeting() = (name: String) => {"hello" + " " + name}
```

On the left side of the = symbol you have a normal method declaration:

```
def greeting()
```

On the right side of the = is a function literal (an anonymous function):

```
(name: String) => {"hello" + " " + name}
```

```
scala> def greeting() = (name: String) => {"hello" + " " + name}
greeting: ()String => String
```

Now you can assign greeting() to a variable:

```
val greet= greeting()
```

```
scala>  val greet= greeting()
greet: String => String = <function1>
```

The greet function is now equivalent to your anonymous function (name: String) =>
{"hello" + " " + name}.

Because the anonymous function takes a String parameter name, you can pass it a name:

```
greet("Reader")
```

```
scala> greet("Reader")
res26: String = hello Reader
```

Closure

A *closure* is a function, whose return value depends on the value of one or more variables declared outside this function. Consider the following multiplier function:

```
val multiplier = (x:Int) => x * 3
```

In the multiplier function, i is the variable used in the function body. x is defined as a parameter to the function. Now let's modify the multiplier function as illustrated here:

```
val multiplier = (x:Int) => x * y
```

Because is a formal parameter to the function, it is bound to a new value each time multiplier is called. However, j is not a formal parameter. Let's further modify the multiplier function as illustrated:

```
var y = 3
val multiplier = (x:Int) => x * y
```

Now, y has a reference to a variable outside the function but in the enclosing scope.

```scala
scala> var y = 3
y: Int = 3
scala> val multiplier = (x:Int) => x * y
multiplier: Int => Int = <function1>
```

Now you can invoke the multiplier function as illustrated here:

```scala
multiplier(3)
```

```scala
scala> multiplier(3)
res37: Int = 9
```

The multiplier function references j and reads its current value each time. The Scala compiler creates a closure (closes over) that encompasses the variable in the enclosing scope.

Partially Applied Function

In functional programming languages, when you call a function that has parameters, you are said to be applying the function to the parameters. When all the parameters are passed to the function you have fully applied the function to all the parameters.

A simple add function:

```scala
val add = (x: Int, y: Int) => x + y
```

```scala
scala> val add = (x: Int, y: Int) => x + y
add: (Int, Int) => Int = <function2>
```

<function2> indicates it is a function of two parameters.

```scala
scala> add(1,2)
res01: Int = 3
```

But when you give only a subset of the parameters to the function, the result of the expression is a partially applied function.

```scala
val partiallyAdd = add(1, _:Int)
```

Because you haven't provided a value for the second parameter, the variable partiallyAdd is a partially applied function. You can see this in the REPL:

```scala
scala> val partiallyAdd = add(1, _:Int)
partiallyAdd: Int => Int = <function1>
```

The output in the REPL shows that partiallyAdd is a function that implements the Function1 trait. Implemeting a Function1 trait indicates that partiallyAdd function takes one argument. When you give partiallyAdd an Int value 2, you get the sum of the Int number passed into the add and partiallyAdd functions:

```
scala> partiallyAdd(2)
res02: Int = 3
```

The first argument 1 was passed into the original add function and the new function named partiallyAdd was created, which is a partially applied function; then, the second argument 2 was passed into partiallyAdd. When you provide all the parameters, the original function is executed, yielding the result.

Curried Function

Currying converts a function with multiple parameters creating a chain of function, each expecting a single parameter.

Let's look at a simple add function that adds two Int parameters, a and b, as illustrated here:

```
val add = (x: Int, y: Int) => x + y
```

```
scala> val add = (x: Int, y: Int) => x + y
add: (Int, Int) => Int = <function2>
scala> add(3,3)
res38: Int = 6
```

In Scala, curried functions are defined with multiple parameter lists, as follows:

```
def add(x: Int)(y: Int) = x + y
```

You can also use the following syntax to define a curried function:

```
def add(x: Int) = (y: Int) => x + y
```

As you can see, instead of one list of two Int parameters, you apply the curried add function to two lists of one Int parameter. Thus the curried add function looks like this:

```
scala> def curriedAdd(a: Int)(b: Int) = a + b
curriedAdd: (a: Int)(b: Int)Int
scala> curriedAdd(2)(2)
res1: Int = 4
```

You could define more than two parameters on a curried function. Our add function that takes two arguments, is transformed into its curried equivalent.

Function Composition

In functional programming, you can compose functions from other functions. For example, tan(x) = sin(x)/cos(x). An implication of composability is that functions can be treated as values. So far, we've created simple functions and manipulated the function instances. However, we can also build functions from other functions. Functional composition provides the basis for a lot of cool things in Scala, including the parser combinator, which we will explore in Chapter 8. But for now, let's see the difference between interpreting a series of commands and "compiling" a function that interprets them. First, let's define a grammar. In our grammar, we have expressions, which can be constant values or named variables. Expressions can also be addition or multiplication of other expressions. Here's a collection of case classes that describes our grammar (recall that we covered case classes in Chapter 2):

```
sealed trait Expr
case class Add(left: Expr, right: Expr) extends Expr
case class Mul(left: Expr, right: Expr) extends Expr
case class Val(value: Int) extends Expr
case class Var(name: String) extends Expr
```

We can build expressions like 1 + 1, Add(Val(1), Val(1)), 3 * (1 + 1), Mul(Val(3), Add(Val(1), Val(1))), and a * 11, Mul(Var("a"), Val(11)).

We can evaluate an expression by interpreting the expression:

```
def calc(expr: Expr, vars: Map[String, Int]): Int = expr match {
case Add(left, right) => calc(left, vars) + calc(right, vars)
case Mul(left, right) => calc(left, vars) * calc(right, vars)
case Val(v) => v
case Var(name) => vars(name)
}
```

Let's look at how this method works. expr is the expression to evaluate, and vars is a Map that contains our variables. We use pattern matching to determine what to do based on the case class. If expr is an Add, we extract the left and right parameters, which are themselves Exprs. We call calc to calculate the value of the left and right parameters and add the results. If expr is Mul, we do the same thing (except we multiply things rather than adding them). If expr is Val, we simply extract the value and return it. If expr is Var, we extract the name and return the lookup of the name in the vars Map. We can turn this from a method call into a function. Having a function allows us to pass around the logic that the expression represents. It also means that we don't have to interpret the tree of Exprs each time. Let's see how we can compose a function based on the Expr.

```
def buildCalc(expr: Expr): Map[String, Int] => Int = expr match {
case Add(left, right) =>
val lf = buildCalc(left)
val rf = buildCalc(right)
m => lf(m) + rf(m)
case Mul(left, right) =>
val lf = buildCalc(left)
val rf = buildCalc(right)
m => lf(m) * rf(m)
case Val(v) => m => v
case Var(name) => m => m(name)
}
```

The buildCalc method returns a function that can be passed to other functions. Also, the JVM can optimize the composed functions so that they perform better than the interpreted version. The performance of the composed function is better because there is no overhead associated with pattern matching each element. The function is evaluated by repeatedly calling the function's apply method. Thus, the cost of each node is one or two method dispatches rather than the cost of the pattern matching. Let's turn to other ways that functions can help us improve performance and readability.

Tail Calls and Tail Call Optimization

A *recursive function* is one that may invoke itself. Recursion plays a crucial role in functional programming because it offers a way to iterate over data structures using mutable data, since each function call has its own stack for storing function parameters. One classic example of a recursion can be seen in the implementation of factorial as shown:

```
scala> def factorial(number:Int) : Int = {
     |     if (number == 1)
     |         return 1
     |     number * factorial (number - 1)
     | }
factorial: (number: Int)Int
```

You can call this function as shown here:

```
scala> println(factorial(3))
6
```

One problem associated with using recursive functions is that invoking a recursive function too many times leads to stack-overflow error. The Scala compiler can optimize recursive functions with tail recursion so that recursive calls do not use all the stack space, therefore not running into stack-overflow error. The tail-recursion is a specific kind of recursion that occurs when a function calls itself as its final operation. With tail-recursion-optimized functions, recursive invocation doesn't create a new stack but instead uses the current function's stack. Only functions whose last statement is the recursive invocation can be optimized for tail-recursion by the Scala compiler.

Next is the implementation of factorial, calculated with tail-call recursion. To facilitate tail-call optimization, Scala provides an annotation available to mark a function to be optimized for tail-recursion. A function marked with the tail-recursion function annotation causes an error at compilation time if it cannot be optimized for tail-recursion. To mark a function to be optimized for tail-recursion, add @annotation.tailrec before the function definition.

Now mark the `factorial` function shown earlier with `@annotation.tailrec` to instruct the Scala compiler that this function must be optimized for tail-recursion and that if annotated function cannot be optimized for tail-recursion, the compiler should treat it as an error.

```
scala> @annotation.tailrec
     | def factorial(number:Int) : Int = {
     |     if (number == 1)
     |         return 1
     |     number * factorial (number - 1)
     | }
<console>:12: error: could not optimize @tailrec annotated method factorial: it contains a
recursive call not in tail positionnumber * factorial (number - 1)^
```

As you can see, Scala compiler throws an error. The `factorial` method can't be optimized because the recursive call is not the last statement in the function; the factorial calls itself and then performs multiplication with the result, so actually multiplication is the last statement in the function, not the recursive call. A function can't be optimized for tail-recursion if the result of invoking itself is used for anything but the direct return value

The factorial method marked with `@annotation.tailrec` will not compile successfully until recursion is the final operation. So we need to perform the multiplication operation before invoking the `factorial` method for which we use accumulator argument to hold the computation in progress. This argument is computed with a multiplication before the recursive call. Thus recursion is a final operation.

```
scala> @annotation.tailrec
     | def factorial(accumulator: Int, number: Int) : Int = {
     |   if(number == 1)
     |     return accumulator
     |   factorial(number * accumulator, number - 1)
     | }
factorial: (accumulator: Int, number: Int)Int
```

A successful compile guarantees that the function will be optimized with tail recursion, so that each successive call will not add new stack frames.

```
scala> println(factorial(1,3))
6
```

Call-by-Name, Call-by-Value, and General Laziness

In Java programs, when you call a method with parameters, the value of the parameters are all calculated before the method is called. Thus, in

```
foo(1 + 1, "A String".length());
```

The expressions 1 + 1 and "A String".length() are both evaluated before the call to foo is made. This is usually what you want. However, there are some cases when you want to parameters to be optionally evaluated or repeatedly evaluated. In these cases, Scala provides the call-by-name mechanism. There's no syntactic difference to the caller for call-by-name parameters.

The first example for call-by-name is the logging example. It's computationally costly to calculate log messages simply to discard them if the message is not going to be logged. This is very common in Java code:

```
if (logger.level().intValue() >= INFO.intValue()) {
logger.log(INFO, "The value is "+value);
}
```

In this code, we have to push the decision to evaluate logger.log(INFO, "The value is "+value); into the place where we call logger. This means we need to wrap the call to logger in an if statement. It would be much better from a coding perspective if the cost of evaluating the String to be logged were incurred only if the String is going to be logged *and* if the current log level is known to and tested by the code inside logger rather than in the call to logger. Call-by-name gives us the ability to delay the evaluation of the String to log only if that String will actually be logged.

In Scala, we can define a log method that takes the thing to log as call-by-name:

```
def log(level: Level, msg: => String) =
if (logger.level.intValue >= level.intValue) logger.log(level, msg)
```

And you would call this code:

```
log(INFO, "The value is "+value)
```

The Scala version passes "The value is "+value as a function that is evaluated each time it is accessed in the log method. The log method will access it only if the log message is going to be printed. Your code is cleaner because you don't have to repeatedly test the log level, but it performs as well as the previous Java code that has the inline test. In order to make something call-by-name, just put => before the type. So, foo(s: String) is call-by-reference, and foo(s: => String) is call-by-name.

You may be wondering how the code could possibly perform as well if a function object is being created and handed off to the log method. In the JVM, the cost of creating an object that never escapes the current thread and is very short-lived is zero or very near zero. The JVM may also inline the log method such that the test is performed without an actual method call. The result is that your code will run as quickly with the Scala code as it will with the Java code that has the repeated test for log level. The first use of call-by-name is passing an expression that takes a long time to evaluate that may not be evaluated. The second use for call-by-name is the situation where we want to evaluate the expression many times in the target method, for example, if we want to evaluate an expression until some condition is met. That condition could be until the expression returns false or until the expression returns null. For example, we could collect all the Strings returned from an expression until we encounter a null:

```
def allStrings(expr: => String): List[String] = expr match {
case null => Nil
case s => s :: allStrings(expr)
}
```

We can test this method:

```
scala> import java.io._
```

```
import java.io._
```

```
scala> val br = new BufferedReader(new FileReader("foo.txt"))
```

```
br: java.io.BufferedReader = jaferedReva.io.Bufader@2bfa91
```

```
scala> allStrings(br.readLine)
```

```
res0: List[String] = List(import scala.xml._, , object Morg {,...)
```

Each time the call-by-name parameter, expr, is accessed, it is applied. If it is passed as a parameter that is also call-by-name, it will be passed without evaluation. In the previous code, you pattern match against the application of expr. If it's null, return an empty List, a Nil. If it's not null, return a List that is the current String and the result of allStrings(expr).

Summary

You saw Scala functions in action in the Chapter 2 where you declared, defined and called functions. As a continuation to the brief introduction in Chapter 2, this chapter provided a detailed treatment on functional programming in Scala, introducing several functional constructs of Scala as a functional programming language. In the next chapter you will learn pattern matching with Scala.

CHAPTER 5

■ ■ ■

Pattern Matching

So far, we've explored some of the basic functional cornerstones of Scala: immutable data types and the passing of functions as parameters. The third cornerstone of functional programming is pattern matching. Pattern matching provides a powerful tool for declaring business logic in a concise and maintainable way. Scala blends traditional functional programming pattern matching with object-oriented concepts to provide a very powerful mechanism for writing programs. In this chapter, we're going to explore the basics of pattern matching. Then we're going to see how Scala's case classes bridge between object-oriented data encapsulation and function decomposition. Next, we'll see how Scala's pattern-matching constructs become functions that can be passed around and composed. Let's look at the simple example first.

Basic Pattern Matching

Pattern matching allows you to make a programmatic choice between multiple conditions, such as, in the case boolean x is true, print a "true" message; in the case that x is false, print a "false" message. However, let this simple example not beguile you into underestimating the true power of Scala's pattern matching. Scala's pattern matching allows your cases to be far more complex than merely the case whether x is true or false. In Scala, your cases can include types, wildcards, sequences, regular expressions, and so forth. Let's start with a simple example: printing numbers as shown in Listing 5-1.

Listing 5-1. Printing Numbers

```
def printNum(int: Int) {
  int match {
    case 0 => println("Zero")
    case 1 => println("One")
    case _ => println("more than one")
  }
}
```

```
scala> printNum(0)
Zero
scala> printNum(1)
One
scala> printNum(2)
more than one
```

As you can see, there are no big ideas in Listing 5-1—it just prints numbers zero, one, or more than one. However, one thing you notice is the last case with the underscore (_) wildcard. It matches anything not defined in the cases above it, so it serves the same purpose as the default keyword in Java and C# switch statements. However, if you are unfamiliar with switch statement in Java or C#, don't worry, it just means that if you try to put a case _before any other case clauses, the compiler will throw an unreachable code error on the next clause as shown in Listing 5-2, because nothing will get past the case _clause so case _serves as default.

Listing 5-2. case _Before Any Other Case Clauses

```
def printNum(int: Int) {
 int match {
  case _ => println("more than one")
  case 0 => println("Zero")
  case 1 => println("One")

 }
}
```

```
<console>:10: warning: unreachable code
          case 0 => println("Zero")
                    ^
```

If you're curious about how the Scala compiler expands a pattern into code, you can use the -print option in the Scala compiler. Create the PrintNum.scala program (see Listing 5-3).

Listing 5-3. PrintNum.scala

```
object PrintNum {
def printNum(int: Int) {
 int match {
  case 0 => println("Zero")
  case 1 => println("One")
  case _ => println("more than one")
  }
}

}
```

Compile it with the following line:

```
scalac -print PrintNum.scala
```

The result follows:

```
package <empty> {
  object PrintNum extends Object {
    def printNum(int: Int): Unit = {
      case <synthetic> val x1: Int = int;
      (x1: Int) match {
        case 0 => scala.this.Predef.println("Zero")
        case 1 => scala.this.Predef.println("One")
        case _ => scala.this.Predef.println("more than one")
      }
    };
    def <init>(): PrintNum.type = {
      PrintNum.super.<init>();
      ()
    }
  }
}
```

Pattern matching, at its core, is a complex set of if/else expressions that lets you select from a number of alternatives. At first glance, if we are allowed to unabashedly assume that you are from Java background, pattern matching looks a lot like Java's switch statement but you will notice several key differences in even a simplest case. Let's analyze this by writing one example using both Scala's pattern matching and Java's switch statement. Listing 5-4 illustrates the example of calculating Fibonacci numbers.

Listing 5-4. Fibonacci Numbers Using Scala's Pattern Matching

```
def fibonacci(in: Int): Int = in match {
  case 0 => 0
  case 1 => 1
  case n => fibonacci(n - 1) + fibonacci(n - 2)
}
```

Let's write the same code in Java as illustrated in Listing 5-5.

Listing 5-5. Java Equivalent of Listing 5-4

```
public int fibonacci(int in) {
  switch (in) {
    case 0:
     return 0;

    case 1:
     return 1;
    default:
     return fibonacci(in - 1) + fibonacci(in - 2);
  }
}
```

You will notice the following differences bewteen Listing 5-4 and Listing 5-5.

- There's no break statement between cases in Scala, where you need break or return at the end of the case in Java.

- The last case in Scala assigns the default value to the variable n. Pattern matching in Scala is also an expression that returns a value.

- In Scala, we can have multiple tests on a single line:

```
case 0 | -1 | -2 => 0
```

That code corresponds to the following in Java:

```
case 0:
case -1:
case -2:
return 0;
```

We just pointed out several key differences in the Fibonacci example written using both Scala's pattern matching and Java's switch statement.

We will now show it gets even better with Scala's pattern matching by modifying Listing 5-4.

Scala allows guards to be placed in patterns to test for particular conditions that cannot be tested in the pattern declaration itself. Thus, we can write our Fibonacci calculator to return 0 if a negative number is passed in as in Listing 5-6.

Listing 5-6. Using Guards in Pattern Matching

```
def fib2(in: Int): Int = in match {
  case n if n <= 0 => 0
  case 1 => 1
  case n => fib2(n - 1) + fib2(n - 2)
}
```

case n if n <= 0 => 0is the first test in the pattern. The test extracts the value into the variable n and tests n to see whether it's zero or negative and returns 0 in that case. Guards are very helpful as the amount of logic gets more complex. Note that the case statements are evaluated in the order that they appear in the code. Thus, case n if n <= 0 => is tested before case n =>. Under the hood, the compiler may optimize the pattern and minimize the number of tests, cache test results, and even cache guard results.

Matching Any Type

Let's consider a list of Any type of element, containing a String, a Double, an Int, and a Char (see Listing 5-7).

Listing 5-7. List of Any Types

```
val anyList= List(1, "A", 2, 2.5, 'a')
```

We decide to let the user know of the Int, String, and Double type from the List using the code in Listing 5-8.

Listing 5-8. Matching Elements of Different Types in a List

```scala
scala> for (m <- anyList) {
 m match {
 case i: Int => println("Integer: " + i)
 case s: String => println("String: " + s)
 case f: Double => println("Double: " + f)
case other => println("other: " + other)
 }
 }
```

```
Integer: 1
String: A
Integer: 2
Double: 2.5
other: a
```

Listing 5-8 has a deep implication as you will learn in the section that follows.

Testing Data Types

Let's write a method that tests an incoming Object to see whether it's a String, an Integer, or something else. Depending on what type it is, different actions will be performed as illustrated in Listing 5-9.

Listing 5-9. Matching Elements of Different Types in a List

```scala
def test2(in: Any) = in match {
case s: String => "String, length "+s.length
case i: Int if i > 0 => "Natural Int"
case i: Int => "Another Int"
case a: AnyRef => a.getClass.getName
case _ => "null"
}
```

The first line tests for a `String`. If it is a `String`, the parameter is cast into a String and assigned to the s variable, and the expression on the right of the => is returned. Note that if the parameter is null, it will not match any pattern that compares to a type. On the next line, the parameter is tested as an `Int`. If it is an `Int`, the parameter is cast to an `Int`, assigned to i, and the guard is tested. If the `Int` is a natural number (greater than zero), "`Natural Int`" will be returned. In this way, Scala pattern matching replaces Java's test/cast paradigm. Now to fully appreciate the power of pattern matching in Scala, we will see the Java equivalent of Listing 5-9.

Listing 5-10. Java Equivalent of Listing 5-9

```java
public String test2(Object in) {
if (in == null) {
return "null";
}
if (in instanceof String) {
String s = (String) in;
return "String, length " + s.length();
}
```

```
if (in instanceof Integer) {
int i = ((Integer) in).intValue();
if (i > 0) {
return "Natural Int";
}
return "Another Int";
}
return in.getClass().getName();
}
```

In the Java equivalent code in Listing 5-10, there is a separation between the instance of test and the casting operation. This often results in bugs when a block of test/cast code is copied and pasted. There's no compiler check that the instance of test matches the cast, and it's not uncommon to have a mismatch between the test and the cast in Java code that's been copied and pasted. The same code in Scala is shorter, and there's no explicit casting. Pattern matching is a powerful way to avoid explicit casting.

Pattern Matching in Lists

Scala's pattern matching can also be applied to Lists. Scala's List collection is implemented as a linked list where the head of the list is called a cons cell.

Note   The naming of the cons cell traces its roots back to Lisp and came from the act of constructing a list. One constructs a list by linking a cons cell to the head of the list.

It contains a reference to its contents and another reference to the tail of the list, which may be another cons cell or the Nil object. Lists are immutable, so the same tail can be shared by many different heads. In Scala, the cons cell is represented by the ::case class. Perhaps you have just said, "Ah hah!" Creating a List is Scala is as simple as this:

```
1 :: Nil
```

:: is the name of the method and the name of a case class. By keeping the creation method, ::, and the case class name the same, we can construct and pattern match Lists in a syntactically pleasing way. And as we've just seen, case classes can be used in pattern matching to either compare or extract values. This holds for Lists as well and leads to some very pleasing syntax.

We construct a List with

```
scala> val x = 1
```

```
x: Int = 1
```

```
scala> val rest = List(2,3,4)
```

```
rest: List[Int] = List(2, 3, 4)
```

```
scala> x :: rest
```

```
res1: List[Int] = List(1, 2, 3, 4)
```

```
scala> (x :: rest) match { // note the symmetry between creation and matching
         case xprime :: restprime => println(xprime); println(restprime)
         }
```

```
1
List(2, 3, 4)
```

Then we can extract the head (x) and tail (rest) of the List in pattern matching.

Pattern Matching and Lists

Pattern matching and Lists go hand in hand. We can start off using pattern matching to sum up all the odd Ints in a List[Int] (see Listing 5-11).

Listing 5-11. Using Pattern Matching to Sum Up All the Odd Ints

```
def sumOdd(in: List[Int]): Int = in match {
  case Nil => 0
  case x :: rest if x % 2 == 1 => x + sumOdd(rest)
  case _ :: rest => sumOdd(rest)
}
```

If the list is empty, Nil, then we return 0. The next case extracts the first element from the list and tests it to see whether it's odd. If it is, we add it to the sum of the rest of the odd numbers in the list. The default case is to ignore the first element of the list (a match with the _wildcard) and return the sum of the odd numbers in the rest of the list.

Extracting the head of a list is useful, but when pattern matching against List, we can match against any number of elements in the List. In this example, we will replace any number of contiguous identical items with just one instance of that item:

```
def noPairs[T](in: List[T]): List[T] = in match {
  case Nil => Nil
  case a :: b :: rest if a == b => noPairs(a :: rest)
    // the first two elements in the list are the same, so we'll
    // call noPairs with a List that excludes the duplicate element
  case a :: rest => a :: noPairs(rest)
    // return a List of the first element followed by noPairs
    // run on the rest of the List
}
```

Let's run the code and see whether it does what we expect:

```
scala> noPairs(List(1,2,3,3,3,4,1,1))
```

```
res6: List[Int] = List(1, 2, 3, 4, 1)
```

Pattern matching can match against constants as well as extract information. Say we have a List[String] and we want to implement a rule that says that we discard the element preceding the "ignore" String. In this case, we'll use pattern matching to test as well as extract:

```
def ignore(in: List[String]): List[String] = in match {
  case Nil => Nil
  case _ :: "ignore" :: rest => ignore(rest)
    // If the second element in the List is "ignore" then return the ignore
    // method run on the balance of the List
  case x :: rest => x :: ignore(rest)
    // return a List created with the first element of the List plus the
    // value of applying the ignore method to the rest of the List
}
```

We've seen how to use pattern matching and Lists with extraction and equality testing. We can also use the class test/cast mechanism to find all the Strings in a List[Any]:

```
def getStrings(in: List[Any]): List[String] = in match {
  case Nil => Nil
  case (s: String) :: rest => s :: getStrings(rest)
  case _ :: rest => getStrings(rest)
}
```

However, the paradigmatic way of filtering a List[Any] into a List of a particular type is by using a pattern as a function. We'll see this in the "Pattern Matching As Functions" section.

In this section, we've explored how to do pattern matching. We've seen extraction and pattern matching with Lists. It may seem that List is a special construct in Scala, but there's nothing special about List in Scala.

Pattern Matching and Case Classes

Case classes are classes that get to String, hashCode, and equals methods automatically. It turns out that they also get properties and extractors. Case classes also have properties and can be constructed without using the new keyword.

Let's define a case class:

```
case class Person(name: String, age: Int, valid: Boolean)
```

Let's create an instance of Person:

```
scala> val p = Person("David", 45, true)
```

```
p: Person = Person(David,45,true)
```

You may use new to create a person as well:

```
scala> val m = new Person("Martin", 44, true)
```

```
m: Person = Person(Martin,44,true)
```

Each of the Person instances has properties that correspond to the constructor parameters:

```
scala> p.name
```

```
res0: String = David
```

```
scala> p.age
```

```
res1: Int = 45
```

```
scala> p.valid
```

```
res2: Boolean = true
```

By default, the properties are read-only, and the case class is immutable.

```
scala> p.name = "Fred"
```

```
<console>:7: error: reassignment to val
p.name = "Fred"
```

You can also make properties mutable:

```
scala> case class MPerson(var name: String, var age: Int)
```

```
defined class MPerson
```

```
scala> val mp = MPerson("Jorge", 24)
```

```
mp: MPerson = MPerson(Jorge,24)
```

```
scala> mp.age = 25
scala> mp
```

```
res3: MPerson = MPerson(Jorge,25)
```

So far, this is just some syntactic sugar. How, you ask, does it work with pattern matching?

Pattern matching against case classes is syntactically pleasing and very powerful. We can match against our Person class, and we get the extractors for free:

```
def older(p: Person): Option[String] = p match {
  case Person(name, age, true) if age > 35 => Some(name)
  case _ => None
}
```

Our method matches against instances of Person. If the valid field is true, the age is extracted and compared against a guard. If the guard succeeds, the person's name is returned, otherwise None is returned. Let's try it out:

```
scala> older(p)
```

```
res4: Option[String] = Some(David)
```

```
scala> older(Person("Fred", 73, false))
```

```
res5: Option[String] = None
```

```
scala> older(Person("Jorge", 24, true))
```

```
res6: Option[String]
```

Nested Pattern Matching in Case Classes

Case classes can contain other case classes, and the pattern matching can be nested. Further, case classes can subclass other case classes. For example, let's create the MarriedPerson subclass of Person:

```
case class MarriedPerson(override val name: String,
override val age: Int,
override val valid: Boolean,
spouse: Person) extends Person(name, age, valid)
```

We've defined the class. Note that the override val syntax is ugly. It's one of the ugliest bits in Scala. And let's create a new instance of MarriedPerson:

```
scala> val sally = MarriedPerson("Sally", 24, true, p)
```

```
sally: MarriedPerson = MarriedPerson(Sally,24,true,Person(David,45,true))
```

Let's create a method that returns the name of someone who is older or has a spouse who is older:

```
def mOlder(p: Person): Option[String] = p match {
case Person(name, age, true) if age > 35 => Some(name)
case MarriedPerson(name, _, _, Person(_, age, true))
if age > 35 => Some(name)
case _ => None
}
```

Let's see the new method in action:

```
scala> mOlder(p)
```

```
res7: Option[String] = Some(David)
```

```
scala> mOlder(sally)
```

```
res8: Option[String] = Some(Sally)
```

Scala's case classes give you a lot of flexibility for pattern matching, extracting values, nesting patterns, and so on. You can express a lot of logic in pattern declarations. Further, patterns are easy for people to read and understand, which makes code maintenance easier. And because Scala is statically typed, the compiler will help detect some code problems.

Pattern Matching As Functions

Scala patterns are syntactic elements of the language when used with the match operator. However, you can also pass pattern matching as a parameter to other methods. Scala compiles a pattern match down to a PartialFunction[A,B], which is a subclass of Function1[A,B]. So a pattern can be passed to any method that takes a single parameter function. This allows us to reduce this code snippet:

```
list.filter(a => a match {
    case s: String => true
    case _ => false
})
```

into the following snippet:

```
list.filter {
    case s: String => true
    case _ => false
}
```

Because patterns are functions and functions are instances, patterns are instances. In addition to passing them as parameters, they can also be stored for later use.

In addition to Function1's apply method, PartialFunction has an isDefinedAt method so that you can test to see whether a pattern matches a given value. If you try to apply a PartialFunction that's not defined for the value, a MatchError will be raised. How is this useful?

If you're building a web application, you might have particular URLs that need special handling while others get handled in the default manner. The URL can be expressed as a List[String]. We can do the following:

```
def handleRequest(req: List[String])(
  exceptions: PartialFunction[List[String], String]): String =
  if (exceptions.isDefinedAt(req)) exceptions(req) else
  "Handling URL "+req+" in the normal way"
```

So, if the partial function exceptions (the pattern) matches the request req according to the isDefinedAt method, then we allow the request to be handled by the exceptions function. Otherwise, we do default handling. We can call handleRequest and handle any "api" requests by a separate handler:

```
handleRequest("foo" :: Nil) {
  case "api" :: call :: params => doApi(call, params)
}

def doApi(call: String, params: List[String]): String =
"Doing API call "+call
```

Partial functions can be composed into a single function using the orElse method. So, we can define a couple of partial functions:

```
val f1: PartialFunction[List[String], String] = {
  case "stuff" :: Nil => "Got some stuff"
}

val f2: PartialFunction[List[String], String] = {
  case "other" :: params => "Other: "+params
}
```

And we can compose them:

```
val f3 = f1 orElse f2
```

And we can pass them into the handleRequest method:

```
handleRequest("a" :: "b" :: Nil)(f3)
```

In this way, Scala gives you a very nice, declarative way of handling complex filtering tasks. Partial functions can match on data and can be passed around like any other instances in Scala. Partial functions replace a lot of the XML configuration files in Java because pattern matching gives you the same declarative facilities as a configuration file, but they are type-safe, high-performance, and they can have guards and generally take advantage of any method in your code. Here's an example of using pattern matching to dispatch REST request in the ESME[1] code:[2]

```
def dispatch: LiftRules.DispatchPF = {
  case Req("api" :: "status"    :: Nil, "", GetRequest) => status
  case Req("api" :: "messages"  :: Nil, "", GetRequest) => getMsgs
  case Req("api" :: "messages"  :: "long_poll" :: Nil, "", GetRequest) =>
    waitForMsgs
  case Req("api" :: "messages"  :: Nil, "", PostRequest) =>
    () => sendMsg(User.currentUser.map(_.id.is), S)

  case Req("api" :: "follow"    :: Nil, _, GetRequest) =>
      following(calcUser)
  case Req("api" :: "followers" :: Nil, _, GetRequest) =>
      followers(calcUser)
  case Req("api" :: "follow"    :: Nil, _, PostRequest) =>
      performFollow(S.param("user"))
}
```

Object-Oriented and Functional Tensions

At this point, the hard-core object-oriented designer folks may be somewhat unhappy about Scala case class's exposure of lots of internal information. Data hiding is an important part of OOP's abstraction. But in fact, most of the Java classes we define have getters and setters, so there is data exposed in OOP. But there is a tension between the amount of internal state that's exposed in our program and the amount of state that's hidden. In this section, we'll explore OOP and functional programming (FP) patterns for data hiding and exposure.

Another tension in OOP is how to define methods on class and interface hierarchies. Where does a method definition belong? What happens when a library is deployed but it's necessary to add new functionality to subclasses? How do we retrofit the defined-in-stone library classes to add this functionality? Put more concretely, if we have a library of shapes—circle, square, rectangle—that each have an area method but hide all their other data, how do we add a perimeter method to the shapes? Let's explore the tension and the tools Scala and FP give us to address the tension.

Shape Abstractions

If we have a collection of shapes that derive from the common trait OShape that has an area method on it, our object definitions would look something like the following if we used a traditional OOP approach:

```
trait OShape {
  def area: Double
}

class OCircle(radius: Double) extends OShape {
  def area = radius * radius * Math.Pi
}
```

---

[1]ESME is the Enterprise Social Messaging Experiment (http://blog.esme.us).
[2]This code will not compile without the rest of the ESME code, but it serves as an illustration of using pattern matching as an alternative to XML configuration files or annotations.

```
class OSquare(length: Double) extends OShape {
    def area = length * length
}
class ORectangle(h: Double, w: Double) extends OShape {
    def area = h * w
}
```

Let's compare this with the pattern-matching implementation:

```
trait Shape

    case class Circle(radius: Double) extends Shape
    case class Square(length: Double) extends Shape
    case class Rectangle(h: Double, w: Double) extends Shape

object Shape {
  def area(shape: Shape): Double = shape match {
     case Circle(r) => r * r * Math.Pi
     case Square(l) => l * l
     case Rectangle(h, w) => h * w
  }
}
```

In the pattern-matching example, all the logic for calculating area is located in the same method, but the fact that the method exists is not obvious from looking at the Shape trait. So far, the OOP methodology seems to be the right answer because it makes it obvious what shapes can do.

However, if we have a shape library and we want to calculate the perimeter of each of the shapes, there's a benefit to pattern matching:

```
def perimeter(shape: Shape) = shape match {
  case Circle(r) => 2 * Math.Pi * r
  case Square(l) => 4 * l
  case Rectangle(h, w) => h * 2 + w * 2
}
```

In this case, the open data makes implementing the perimeter method possible. With the OOP implementation, we would have to expose data to make the perimeter method possible to implement. So our OOP implementation would look like

```
trait OShape {
    def area: Double
}

class OCircle(radius: Double) extends OShape {
  def area = radius * radius * Math.Pi
  def getRadius = radius
}
class OSquare(length: Double) extends OShape {
  def area = length * length
  def getLength = length
}
```

86

```
class ORectangle(h: Double, w: Double) extends OShape {
  def area      = h * w
  def getHeight = h
  def getWidth  = w
}
```

In a broader sense it's rare that the designer of an object hierarchy implements all the methods that a library consumer is going to need.

The visitor pattern is a design pattern that allows you to add functionality to a class hierarchy after the hierarchy is already defined. Let's look at a typical visitor pattern implementation. Following is the interface that defines the visitor. The code contains circular class references and will not work at the REPL. So, first the code, and then a walk-through of the code:

```
trait OCarVisitor {
   def visit(wheel: OWheel): Unit
   def visit(engine: OEngine): Unit
   def visit(body: OBody): Unit
   def visit(car: OCar): Unit
}

trait OCarElement {
  def accept(visitor: OCarVisitor): Unit
}

class OWheel(val name: String) extends OCarElement {
  def accept(visitor: OCarVisitor) = visitor.visit(this)
}

class OEngine extends OCarElement {
  def accept(visitor: OCarVisitor) = visitor.visit(this)
}

class OBody extends OCarElement {
  def accept(visitor: OCarVisitor) = visitor.visit(this)
}

class OCar extends OCarElement {
  val elements = List(new OEngine, new OBody, new OWheel("FR"),
                  new OWheel("FL"), new OWheel("RR"), new OWheel("RL"))

  def accept(visitor: OCarVisitor) =
  (this :: elements).foreach(_.accept(visitor))
}
```

The library author has to think about extensibility and implement the visitor pattern. Note also that the class hierarchy is fixed in the visitor because the visitor has to implement an interface that defines all the possible classes that the visitor can handle:

```
trait OCarVisitor {
  def visit(wheel: OWheel): Unit
  def visit(engine: OEngine): Unit
  def visit(body: OBody): Unit
  def visit(car: OCar): Unit
}
```

Each element derives from a trait that creates a contract, which requires that the class implement the accept method:

```
trait OCarElement {
  def accept(visitor: OCarVisitor): Unit
}
```

We implement each subclass and implement the accept method:

```
class OWheel(val name: String) extends OCarElement {
  def accept(visitor: OCarVisitor) = visitor.visit(this)
}

class OEngine extends OCarElement {
  def accept(visitor: OCarVisitor) = visitor.visit(this)
}

class OBody extends OCarElement {
  def accept(visitor: OCarVisitor) = visitor.visit(this)
}

class OCar extends OCarElement {
  val elements = List(new OEngine, new OBody, new OWheel("FR"),
                      new OWheel("FL"), new OWheel("RR"), new OWheel("RL"))

  def accept(visitor: OCarVisitor) =
  (this :: elements).foreach(_.accept(visitor))
}
```

That's a lot of boilerplate.[3] Additionally, it violates the data-hiding principles of OOP because the visitor has to access some of the data in each element that it visits. Let's compare the pattern-matching version:

```
trait CarElement
case class Wheel(name: String) extends CarElement
case class Engine() extends CarElement
case classBody() extends CarElement
case class Car(elements: List[CarElement]) extends CarElement
```

---

[3]Here is where a unity ped language such as Ruby or Python has a material advantage over a static language such as Java. In Ruby, you don't need all the boilerplate, and the class hierarchy is not fixed at the time the OCarVisitor interface is defined.

The code is cleaner because there's no boilerplate accept method. Let's see what we do when we want to traverse the object hierarchy:

```
def doSomething(in: CarElement): Unit = in match {
  case Wheel(name) =>
  case Engine() =>
  case Body() =>
  case Car(e) => e.foreach(doSomething)
}
```

Summary

In this chapter, we explored pattern matching and saw how pattern matching provides powerful declarative syntax for expressing complex logic. Pattern matching provides an excellent and type-safe alternative to Java's test/cast paradigm. Pattern matching used with case classes and extraction provides a powerful way to traverse object hierarchies and is an excellent alternative to the visitor pattern. And because patterns are functions and objects, they can be passed as parameters and used wherever functions are used.

In the next chapter, we'll explore Collections. The Scala collections library is the most noteworthy library in the Scala ecosystem.

CHAPTER 6

███ ███ ███

Scala Collections

The collections framework in Scala is a high-performance and type-parametrized framework with support for mutable and immutable type hierarchies. These distinct and independent mutable and immutable type hierarchies enable switching between mutable and immutable implementations much simpler. Scala's object-oriented collections also support functional higher-order operations such as `map`, `filter`, and `reduce` that let you use expression-oriented programming in collections. You can access and use the entire Java collections library from your Scala code because Scala is a JVM language, but this is not recommended because higher-order operations are not available with Java Collections library. Scala has a rich collection library. This chapter gives you a tour of the most commonly used collection types and operations, showing just the types you will use most frequently. The goal of this chapter is to guide you through the myriad of options to find the solutions you need.

Scala Collection Hierarchy

Most collection classes needed by client code exist in three packages, `scala.collection`, `scala.collection.immutable`, and `scala.collection.mutable`. In this section we will explore the three main packages of the collection framework and show you how to use the general and some prevalent features.

package scala.collection

This package is comprised of all high-level abstract classes or traits, which generally have mutable as well as immutable implementations. Figure 6-1 shows all collections in package `scala.collection`.

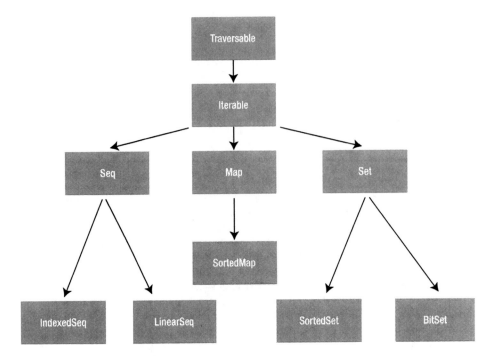

Figure 6-1. *scala.collection package*

The types in scala.collection package shown in Figure 6-1 are implemented in two different ways in the Scala libraries based on whether the implementations are immutable or mutable. To keep these different implementations separate, there are packages called scala.collection.immutable and scala.collection.mutable.

■ **Note** All types in scala.collections package are implemented in different ways in the Scala libraries based on whether the implementations are immutable or mutable. To keep these different implementations separate, there are packages called scala.collection.immutable and scala.collection.mutable.

Sequences

Sequences store a number of different values in a specific order. Because the elements are ordered, you can ask for the first element, second element, and so on.

As shown in Figure 6-1, sequences branch off into two main categories: indexed sequences and linear sequences. By default, Seq creates a List as shown in Listing 6-1.

Listing 6-1. By Default, Seq Creates a List

```
val x = Seq(1,2,3)
```

```
scala> val x = Seq(1,2,3)
x: Seq[Int] = List(1, 2, 3)
```

By default, IndexedSeq creates a Vector as shown in Listing 6-2.

Listing 6-2. By Default, IndexedSeq Creates a Vector

```
val x = IndexedSeq(1,2,3)
```

```
scala> val x = IndexedSeq(1,2,3)
x: IndexedSeq[Int] = Vector(1, 2, 3)
```

Sets

A Scala Set is a collection of unique elements. The common Set classes are shown in Figure 6-1. By default, Set creates an immutable Set as shown in Listing 6-3.

Listing 6-3. collection.immutable package Is Automatically Added to the Current Namespace

```
val x = Set(1,2,3)
```

```
scala> val x = Set(1,2,3)
x: scala.collection.immutable.Set[Int] = Set(1, 2, 3)
```

■ **Note**   While the collection.immutable package is automatically added to the current namespace in Scala, the collection.mutable is not.

Map

Scala Map is a collection of key/value pairs, where all the keys must be unique. The most common map classes are shown in Figure 6-1.When you just need a simple, immutable Map, you can create one without requiring an import as shown in Listing 6-4.

Listing 6-4. Creating an Immutable Map Without Requiring an Import

```
scala> val map = Map(1 -> "a", 2 -> "b", 3 -> "c")
```

```
map: scala.collection.immutable.Map[Int,String] = Map(1 -> a, 2 -> b, 3 -> c)
```

package scala.collection.immutable

The scala.collection.immutable package stores various types of collections that are all immutable. The main classes and traits in this package are shown in Figure 6-2, Figure 6-3, and Figure 6-4 for Seq, Set, and Map, respectively. The top part of the hierarchy looks the same as that shown in Figure 6-1 for the scala.collection package. It begins with Traversable and Iterable, then has three main subtypes in the form of Set, Seq, and Map. The difference is that there are many more subtypes.

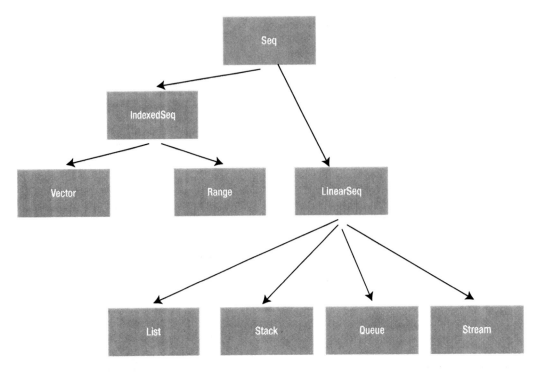

Figure 6-2. *Immutable Seq*

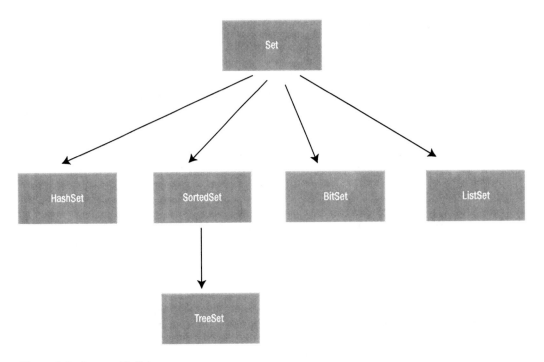

Figure 6-3. *Immutable Set*

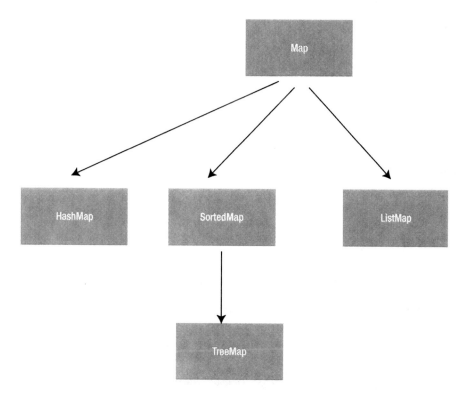

Figure 6-4. *Immutable Map*

Immutable Sequence

Figure 6-2 illustrates the Seq in `scala.collection.immutable` package. The top part of the hierarchy looks the same as that shown in Figure 6-1 for the `scala.collection` package.

If you want an immutable collection that has efficient indexing, your default choice would generally be Vector. An immutable IndexedSeq creates a Vector as shown in Listing 6-5.

Listing 6-5. An Immutable IndexedSeq Creates a Vector

```
val x = scala.collection.immutable.IndexedSeq(1,2,3)
```

```
scala> val x = scala.collection.immutable.IndexedSeq(1,2,3)
x: scala.collection.immutable.IndexedSeq[Int] = Vector(1, 2, 3)
```

An immutable LinearSeq creates as List as seen in Listing 6-6.

Listing 6-6. An Immutable LinearSeq Creates a Vector

```
val x = scala.collection.immutable.LinearSeq(1,2,3)
```

```
scala> val x = scala.collection.immutable.LinearSeq(1,2,3)
x: scala.collection.immutable.LinearSeq[Int] = List(1, 2, 3)
```

An immutable Seq creates a List too as shown in Listing 6-7.

Listing 6-7. An Immutable Seq Creates a List

```
val x = scala.collection.immutable.Seq(1,2,3)
```

```
scala> val x = scala.collection.immutable.Seq(1,2,3)
x: scala.collection.immutable.Seq[Int] = List(1, 2, 3)
```

A collection in package `scala.collection.immutable` is guaranteed to be immutable for everyone. Such a collection will never change after it is created. This means that accessing the same collection value at different points in time will always yield a collection with the same elements.

Immutable Set

Figure 6-3 illustrates the Set in `scala.collection.immutable` package. The top part of the hierarchy looks the same as that shown in Figure 6-1 for the `scala.collection` package.

The difference between root collections and immutable collections is that clients of an immutable collection have a guarantee that nobody can mutate the collection as illustrated in Listings 6-8, through 6-10.

Listing 6-8. Using an Immutable Set

```
val m = collection.immutable.Set(1,2,3)
```

```
m: scala.collection.immutable.Set[Int] = Set(1, 2, 3)
```

Listing 6-9. An Immutable SortedSet creates a TreeSet

```
scala> val m = collection.immutable.SortedSet(1,2,3)
```

```
m: scala.collection.immutable.SortedSet[Int] = TreeSet(1, 2, 3)
```

Listing 6-10. Using an Immutable BitSet

```
scala> val m = collection.immutable.BitSet(1,2,3)
```

```
m: scala.collection.immutable.BitSet = BitSet(1, 2, 3)
```

Immutable Map

Figure 6-4 illustrates the `Map` in `scala.collection.immutable` package. The top part of the hierarchy looks the same as that shown in Figure 6-1 for the `scala.collection` package.

There are base mutable and immutable map classes, Map, that is the base map, with both mutable and immutable implementations as illustrated in Listings 6-11 through 6-13.

Listing 6-11. Using an Immutable Map Without Requiring an Import

```
scala> val m = Map(1 -> "a", 2 -> "b")
```

```
m: scala.collection.immutable.Map[Int,String] = Map(1 -> a, 2 -> b)
```

Listing 6-12. Using an Immutable Map With the Prefix

```
scala> val m = collection.immutable.Map(1 -> "a", 2 -> "b")
```

```
m: scala.collection.immutable.Map[Int,String] = Map(1 -> a, 2 -> b)
```

Listing 6-13. Using an Immutable SortedMap

```
scala> val m = collection.immutable.SortedMap(1 -> "a", 2 -> "b")
```

```
m: scala.collection.immutable.SortedMap[Int,String] = Map(1 -> a, 2 -> b)
```

package scala.collection.mutable

As the name implies, this package includes collections that are mutable. The `scala.collection.mutable` is the most extensive of the three packages. It is worth scanning through the API to look at the various types in this package and to see what they are used for. By default, Scala always picks immutable collections. For instance, if you just write `Set` without any prefix or without having imported `Set` from somewhere, you get an immutable set, and if you write `Iterable` you get an immutable iterable collection, because these are the default bindings imported from the scala package. To get the mutable default versions, you need to write explicitly `collection.mutable.Set`, or `collection.mutable.Iterable`.

▓ **Note**   A useful convention if you want to use both mutable and immutable versions of collections is to import just the `package collection.mutable`.

```
import scala.collection.mutable
```

░ **Note**   Then a word like Set without a prefix still refers to an immutable collection, whereas mutable.Set refers to the mutable counterpart.

Now let's look at Mutable Sequences, Sets, and Maps. It is worth noting that we will go through only the partial implementations. The `scala.collection.mutable` is extensive and it is worth going through the Scala docs for a detailed treatment.

Figure 6-5 illustrates the Sequences in `scala.collection.mutable` package.

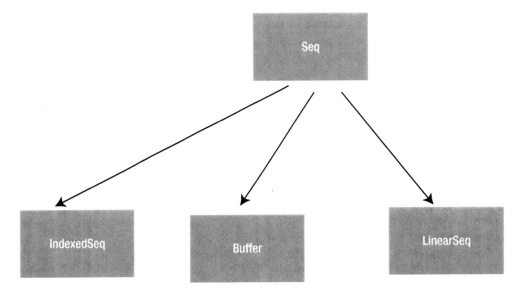

Figure 6-5. *Mutable sequences*

As you can see the difference from Figure 6-1 of the `scala.collection` package is the `Buffer` type. Let's look at that now.

Buffer

The `Buffer` type is implicitly mutable. There is no immutable `Buffer`. There are several subtypes of `Buffer` in the Scala libraries. The two most significant ones are `ArrayBuffer` and `ListBuffer`. You can create a buffer as shown in Listing 6-14.

Listing 6-14. Creating a Buffer

```
val buffer = collection.mutable.Buffer(1,2,3)
```

```
buffer: scala.collection.mutable.Buffer[Int] = ArrayBuffer(1, 2, 3)
```

A mutable Seq creates as `ArrayBuffer` (see Listing 6-15).

Listing 6-15. A Mutable Seq

```
val x = scala.collection.mutable.Seq(1,2,3)
```

```
x: scala.collection.mutable.Seq[Int] = ArrayBuffer(1, 2, 3)
```

A mutable LinearSeq creates as `MutableList` (see Listing 6-16).

Listing 6-16. A Mutable LinearSeq

```
val x = scala.collection.mutable.LinearSeq(1,2,3)
```

```
x: scala.collection.mutable.LinearSeq[Int] = MutableList(1, 2, 3)
```

A mutable `IndexedSeq` creates an `ArrayBuffer` (see Listing 6-17).

Listing 6-17. A Mutable IndexedSeq

```
scala> val x = scala.collection.mutable.IndexedSeq(1,2,3)
```

```
x: scala.collection.mutable.IndexedSeq[Int] = ArrayBuffer(1, 2, 3)
```

You can use a mutable Set as shown in Listing 6-18.

Listing 6-18. A Mutable Set

```
scala> val m = collection.mutable.Set(1,2,3)
```

```
m: scala.collection.mutable.Set[Int] = Set(1, 2, 3)
```

A mutable SortedSet creates a TreeSet as seen in Listing 6-19.

Listing 6-19. A Mutable SortedSet

```
scala> val m = collection.mutable.SortedSet(1,2,3)
```

```
m: scala.collection.mutable.SortedSet[Int] = TreeSet(1, 2, 3)
```

You can use a mutable BitSet as shown in Listing 6-20.

Listing 6-20. A Mutable BitSet

```
scala> val m = collection.mutable.BitSet(1,2,3)
```

```
m: scala.collection.mutable.BitSet = BitSet(1, 2, 3)
```

You can use a mutable Map as shown in Listing 6-21.

Listing 6-21. A Mutable Map

```
scala> val m = collection.mutable.Map(1 -> "a", 2 -> "b")
```

```
m: scala.collection.mutable.Map[Int,String] = Map(2 -> b, 1 -> a)
```

The idea of this section was to give you an overview of Scala collection hierarchy. You learned that there are three basic types Seq, Set, and Map, which are then implemented in mutable and immutable packages. Now we will look at the immutable and mutable collection classes.

Using Immutable Collection Classes

Scala has a wide variety of collections classes. Collections are containers of things. Those containers can be sequenced, linear sets of items as shown in Listing 6-22 and Listing 6-23.

Listing 6-22. A List

```
scala> val x = List(1,2,3,4)
```

```
x: List[Int] = List(1, 2, 3, 4)
```

Listing 6-23. Filtering Through List

```
scala> x.filter(a => a % 2 == 0)
```

```
res14: List[Int] = List(2, 4)
```

```
scala> x
```

```
res15: List[Int] = List(1, 2, 3, 4)
```

They may be indexed items where the index is a zero-based Int (e.g., Array) or any other type (e.g., Map) as illustrated in Listing 6-24.

Listing 6-24. Creating Array

```scala
scala> val a = Array(1,2,3)

a: Array[Int] = Array(1, 2, 3)

scala> a(1)

res16: Int = 2
```

Listing 6-25. Creating a Map

```scala
scala> val m = Map("one" -> 1, "two" -> 2, "three" -> 3)

m: scala.collection.immutable.Map[String,Int] = Map(one -> 1, two -> 2, three ->3)

scala> m("two")

res17: Int = 2
```

The collections may have an arbitrary number of elements or be bounded to zero or one element (e.g., Option). Collections may be strict or lazy.

Lazy collections have elements that may not consume memory until they are accessed (e.g., Range). Let's create a Range (see Listing 6-26).

Listing 6-26. Creating a Range

```scala
scala> 0 to 10

res0: Range.Inclusive = Range(0, 1, 2, 3, 4, 5, 6, 7, 8, 9, 10)
```

The nifty thing about Ranges is that the actual elements in the Range are not instantiated until they are accessed. So we can create a Range for all positive Integers but take only the first five elements. This code runs without consuming many gigabytes of RAM because only the elements that are needed are created (see Listing 6-27).

Listing 6-27. Using Range as Lazy Collection

```scala
scala> (1 to Integer.MAX_VALUE - 1).take(5)

res57: scala.collection.immutable.Range = Range(1, 2, 3, 4, 5)
```

Collections may be mutable (the contents of the reference can change) or immutable (the thing that a reference refers to is never changed). Note that immutable collections may contain mutable items.

Vector

You saw earlier that by default, specifying that you want an IndexedSeq creates a Vector (see Listing 6-28).

Listing 6-28. Creating a Vector

```scala
scala> val x = IndexedSeq(1,2,3)
```

```scala
x: IndexedSeq[Int] = Vector(1, 2, 3)
```

Accessing the vector using index:

```scala
scala> x(0)
```

```scala
res53: Int = 1
```

You can't modify a vector, so you add elements to an existing vector as you assign the result to a new variable:

```scala
scala> val a = Vector(1, 2, 3)
```

```scala
a: scala.collection.immutable.Vector[Int] = Vector(1, 2, 3)
```

```scala
scala> val b = a ++ Vector(4, 5)
```

```scala
b: scala.collection.immutable.Vector[Int] = Vector(1, 2, 3, 4, 5)
```

Use the updated method to replace one element in a vector while assigning the result to a new variable:

```scala
scala> val c = b.updated(0, "x")
```

```scala
c: scala.collection.immutable.Vector[java.lang.String] = Vector(x, b, c)
```

You can also use all the usual filtering methods to get just the elements you want out of a vector:

```scala
scala> val a = Vector(1, 2, 3, 4, 5)
```

```scala
a: scala.collection.immutable.Vector[Int] = Vector(1, 2, 3, 4, 5)
```

```scala
scala> val b = a.take(2)
```

```scala
b: scala.collection.immutable.Vector[Int] = Vector(1, 2)
```

```
scala> val c = a.filter(_ > 2)
```

```
c: scala.collection.immutable.Vector[Int] = Vector(3, 4, 5)
```

In these examples, we created each variable as a val and assigned the output to a new variable just to be clear, but you can also declare your variable as a var and reassign the result back to the same variable:

```
scala> var a = Vector(1, 2, 3)
```

```
a: scala.collection.immutable.Vector[Int] = Vector(1, 2, 3)
```

```
scala> a = a ++ Vector(4, 5)
```

```
a: scala.collection.immutable.Vector[Int] = Vector(1, 2, 3, 4, 5)
```

You may have seen that mixing a mutable variable (var) with an immutable collection causes surprising behavior. For instance, when you create an immutable Vector as a var, it appears you can somehow add new elements to it:

```
scala> var int = Vector(1)
```

```
int: scala.collection.immutable.Vector[Int] = Vector(1)
```

```
scala>int = int :+ 2
```

```
int: scala.collection.immutable.Vector[Int] = Vector(1, 2)
```

```
scala>int = int :+ 3
```

```
int: scala.collection.immutable.Vector[Int] = Vector(1, 2, 3)
```

```
scala>int.foreach(println)
```

```
1
2
3
```

Though it looks like you're mutating an immutable collection, what's really happening is that the int variable points to a new collection each time you use the :+. The int variable (var) is mutable so it's actually being reassigned to a new collection during each step. However, the elements in an immutable collection like Vector cannot be changed. If you want to change the elements in a mutable collection, use ArrayBuffer.

List[T]

Scala's List[T] is a linked list of type T. That means it's a sequential list of any type, including Java's primitives (Int, Float, Double, Boolean, Char) because Scala takes care of boxing (turning primitives into objects) for you. We can build a list using the same syntax we used to build an array with initial values as shown.

```
List(1, 2, 3)
```

```
scala> List(1,2,3)
res0: List[Int] = List(1, 2, 3)
```

Like the array type, the list type is parametric and Scala will figure out the best type if you use this syntax. There is no syntax for making an uninitialized list. That is because lists are immutable. Once you have created a list, the values in it cannot be changed. Changing it would require making a new list. However, there is another way to put lists together when we do not know initially all the values that will be stored in them. We can efficiently build lists one element at a time if we add elements to the front of the list. To add elements to a list we use the "cons" operator, ::. Internally, List is made up of a "cons" cell (the scala.:: class [yes, that's two colons]) with a tail that refers to another cons cell or the Nil object. It's easy to create a List:

```
scala> 1 :: 2 :: 3 :: Nil
```

```
res20: List[Int] = List(1, 2, 3)
```

The previous code creates three cons cells, each with an Int in it. Anything that looks like an operator with a : (colon) as the first character is evaluated right to left. Thus, the previous code is evaluated just like the following:

```
scala> new ::(1, new ::(2, new ::(3, Nil)))
```

```
res21: ::[Int] = List(1, 2, 3)
```

:: takes a "head" which is a single element and a "tail" which is another List. The expression on the left of the :: is the head, and the expression on the right is the tail. To create a List using ::, we must always put a List on the right side. That means that the right-most element has to be a List, and in this case, we're using an empty List, Nil.

We can also create a List using the List object's apply method (which is defined as defapply[T] (param: T*):List[T], which translates to "the apply method of type T takes zero or more parameters of type T and returns a List of type T"):

```
scala> List(1,2,3)
```

```
res22: List[Int] = List(1, 2, 3)
```

The type inferencer is pretty good at figuring out the type of the List, but sometimes you need to help it along:

```scala
scala> List(1, 44.5, 8d)
```

```scala
res27: List[AnyVal] = List(1, 44.5, 8.0)
```

```scala
scala> List[Number](1, 44.5, 8d)
```

```scala
res28: List[java.lang.Number] = List(1, 44.5, 8.0)
```

If you want to prepend an item to the head of the List, you can use ::, which actually creates a new cons cell with the old list as the tail:

```scala
scala> val x = List(1,2,3)
scala> 99 :: x
```

```scala
res0: List[Int] = List(99, 1, 2, 3)
```

Note that the list referred to by the variable x is unchanged, but a new List is created with a new head and the old tail. This is a very fast, constant-time, O(1), operation.

You can also merge two lists to form a new List. This operation is O(n) where n is the number of elements in the first List:

```scala
scala> val x = List(1,2,3)
scala> val y = List(99, 98, 97)
scala> x ::: y
```

```scala
res3: List[Int] = List(1, 2, 3, 99, 98, 97)
```

Getting Functional

The power of List and other collections in Scala come when you mix functions with the collection operators. Let's say we want to find all the odd numbers in a List. It's easy:

```scala
scala> List(1,2,3).filter(x => x % 2 == 1)
```

```scala
res4: List[Int] = List(1, 3)
```

The filter method iterates over the collection and applies the function, in this case, an anonymous function, to each of the elements. If the function returns true, the element is included in the resulting collection. If the function returns false, the element is not included in the resulting collection. The resulting collection is the same type of collection that filter was invoked on. If you invoke filter on a List[Int], you get a List[Int]. If you invoke filter on an Array[String], you get an Array[String] back. In this case, we've written a function that performs mod 2 on the parameter and tests to see whether the result is 1, which indicates that the parameter is odd.

We can also write a method called isOdd and pass the isOdd method as a parameter (Scala will promote the method to a function):

```scala
scala> def isOdd(x: Int) = x % 2 == 1
```

```
isOdd: (Int)Boolean
```

```scala
scala> List(1,2,3,4,5).filter(isOdd)
```

```
res6: List[Int] = List(1, 3, 5)
```

filter works with any collections that contain any type. For example:

```scala
scala> "99 Red Balloons".toList.filter(Character.isDigit)
```

```
res9: List[Char] = List(9, 9)
```

In this case, we're converting a String to a List[Char] using the toList method and filtering the numbers. The Scala compiler promotes the isDigit static method on Character to a function, thus demonstrating interoperability with Java and that Scala methods are not magic.

Another useful method for picking the right elements out of a List is takeWhile, which returns all the elements until it encounters an element that causes the function to return false. For example, let's get all the characters up to the first space in a String:

```scala
scala> "Elwood eats mice".takeWhile(c => c != ' ')
```

```
res12: Seq[Char] = ArrayBuffer(E, l, w, o, o, d)
```

Transformation

The map method on List (and Seq), transforms each element of a collection based on a function. For example, if we have a List[String] and want to convert it to all lowercase:

```scala
scala> List("A", "Cat").map(s => s.toLowerCase)
```

```
res29: List[java.lang.String] = List(a, cat)
```

We can shorten the function so the code reads:

```scala
scala> List("A", "Cat").map(_.toLowerCase)
```

```
res30: List[java.lang.String] = List(a, cat)
```

The number of elements in the returned collection is the same as the number of elements in the original collection, but the types may be different. If the function passed into map returns a different type, then the resulting collection is a collection of the type returned from the function. For example, we can take a List[String] and calculate the length of each String, which will result in a List[Int]:

```
scala> List("A", "Cat").map(_.length)
```

```
res31: List[Int] = List(1, 3)
```

map provides a very powerful and uniform way to transform data from one type to another. We can transform our Strings to lowercase, to a List of their length, and we can extract data from a collection of complex objects. For example, if we have a database query that returns records of type Person defined as having a first method that returns a String containing the person's first name, we can create a List of the first names of the people in the List:

```
scala> trait Person {def first: String }
```

```
defined trait Person
```

```
scala> val d = new Person {def first = "David" }
scala> val e = new Person {def first = "Elwood"}
scala> val a = new Person {def first = "Archer"}
scala> List(a, d, e).map(_.first)
```

```
res35: List[String] = List(Archer, David, Elwood)
```

Or, if we're writing a web app, we can create an <li> (an HTML list element) containing the first name of each Person in our List:

```
scala> List(a,d,e).map(n =><li>{n.first}</li>)
```

```
List(<li>Archer</li>, <li>David</li>, <li>Elwood</li>)
```

We can combine the operations. Let's update our Person trait:

```
trait Person {
    def first: String
    def valid: Boolean
}
```

Now we can write the code shown in Listing 6-29 to find all the valid Person records, sort by age, and return the first names.

Listing 6-29. First Name of Valid Persons

```
def validByAge(in: List[Person]) =
  in.filter(_.valid).
  map(_.first)
```

Reduxio

Scala has other abstractions for common collections operations. reduceLeft allows you to perform an operation on adjacent elements of the collection where the result of the first operation is fed into the next operation. For example, if we want to find the biggest number in a List[Int]:

```
scala> List(8, 6, 22, 2).reduceLeft(_ max _)
```

```
res50: Int = 22
```

In this case, reduceLeft takes 8 and 6 and feeds them into our function, which returns the maximum value of the two numbers: 8. Next, reduceLeft feeds 8 (the output of the last iteration) and 22 into the function, resulting in 22. Next, reduceLeft feeds 22 and 2 into the function, resulting in 22. Because there are no more elements, reduceLeft returns 22.

We can use reduceLeft to find the longest word:

```
scala> List("moose", "cow", "A", "Cat").
        reduceLeft((a, b) => if (a.length > b.length) a else b)
```

```
res41: java.lang.String = moose
```

Because Scala's if expression works like Java's ternary operator, the if in the previous code returns a if it's longer than b. We can also find the shortest word:

```
scala> List("moose", "cow", "A", "Cat").
        reduceLeft((a, b) => if (a.length < b.length) a else b)
```

```
res42: java.lang.String = A
```

reduceLeft throws an exception on an Nil (empty) List. This is correct behavior as there is no way to apply the function on the members of the List as a Nil List has no elements.

foldLeft is similar to reduceLeft, but it starts with a seed value. The return type of the function and the return type of foldLeft must be the same type as the seed. The first example is summing up List[Int]:

```
scala> List(1,2,3,4).foldLeft(0) (_ + _)
```

```
res43: Int = 10
```

In this case, the seed value is 0. Its type is Int. foldLeft feeds the seed and the first element of the List, 1, into the function, which returns 1. Next, foldLeft feeds 1 (the result of the previous iteration) and 2 (the next element) into the function, resulting in 3. The process continues, and the sum of the List[Int] is generated: 10. We can generate the product of the List the same way:

```
scala> List(1,2,3,4).foldLeft(1) (_ * _)
```

```
res44: Int = 24
```

But because the return type of foldLeft is the type of the seed, not the type of the List, we can figure out the total length of a List[String]:

```
scala> List("b", "a", "elwood", "archer").foldLeft(0)(_ + _.length)
```

```
res51: Int = 14
```

I find that sometimes I need to work with more than one collection at a time. For example, if we want to generate the List of products of the numbers from 1 to 3:

```
scala> val n = (1 to 3).toList
```

```
n: List[Int] = List(1, 2, 3)
```

```
scala> n.map(i => n.map(j => i * j))
```

```
res53: List[List[Int]] = List(List(1, 2, 3), List(2, 4, 6), List(3, 6, 9))
```

We have nested map invocations, and that results in a List[List[Int]]. In some cases, this may be what we want. In other cases, we want the results in a single List[Int]. In order to nest the map operations but flatten the results of nested operations, we use the flatMap method:

```
scala> n.flatMap(i => n.map(j => i * j))
```

```
res58: List[Int] = List(1, 2, 3, 2, 4, 6, 3, 6, 9)
```

Look Ma, No Loops

So far, we've written a bunch of code that manipulates collections without explicit looping. By passing functions, that is, logic, to methods that control the looping, we let the library writers define the looping, and we define the logic in our app. However, syntactically, nested map, flatMap, and filter can get ugly. For example, if we want to find the product of the odd numbers from 1 to 10 times the even numbers from 1 to 10, we could write the following:

```
scala> def isOdd(in: Int) = in % 2 == 1
scala> def isEven(in: Int) = !isOdd(in)
scala> val n = (1 to 10).toList
scala> n.filter(isEven).flatMap(i => n.filter(isOdd).map(j => i * j))
```

```
res60: List[Int] = List(2, 6, 10, 14, 18, ... 10, 30, 50, 70, 90)
```

Scala provides the for comprehension, which provides syntactically pleasing nesting of map, flatMap, and filter. We can convert the nested statements from the previous example into a syntactically pleasing statement:

```
scala> for {i <- n if isEven(i); j <- n if isOdd(j)} yield i * j
```

```
res59: List[Int] = List(2, 6, 10, 14, 18, ... 10, 30, 50, 70, 90)
```

The for comprehension is not a looping construct but is a syntactic construct that the compiler reduces to map, flatMap, and filter. In fact, the two lines

```
n.filter(isEven).flatMap(i => n.filter(isOdd).map(j => i * j))
```

and

```
for {i <- n if isEven(i); j <- n if isOdd(j)} yield i * j
```

result in the same bytecode. The for comprehension can be used with any class, including user-generated classes, that implement map, flatMap, filter, and foreach. This means you can create your own classes that work with the for comprehension.

Lists also work well with Scala's pattern matching and recursive programming. We'll be exploring pattern matching in depth in Chapter 5. For this example, pattern matching is a lot like Java's switch statement, but it can be used to compare things that are more complex than Ints, and Scala's pattern matching allows you to match some elements and extract, or capture, others into variables.

The pattern-matching syntax is the same as List construction syntax. For example, if we are matching against List[Int], case 1 :: Nil =>will match List(1). case 1 :: 2 :: Nil => will match List(1,2). case 1 :: rest => will match any List that starts with 1 and will put the tail of the List into the variable rest.

Our example converts a List[Char] of Roman numerals to their Arabic numeral equivalent. The code matches the List to a series of patterns. Based on the matched pattern, a value is returned. The patterns are matched in order of appearance. However, the compiler may optimize the patterns by eliminating duplicate tests[1]. The code to convert from Roman numerals to Int is in Listing 6-30.

Listing 6-30. Roman Numerals

```
def roman(in: List[Char]): Int = in match {
    case 'I' :: 'V' :: rest => 4 + roman(rest)
    case 'I' :: 'X' :: rest => 9 + roman(rest)
    case 'I' :: rest => 1 + roman(rest)
    case 'V' :: rest => 5 + roman(rest)
    case 'X' :: 'L' :: rest => 40 + roman(rest)
    case 'X' :: 'C' :: rest => 90 + roman(rest)
    case 'X' :: rest => 10 + roman(rest)
    case 'L' :: rest => 50 + roman(rest)
    case 'C' :: 'D' :: rest => 400 + roman(rest)
    case 'C' :: 'M' :: rest => 900 + roman(rest)
    case 'C' :: rest => 100 + roman(rest)
    case 'D' :: rest => 500 + roman(rest)
    case 'M' :: rest => 1000 + roman(rest)
    case _ => 0
}
```

---

[1]You can see exactly how Scala turns patterns into code by typing **scalac -print FileName.scala**. This will cause the Scala compiler to emit desugared code that looks strangely like Java code.

case 'I' :: 'V' :: rest => 4 + roman(rest) tests the first two characters, and if they are IV, the method returns 4 plus the Roman numeral conversion of the rest of the List[Char]. If the test falls through to case _ => 0, there are no more Roman numerals, 0 is returned, and there's no more recursion—no more calls back into the roman() method. Without explicit looping or length testing or explicit branching logic, we've written a concise, readable method.

Scala's List and other sequential collections provide powerful ways to define business logic in a concise, maintainable way. In the next section, we're going to explore Tuples, which are fixed-length collections where each element can be a different type.

Range

Ranges are often used to populate data structures, and to iterate over for loops. Ranges provide a lot of power with just a few methods, as shown in these examples:

```
scala> 1 to 10
```

```
res0: scala.collection.immutable.Range.Inclusive =Range(1, 2, 3, 4, 5, 6, 7, 8, 9, 10)
```

```
scala> 1 until 10
```

```
res1: scala.collection.immutable.Range = Range(1, 2, 3, 4, 5, 6, 7, 8, 9)
```

```
scala> 1 to 10 by 2
```

```
res2: scala.collection.immutable.Range = Range(1, 3, 5, 7, 9)
```

```
scala> 'a' to 'c'
```

```
res3: collection.immutable.NumericRange.Inclusive[Char] = NumericRange(a, b, c)
```

You can use ranges to create and populate sequences:

```
scala> val x = (1 to 10).toList
```

```
x: List[Int] = List(1, 2, 3, 4, 5, 6, 7, 8, 9, 10)
```

Stream

A Stream is like a List, except that its elements are computed lazily, in a manner similar to how a view creates a lazy version of a collection. Because Stream elements are computed lazily, a Stream can be long ... infinitely long. Like a view, only the elements that are accessed are computed. Other than this behavior, a Stream behaves similar to a List.

Just like a List can be constructed with ::, a Stream can be constructed with the #:: method, using Stream.empty at the end of the expression instead of Nil:

```scala
scala> val stream = 1 #:: 2 #:: 3 #:: Stream.empty
```

```
stream: scala.collection.immutable.Stream[Int] = Stream(1, ?)
```

The REPL output shows that the stream begins with the number 1 but uses a ? to denote the end of the stream. This is because the end of the stream hasn't been evaluated yet.

For example, given a Stream:

```scala
scala> val stream = (1 to 100000000).toStream
```

```
stream: scala.collection.immutable.Stream[Int] = Stream(1, ?)
```

you can attempt to access the head and tail of the stream. The head is returned immediately:

```scala
scala> stream.head
```

```
res0: Int = 1
```

but the tail isn't evaluated yet:
```scala
scala> stream.tail
```

```
res1: scala.collection.immutable.Stream[Int] = Stream(2, ?)
```

The ? symbol is the way a lazy collection shows that the end of the collection hasn't been evaluated yet.

Tuples

Have you ever written a method that returns two or three values? Let's write a method that takes a List[Double] and returns the count, the sum, and the sum of squares returned in a three-element Tuple, a Tuple3[Int, Double, Double]:

```scala
def sumSq(in: List[Double]): (Int, Double, Double) =
    in.foldLeft((0, 0d, 0d))((t, v) => (t._1 + 1, t._2 + v, t._3 + v * v))
```

The sumSq method takes a List[Double] as input and returns a Tuple3[Int, Double, Double]. The compiler desugars (Int, Double, Double) into Tuple3[Int, Double, Double]. The compiler will treat a collection of elements in parentheses as a Tuple. We seed the foldLeft with (0, 0d, 0d), which the compiler translates to a Tuple3[Int, Double, Double]. The function takes two parameters: t and v. t is a Tuple3, and v is a Double. The function returns a new Tuple3 by adding 1 to the first element of the Tuple, adding v to the second element of the Tuple, and adding the square of v to the third element of the Tuple. Using Scala's pattern matching, we can make the code a little more readable:

```scala
def sumSq(in: List[Double]) : (Int, Double, Double) =
    in.foldLeft((0, 0d, 0d)){
      case ((cnt, sum, sq), v) => (cnt + 1, sum + v, sq + v * v)}
```

You can create Tuples using a variety of syntax:

```scala
scala> Tuple2(1,2) == Pair(1,2)
scala> Pair(1,2) == (1,2)
scala> (1,2) == 1 -> 2
```

The last example, 1 -> 2, is a particularly helpful and syntactically pleasing way for passing pairs around. Pairs appear in code very frequently, including name/value pairs for creating Maps.

Map[K, V]

A Map is a collection of key/value pairs. Any value can be retrieved based on its key. Keys are unique in the Map, but values need not be unique. In Java, Hashtable and HashMap are common Map classes. The default Scala Map class is immutable. This means that you can pass an instance of Map to another thread, and that thread can access the Map without synchronizing. The performance of Scala's immutable Map is indistinguishable from the performance of Java's HashMap.

We can create a Map:

```scala
scala> var p = Map(1 -> "David", 9 -> "Elwood")
```

```
p: ... Map[Int,String] = Map(1 -> David, 9 -> Elwood)
```

We create a new Map by passing a set of Pair[Int, String] to the Map object's apply method. Note that we created a var p rather than a val p. This is because the Map is immutable, so when we alter the contents on the Map, we have to assign the new Map back to p.

We can add an element to the Map:

```scala
scala> p + 8 -> "Archer"
```

```
res4: ... Map[Int,String] = Map(1 -> David, 9 -> Elwood, 8 -> Archer)
```

But we haven't changed the immutable Map:

```scala
scala> p
```

```
res5: ... Map[Int,String] = Map(1 -> David, 9 -> Elwood)
```

In order to update p, we have to assign the new Map back to p:

```scala
scala> p = p + 8 -> "Archer"
```

or:

```scala
scala> p += 8 -> "Archer"
```

And we can see that p is updated:

```
scala> p
```

```
res7: Map[Int,String] = Map(1 -> David, 9 -> Elwood, 8 -> Archer)
```

We can get elements out of the Map:

```
scala> p(9)
```

```
res12: java.lang.String = Elwood
```

What happens when we ask for an element that doesn't exist?

```
scala> p(88)
```

```
java.util.NoSuchElementException: key not found: 88
```

This is mighty inconvenient. If you try to get an element that's not in the Map, you get an exception. That's kind of jarring. So far, we haven't seen much in Scala that results in exceptions being thrown, but it makes logical sense. If you request something that doesn't exist, that's an exceptional situation. Java's Map classes handle this situation by returning null, which has two drawbacks. First, you have to null-test the result of every Map access. Second, it means you can't store a null in a Map. Scala has a kinder and gentler mechanism for dealing with this situation. The get() method on Map returns an Option (Some or None) that contains the result:

```
scala> p.get(88)
```

```
res10: Option[java.lang.String] = None
```

```
scala> p.get(9)
```

```
res11: Option[java.lang.String] = Some(Elwood)
```

You can return a default value if the key is not found:

```
scala> p.getOrElse(99, "Nobody")
```

```
res55: java.lang.String = Nobody
```

```
scala> p.getOrElse(1, "Nobody")
```

```
res56: java.lang.String = David
```

We can also use `flatMap` with `Options` to find all the values with keys between 1 and 5:

```scala
scala> 1 to 5 flatMap(p.get)
```

```
res53: Seq.Projection[java.lang.String] = RangeG(David)
```

In this case, we create a range of numbers from 1 to 5. We `flatMap` this collection, passing in a function, `p.get`. Wait, you say, `p.get` isn't a function, it's a method, but you didn't include the parameter. Scala is very cool, because if it's expecting a function with parameters of a particular type and you pass a method that takes those parameters, Scala will promote the method with its missing parameters to a function. We'll explore `Options` in the next subsection.

Let's continue exploring `Map`. We can remove elements from our `Map`:

```scala
scala> p -= 9
scala> p
```

```
res20: Map[Int,String] = Map(1 -> David, 8 -> Archer)
```

We can test the `Map` to see whether it contains a particular key:

```scala
scala> p.contains(1)
```

```
res21: Boolean = true
```

We can operate on the collection of keys. We get a collection of keys from our `Map` and use `reduceLeft` to find the largest key:

```scala
scala> p.keys.reduceLeft(_ max _)
```

```
res22: Int = 8
```

And we can use `reduceLeft` on the collection of values to find the largest `String`:

```scala
scala> p.values.reduceLeft((a, b) => if (a > b) a else b)
```

```
res23: java.lang.String = David
```

We can test whether any of the values contains the letter "z":

```scala
scala> p.values.exists(_.contains("z"))
```

```
res28: Boolean = false
```

You can also add a bunch of elements to a Map using the ++ method:

```
scala> p ++= List(5 -> "Cat", 6 -> "Dog")
```

```
p: Map[Int,String] = Map(1 -> David, 8 -> Archer, 5 -> Cat, 6 -> Dog)
```

And you can remove a bunch of keys with the -- method:

```
scala> p --= List(8, 6)
```

```
res40: Map[Int, String] = Map(1 -> David, 5 -> Cat)
```

Maps are Scala collections and have collection manipulation methods. This means we can use methods, including map, filter, and foldLeft. One of the tricky parts of using Java's immutable collections is iterating over the collection and simultaneously removing elements. In my code, I have to create an accumulator for the keys I'm going to remove, loop over the collection, find all the keys to remove, and then iterate over the collection of keys to remove and remove them from the collection. Not only that, but I frequently forget how brittle Hashtable is and inevitably forget this sequence and get some nasty runtime errors. In Scala, it's much easier. But there's a simpler way to remove unwanted elements from a Map:

```
def removeInvalid(in: Map[Int, Person]) = in.filter(kv => kv._2.valid)
```

Pretty cool, huh? Map has a filter method that works just like List's filter method. The kv variable is a Pair representing the key/value pair. The filter method tests each key/value pair by calling the function and constructs a new Map that contains only the elements that passed the filter test.

Mutable Collections

The List, Set, and Map immutable collections we are familiar with cannot be changed after they have been created. They can, however, be transformed into new collections. For example, we can create an immutable map, and then transform it by removing one mapping and adding another.

```
val immutableMap = Map(1 -> "a", 2 -> "b", 3 -> "c")
```

```
scala> val immutableMap = Map(1 -> "a", 2 -> "b", 3 -> "c")
immutableMap: scala.collection.immutable.Map[Int,String] = Map(1 -> a, 2 -> b, 3 -> c)
```

```
val newMap = immutableMap - 1 + (4 -> "d")
```

```
scala> val newMap = immutableMap - 1 + (4 -> "d")
newMap: scala.collection.immutable.Map[Int,String] = Map(2 -> b, 3 -> c, 4 -> d)
```

Removing "a" and adding "d" gives us a different collection, while the original collection immutableMap remains the same.

```scala
scala> println(newMap)
Map(2 -> b, 3 -> c, 4 -> d)
scala> println(immutableMap)
Map(1 -> a, 2 -> b, 3 -> c)
```

What you end up with is a completely new collection stored in newMap. The original collection immutableMap, remains untouched.

However, there are times when you do want mutable data. For example, creating a mutable data structure that is only used within a function.

You can create mutable collections by directly from immutable collections. The List, Map, and Set immutable collections can all be converted to the mutable collection.mutable.Buffer type with the toBuffer method. Here is an example of converting an immutable map to a mutable one and then changing it back.

```scala
scala> val m = Map(1->"a", 2 -> "b")
```

```scala
m: scala.collection.immutable.Map[Int,String] = Map(1 -> a, 2 -> b)
```

```scala
scala> val b = m.toBuffer
```

```scala
b: scala.collection.mutable.Buffer[(Int, String)] = ArrayBuffer((1,a), (2,b))
```

The map, containing key-value pairs, is now a sequence of tuples. We can now add a new entry.

```scala
scala> b += (3 ->"c")
```

```scala
res56: b.type = ArrayBuffer((1,a), (2,b), (3,c))
```

After adding new entry, you can now change the buffer to map again.

```scala
scala> val newMap = b.toMap
```

```scala
newMap: scala.collection.immutable.Map[Int,String] = Map(1 -> a, 2 -> b, 3 -> c)
```

The buffer methods toList and toSet can be used in addition to toMap to convert a buffer to an immutable collection. The most straightforward way to modify collections is with a mutable collection type. We will look at some mutable collection classes in the following sections.

Mutable Queue

A queue is a first-in, first-out (FIFO) data structure. Scala offers both an immutable queue and mutable queue. You can create an empty, mutable queue of any data type. Listing 6-31 shows mutable queue for int.

Listing 6-31. Creating a Queue

```
import scala.collection.mutable.Queue
var ints = Queue[Int]()
```

```
scala> import scala.collection.mutable.Queue
import scala.collection.mutable.Queue
scala> var ints = Queue[Int]()
ints: scala.collection.mutable.Queue[Int] = Queue()
```

■ **Note**   While the collection.immutable package is automatically added to the current namespace in Scala, the collection.mutable is not. When creating mutable collections, make sure to include the full package name for the type.

Once you have a mutable queue, add elements to it using +=, ++=, and enqueue, as shown in Listings 6-32 through 6-34.

Listing 6-32. Adding Elements to the Queue

```
scala> ints += 1
```

```
res46: scala.collection.mutable.Queue[Int] = Queue(1)
```

Listing 6-33. Adding Multiple Elements to the Queue

```
scala> ints += (2, 3)
```

```
res47: scala.collection.mutable.Queue[Int] = Queue(1, 2, 3)
```

Listing 6-34. Using enqueue

```
scala> ints.enqueue(4)
```

```
scala> ints
```

```
res49: scala.collection.mutable.Queue[Int] = Queue(1, 2, 3, 4)
```

Because a queue is a FIFO, you typically remove elements from the head of the queue, one element at a time, using dequeue (see Listing 6-35).

Listing 6-35. Using dequeue

```
ints.dequeue
```

```
scala> ints.dequeue
res50: Int = 1
scala> ints
res51: scala.collection.mutable.Queue[Int] = Queue(2, 3, 4)
```

A Queue is a collection class that extends from Iterable and Traversable, so it has all the usual collection methods, including foreach, map, and so on.

Mutable Stack

A stack is a last-in, first-out (LIFO) data structure. Scala has both immutable and mutable versions of a stack. The following examples demonstrate how to use the mutable Stack class.

Listing 6-36 creates an empty, mutable stack of int data type.

Listing 6-36. Creating a Stack

```
import scala.collection.mutable.Stack
var ints = Stack[Int]()
```

```
scala> import scala.collection.mutable.Stack
import scala.collection.mutable.Stack
scala> var ints = Stack[Int]()
ints: scala.collection.mutable.Stack[Int] = Stack()
```

You can also populate a stack with initial elements when you create it as seen in Listing 6-37.

Listing 6-37. Creating a Stack

```
val ints = Stack(1, 2, 3)
```

```
scala> val ints = Stack(1, 2, 3)
ints: scala.collection.mutable.Stack[Int] = Stack(1, 2, 3)
```

You can now push elements onto the stack with push:

Listing 6-38. Creating a Stack

```
scala> ints.push(4)
```

```
res41: ints.type = Stack(4, 1, 2, 3)
```

Listing 6-39. Creating a Stack

```
scala>ints.push(5, 6,7)
```

```
scala> ints.push(5, 6 ,7)
res42: ints.type = Stack(7, 6, 5, 4, 1, 2, 3)
```

To take elements off the stack, pop them off the top of the stack (see Listing 6-40).

Listing 6-40. Creating a Stack

```
scala> val lastele = ints.pop
lastele: Int = 7
```

With this we complete the discussion of mutable collections and this chapter. The scala collections framework is broad, rather than deep, and deserves a book of its own. Nevertheless, this chapter tried to show you how to use a variety of Scala's collection types.

Summary

This chapter gave you the tour of scala collections framework and showed you three main packages of the framework. This chapter has delved deeply into how to use lists. You have seen many ways to work with lists. You have seen the basic operations like head and tail, the higher-order operations like map, and the utility methods in the List object. Lists are just one kind of collection that Scala supports, however. This chapter has given an overview of the Scala collections library and the most important classes and traits in it. With this foundation you should be able to work effectively with Scala collections, and know where to look in Scaladoc when you need more information. For now we'll turn our attention to the internals of Scala traits in the next chapter.

CHAPTER 7

▨ ▨ ▨

Traits

In this chapter you will learn how to construct reusable parts of a program and deal with the tribulations of multiple inheritance, sidestepping the disadvantages of single inheritance by means of the mixing of compositions made possible by traits.

A *trait* provides code reusability in Scala by encapsulating method and state and then offering the possibility of mixing them into classes thus allowing code reuse. In this way a class can be mixed in with a myriad of traits unlike inheritance where each class is allowed to inherit from just one superclass. Moreover, other than using the keyword trait a trait definition resembles a class definition as illustrated in Listing 7-1.

Listing 7-1. The Definition of Trait Gliding

```
trait Gliding {
def gliding() {
println("gliding")
}
}
```

This trait is named Gliding. It does not declare a superclass, so like a class, it has the default superclass of AnyRef. It defines one concrete method, named gliding.

```
scala> trait Gliding {
     | def gliding() {
     | println("gliding")
     | }
     | }
defined trait Gliding
```

The Gliding trait is a simple example but adequate to show how traits works. Now we will explore how mixin composition is made possible by trait.

Using Traits as Mixins

With single inheritance a class can inherit methods and fields from only one class. Multiple inheritance enables the class to inherit methods and fields from more than one class; however, multiple inheritance can be problematic as the order of inheriting classes may affect the behavior of the subclass inadvertently. The mixin composition is a better approach toward solving the problems of multiple inheritance, sidestepping the drawbacks of single inheritance. In Java, a class can implement any arbitrary number of interfaces toward multiple abstractions. Unlike Java, Scala provides a mechanism for defining and using reusable code in interfaces, which will be valid for all the classes implementing the interface. You have abstract classes for defining and using such reusable code but a class can extend only one abstract class eliminating the possibility of multiple inheritance. The term mixin is used for such reusable code that could be independently maintained. You can use traits in a way similar to the way in which Java interfaces are used. When you add implementation to traits they become Mixins. You can create a trait that inherits from a Class, as well as a Class that extends a trait. Once a trait is defined, it can be mixed in to a class using either the extends or with keywords. Listing 7-2 shows a class that mixes in the Gliding trait using extends.

Listing 7-2. Mixin by Extending the Trait

```
class Glider extends Gliding {
override def toString = "glider"
}
```

```
scala> class Glider extends Gliding {
     | override def toString = "glider"
     | }
defined class Glider
```

You can use the extends keyword to mix in a trait; in that case you implicitly inherit the trait's superclass. In Listing 7-2, class Glider mixes in Gliding. You can use the methods inherited from a trait as following:

```
scala> val glider = new Glider
glider: Glider = glider
scala> glider.gliding()
gliding
```

A trait also defines a type. Here's an example in which Gliding is used as a type as illustrated in the following example:

```
scala> val g: Glider = glider
g: Glider = glider
scala> g.gliding()
gliding
```

In the example shown earlier the type of g is a Glider trait, and so g could be initialized with any object whose class mixes in Glider.

In the Listing 7-3, class `Glider` has inherited an implementation of `gliding` from trait `Glider`. The class `Glider` could override `gliding` as illustrated in Listing 7-3.

Listing 7-3. Overriding the Trait's Method

```
class Glider extends Gliding {
override def toString = "glider"
override def gliding() {
println("race for now "+ toString )
}
}
```

Because `Glider` overrides `Gliding`'s implementation of `gliding`, you'll get a new behavior when you call it:

```
scala> class Glider extends Gliding {
     | override def toString = "glider"
     | override def gliding() {
     | println("race for now "+ toString )
     | }
     | }
defined class Glider
scala> val glider = new Glider
glider: Glider = glider
scala> glider.gliding()
race for now glider
```

Fundamentally, traits are akin to Java interfaces. As with interfaces, you could just declare the methods in your trait that you want your extending classes to implement as illustrated in Listing 7-4.

Listing 7-4. Declaring Methods in a Trait

```
trait TraitA {
def methodA
def methodAWithParam(param :String)
def methodWithReturnType: String
}
```

Listing 7-4 shows a trait that declares the methods that don't take any argument. The methods without argument can be declared with a `def` keyword followed by the method name as illustrated in the first method `def methodA` in Listing 7-4. If a method requires parameter, you could list them as usual as illustrated in Listing 7-4.

One trait can extend another trait as illustrated in Listing 7-5. `TraitA` can extend `TraitB`.

Listing 7-5. Trait Extending Another Trait

```
trait TraitB extends TraitA{
def methodB
}
```

When a class extends a trait, it uses the extends and with keywords based on whether the class extends one trait or several traits. When a class extends one trait, use the extends keyword as illustrated in Listing 7-6.

Listing 7-6. Extending One Trait

```
class ClassA extends TraitA{
// code
}
```

If a class extends more than one trait, use extends for the first trait and with to mix in the other traits as illustrated in Listing 7-7.

Listing 7-7. Extending Multiple Traits

```
class ClassA extends TraitA with TraitB{
// code
}
```

If a class extends a class and a trait, always use extends before the class name, and use with before the trait's name as illustrated in Listing 7-8.

Listing 7-8. Extending Class and Traits

```
class ClassA extends ClassB withTraitA with TraitB{
// code
}
```

A class extending the trait must implement all the abstract methods of trait, unless the class extending a trait is itself abstract, as illustrated in Listing 7-9.

Listing 7-9. Concrete Class Must Implement All Abstract Methods of Trait

```
class ClassA extends TraitA {
def methodA { // code... }
def methodAWithParam(param :String){ // code... }
def methodWithReturnType: String{ // code... }
}
```

In Listing 7-9, ClassA is not declared abstract and therefore implements all abstract methods of trait TraitA.

■ **Note** A trait can be comprised of both abstract and concrete methods.

However, if a class extends a trait but does not implement the abstract methods defined in the trait, the class extending the trait must be declared abstract as illustrated in Listing 7-10.

Listing 7-10. Extending Class Not Implementing Abstract Methods of Trait Must Be Abstract

```
abstract class ClassA extends TraitA {
def methodA { // code... }
def methodAWithParam(param :String){ // code... }
}
```

In Listing 7-10, ClassA does not implement the methodWithReturnType method of TraitA shown in Listing 7-4.

The subclass of a trait can choose, if it prefers, to override the trait's method.

Listing 7-11 illustrates a Vehicle trait that provides an implementation for the drive method.

Listing 7-11. Trait with Implementation

```
trait Vehice {
def drive { println("Driving") }
def race
}
```

In Listing 7-12, drive is a concrete method and race is an abstract method.

The Car class in Listing 7-12 does not override the drive method of Vehicle trait.

Listing 7-12. Subclass Does Not Override the Trait's DriveMethod

```
class Car extends Vehicle {
def race { ("Racing the car") }
}
```

The Boat class in Listing 7-13 overrides the drive method of Vehicle trait.

Listing 7-13. Subclass Overridesthe Trait's DriveMethod

```
class Boat extends Vehicle {
override def drive { ("float") }
def race { ("Racing boat.") }
}
```

▒ **Note** Although Scala has abstract classes, it's recommended to use traits instead of abstract classes to implement base behavior because a class can extend only one abstract class, but it can implement multiple traits. If you want the base behavior to be inherited in Java code, use an abstract class.

You can also use fields in your traits. The fields of a trait can be declared as either var or val and can be concrete by defining the field with an initial value or the field can be made abstract by not assigning the initial value. Listing 7-14 illustrates a trait CarTrait with abstract field door and concrete field seat.

Listing 7-14. Trait with Abstract and Concrete Fields

```
trait CarTrait {
var door: Int
var seat = 4
}
```

Listing 7-15 illustrates Car class that extends the CarTrait. As you can see you don't need to use the override keyword to override var fields door and seat.

Listing 7-15. Override Keyword Not Necessary for var Field

```
class Car extends CarTrait {
var door = 4
seat = 5
}
```

You need to use the override keyword in a subclass of a trait to override a val field as illustrated in Listing 7-16.

Listing 7-16. Override Keyword Necessary for val Field

```
trait CarTrait {
val door: Int
}
class Car  extends CarTrait {
override val door = 5
}
```

In the class Car that extends the CarTrait trait, you'll need to define the values for the abstract fields, otherwise you need to define the class as abstract.

As you can see traits can declare fields and maintain state. The syntax of class definition and trait definition is exactly the same except that a class definition can have the parameters passed to the primary constructor of a class but a trait definition cannot have such parameters.

Listing 7-17. Trait Definition Cannot Have Parameters

```
class Car(door: Int )trait Car (door: Int) // does not compile
```

In the next section we will explore using traits for modelling complex class hierarchies that you cannot model in Java.

Traits and Class Hierarchies

One of the big challenges with developing a class hierarchy when you are constrained by single inheritance is figuring out what things should be base classes and where things should go in the class hierarchy. If we're modeling living things, how do you model things with legs when that can include any animal? Should there be LeggedAnimals and LeglessAnimals? But then, how do you deal with Mammals and Reptiles? Maybe we can make HasLegs an interface, but then I can give a Plant legs. Scala to the rescue.

We've already seen that traits can implement methods. Additionally, traits can have rules about what kind of classes and other traits they can be mixed into. Further, you can declare method parameters that are a consolidation of types, for example:

```
def foo(bar: Baz with Blarg with FruitBat)
```

Only instances of classes that extend Baz, Blarg, and FruitBat may be passed into this method. Let's model some living things.

Listing 7-18. Modelling Living Things

```
abstract class LivingThing
abstract class Plant extends LivingThing
abstract class Fungus extends LivingThing
abstract class Animal extends LivingThing
```

Good so far. A LivingThing must be a plant, fungus, or animal. But, what about legs? Who can have legs?

Listing 7-19. Trait HasLegs

```
trait HasLegs extends Animal {
  def walk() {println("Walking")}
}
```

The HasLegs trait extends Animal. But Animal is a class, so what does it mean for a trait to extend a class? It means that the compiler will only let you mix HasLegs into something that subclasses from Animal. Thus, we've defined that only animals have legs, but any type of animal can have legs. It's the same for HasWings as shown in Listing 7-20.

Listing 7-20. Trait HasWings

```
trait HasWings extends Animal {
  def flap() {println("Flap Flap")}
}
```

But, only things with wings can fly. This is a different notation. We define the rules of the self type with this: HasWings =>. The compiler flags an error if this trait is not mixed into a class that also extends HasWings. So, we can use self types to define the rules for what classes a given trait can be mixed into (see Listing 2-11).[1]

Listing 7-21. Trait Flies

```
trait Flies {
  this: HasWings =>
  def fly() {println("I'm flying")}
}
```

And Birds have wings and legs:

```
abstract class Bird extends Animal with HasWings with HasLegs
```

Let's define a couple of different Birds in Listing 7-22.

Listing 7-22. Concrete Birds

```
class Robin extends Bird with Flies
class Ostrich extends Bird
```

---

[1]Self types can also be used to discover at compile time what class a trait has been mixed into.
See http://www.scala-lang.org/node/124.

All mammals have a bodyTemperature as shown in Listing 7-23.

Listing 7-23. Mammal Behavior

```
abstract class Mammal extends Animal {
  def bodyTemperature: Double
}
```

Some animals know their name, and if they do, they respond to their name (see listing 7-24).

Listing 7-24. KnowsName Trait

```
trait KnowsName extends Animal {
  def name: String
}
```

So, in Listing 7-25 a Dog is a Mammal that has legs and knows (responds to) its name.

Listing 7-25. Dog Has Legs and Knows Its Name

```
class Dog(val name: String) extends Mammal with HasLegs with KnowsName {
  def bodyTemperature: Double = 99.3
}
```

Some cats and children come to mind as mammals that know their own name but will sometimes ignore their name (Listing 7-26).

Listing 7-26. IgnoresNames Trait

```
trait IgnoresName {
  this: KnowsName =>
  def ignoreName(when: String): Boolean

  def currentName(when: String): Option[String] =
    if (ignoreName(when)) None else Some(name)
}
```

Now we can define a Cat class that has legs, knows its name, and ignores its name except at dinner time (Listing 7-27).

Listing 7-27. Cat Ignores Name Except at Dinner Time

```
class Cat(val name: String) extends Mammal with HasLegs with
  KnowsName with IgnoresName {
  def ignoreName(when: String) = when match {
    case "Dinner" => false
    case _       => true
  }
  def bodyTemperature: Double = 99.5
}
```

Some Animals can be Athletes, and Runners are Athletes with legs:

```
trait Athlete extends Animal.
```

Listing 7-28. Runner Trait

```
trait Runner {
  this: Athlete with HasLegs =>
  def run() {println("I'm running")}
}
```

A Person is a Mammal with legs and knows its name (Listing 7-29).

Listing 7-29. Person Is Mammal with Legs and Knows Its Name

```
class Person(val name: String) extends Mammal with
  HasLegs with KnowsName {
  def bodyTemperature: Double = 98.6
}
```

A Biker is a Person but may only be added to an Athlete (listing 7-30).

Listing 7-30. Biker Trait

```
trait Biker extends Person {
  this: Athlete=>
  def ride() {println("I'm riding my bike")}
}
```

And finally, let's define some Genders (Listing 7-31).

Listing 7-31. Defining Gender

```
trait Gender
trait Male extends Gender
trait Female extends Gender
```

We've defined a complex hierarchy of classes and traits. Let's see what we can do with these classes. First, let's try to create a Dog that's also a Biker:

```
scala> val bikerDog = new Dog("biker") with Athlete with Biker
```

```
<console>:4: error: illegal inheritance; superclass Dog
is not a subclass of the superclass Person
of the mixin trait Biker
    val bikerDog = new Dog("biker") with Athlete with Biker
```

Cool, the compiler enforced our rule about Bikers needing to be Persons. Let's create some valid LivingThings. Please note that we can combine different traits as part of the object creation. So, archer is an instance of a class that is a subclass of Dog that implements Athlete, Runner, and Male. The Scala compiler automatically creates this new, anonymous class for you.

```
scala> val archer = new Dog("archer") with Athlete with Runner with Male
```

```
archer: Dog with Athlete with Runner with Male = $anon$1@18bbc98
```

```
scala> val dpp = new Person("David") with Athlete with Biker with Male
```

```
dpp: Person with Athlete with Biker with Male = $anon$1@7b5617
```

```
scala> val john = new Person("John") with Athlete with Runner with Male
```

```
john: Person with Athlete with Runner with Male = $anon$1@cd927d
```

```
scala> val annette = new Person("Annette") with Athlete with Runner with Female
```

```
annette: Person with Athlete with Runner with Female = $anon$1@1ec41c0
```

We've got a bunch of Animals. Let's see what we can do with them:

```
scala> def goBiking(b: Biker) = println(b.name+" is biking")
goBiking: (Biker)Unit
scala> goBiking(dpp)
```

```
David is biking
```

What happens if we try to send Annette on a bike ride?

```
scala> goBiking(annette)
```

```
<console> :7: error: type mismatch;
  found    : Person with Athlete with Runner with Female
  required: Biker
        goBiking(annette)
```

This makes sense. The method requires a Biker, and Annette is not a Biker. However, just as we can compose a class out of traits, we can require that a class implement more than one trait in order to be the parameter to a method:

```scala
scala> def charityRun(r: Person with Runner) = r.run()
```

```
charityRun: (Person with Runner)Unit
```

The charityRun method can only be called with a parameter that is a subclass of Person and also implements the Runner trait.

```scala
scala> charityRun(annette)
```

```
I'm running
```

What if we try to call the method with a Runner that is not a Person?

```scala
scala> charityRun(archer)
```

```
<console> :7: error: type mismatch;
found       : Dog with Athlete with Runner with Male
required    : Person with Runner
      charityRun(archer)
```

We can define the parameter in terms of traits. The womensRun method may only be called with a parameter that's both a Runner and a Female:

```scala
scala> def womensRun(r: Runner with Female) = r.run()
```

```
womensRun: (Runner with Female)Unit
```

```scala
scala> womensRun(annette)
```

```
I'm running
```

```scala
scala> val madeline = new Cat("Madeline") with Athlete with Runner with Female
```

```
madeline: Cat with Athlete with Runner with Female = $anon$1@11dde0c
```

```scala
scala> womensRun(madeline)
```

```
I'm running
```

In this way, we've modeled complex relationships. We've modeled things in a way that you cannot model with Java. Scala's compositional rules are very powerful tools for defining complex class hierarchies and for specifying the rules for composing classes as well as the rules for passing parameters into methods. In this way, we can make sure that the charityRun method can only be called with valid parameters rather than testing for parameter correctness at runtime and throwing an exception if the parameter is not correct. This increased modeling flexibility combined with enhanced type safety gives the architect another tool to help developers write correct code.

Summary

This chapter has shown you how traits work and how to use them. You saw how a trait encapsulates method and field definitions, which can then be reused by mixing them into classes. You saw that traits are similar to multiple inheritance but they avoid some of the difficulties of multiple inheritance. In the next chapter, we'll explore Collections which is the most noteworthy library in the Scala ecosystem.

■ ■ ■

CHAPTER 8

Scala Type System

Types in a programming language are checked at compile time and can be inferred by a compiler. Scala has a strong and statically typed language with a unified Type system. The two fundamental design considerations of a programming language are static versus dynamic typing and strong versus weak typing.

In static typing, a variable is bound to a particular type. In dynamic typing, the type is bound to the value instead of the variable. Scala and Java are statically typed languages, whereas JavaScript, Python, Groovy, and Ruby, are dynamically typed languages.

If a type is static and strongly typed, every variable must have a definite type. If a type is dynamic and strongly typed, every value must have a definite type. However, in the case of weak typing, a definite type is not defined; Scala, Java, and Ruby are principally strongly typed languages. Some languages, such as C and Perl, are weakly typed.

Scala brings the best of two worlds, in that it feels like a dynamically typed language, because of type inference, and at the same time, Scala gives you all the benefits of static typing in terms of an advanced object model and an advanced type system.

This chapter explores venues such as which type parameters should be covariant, contravariant, or invariant under subtyping, using implicits judiciously, and so forth.

Unified Type System

Scala has a unified type system, enclosed by the type Any at the top of the hierarchy and the type Nothing at the bottom of the hierarchy, as illustrated in Figure 8-1. All Scala types inherit from Any. The subtypes of Any are AnyVal (value types, such as Int and Boolean) and AnyRef (reference types, as in Java). As you can see in the Figure 8-1, the primitive types of Java are enclosed under AnyVal and, unlike Java, you can define your own AnyVal. And also unlike Java, Scala does not have Wrapper Types, such as Integer, to be distinguished from the primitive type, such as int.

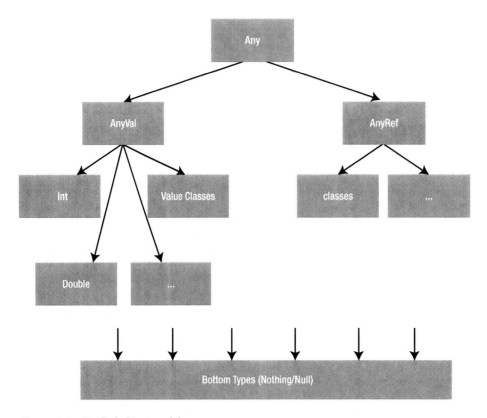

Figure 8-1. *Unified object model*

As you can see in the Figure 8-1, Any is a supertype of both AnyRef and AnyVal. AnyRef corresponds to java.lang.Object, and is the supertype of all objects. AnyVal on the other hand represents the value such as int and other JVM primitives. Because of this hierarchy, it becomes possible to define methods that take Any, thus being compatible with both scala.Int instances as well as java.lang.String (see Listing 8-1).

Listing 8-1. Using Any

```
import scala.collection.mutable.ListBuffer
val list = ListBuffer[Any]()
val x= 2
list += x
class Book
list += new Book()
```

In Listing 8-1, Book extends AnyRef, and x is an Int that extends AnyVal.

```
scala> import scala.collection.mutable.ListBuffer
import scala.collection.mutable.ListBuffer
scala> val list = ListBuffer[Any]()
list: scala.collection.mutable.ListBuffer[Any] = ListBuffer()
scala> val x= 2
x: Int = 2
scala> list += x
res12: list.type = ListBuffer(2)
scala> class Book
defined class Book
scala> list += new Book()
res13: list.type = ListBuffer(2, Book@15e8485)
```

You can limit a method to only be able to work on Value Types as seen in Listing 8-2.

Listing 8-2. Value Types

```
def test(int: AnyVal) = ()
test(5)
test(5.12)
test(new Object)
```

In Listing 8-2, test(5) takes an Int that extends AnyVal and test(5.12) takes a Double that also extends AnyVal. Test(new Object) takes an Object that extends AnyRef. Refer to Figure 8-1. Test(new Object) fails to compile.

```
scala> def test(int: AnyVal) = ()
test: (int: AnyVal)Unit
scala> test(5)
scala> test(5.12)
scala> test(new Object)
<console>:9: error: type mismatch;
 found    : Object
 required: AnyVal
Note that implicit conversions are not applicable because they are ambiguous: both method
ArrowAssoc in object Predef of type [A](self: A)ArrowAssoc[A]and method Ensuring in object
Predef of type [A](self: A)Ensuring[A] are possible conversion functions from Object to
AnyVal
              test(new Object)
                  ^
```

The idea is that this method will only take Value Classes, be it Int or your own Value Type. So, we imply Java code is not as type-safe as Scala code. You're probably thinking, "But Java is a statically typed language, doesn't it give me all the safety that Scala does?" The answer to that is no. Take a look at the Listing 8-3 and spot the problem:

Listing 8-3. Java's Type Unsafety

```
public class Bad {
public static void main(String[] argv) {
Object[] a = argv;
a[0] = new Object();
}
}
```

This is legal Java code, and here's what happens when we run the code:

```
> java Bad Hello
Exception in thread "main" java.lang.ArrayStoreException: java.lang.Object
at Bad.main(Bad.java:4)
```

Java allows us to assign a String[] to Object[]. This is because a String is a subclass of Object, so if the array was read-only, the assignment would make sense. However, the array can be modified. The modification that we've demonstrated shows one of Java's "type-unsafety" features. We'll discuss why this happened and the complex topic of invariant, covariant, and contravariant types later in this chapter. Let's start looking at how Scala makes the architect's job easier and also makes the coder's job easier.

Type Parameterization

Scala's parameterized types are similar to generics in Java. If you are familiar with Java or C# you might already have some understanding of parameterized types. Scala's parametrized types provide the same features as Java generics, but with extended functionalities.

■ **Note** Classes and traits that take type parameters are called generic; the types they generate are called parameterized type.

One straightforward syntactical difference is that Scala uses square brackets ([...]), while Java uses angle brackets (<...>). For example, a list of strings would be declared as shown in Listing 8-4.

Listing 8-4. Scala List of Strings

```
val list : List[String] = List("A", "B", "C")
```

Scala allows angle brackets to be used in the method name. So, to avoid ambiguities, Scala uses square brackets for parameterized types.

Types in Scala are used to define classes, abstract classes, traits, objects, and functions. Type parameterization lets you make these generic. As an example, sets can be defined as generic in the following manner: Set[T]. However, unlike Java which allows raw types, in Scala you are required to specify type parameters, that is to say, the Set[T], is a trait, but not a type because it takes a type parameter.

As a result, you cannot create variables of type Set as illustrated in Listing 8-5.

Listing 8-5. Scala Requires to Specify Type Parameters

```
def test(s: Set) {} // this will not compile
```

```
scala> def test(s: Set) {}
<console>:14: error: type Set takes type parameters
       def test(s: Set) {}
                   ^
```

Instead, trait Set enables you to specify parameterized types, such as Set[String], Set[Int], or Set[AnyRef] as in Listing 8-6.

Listing 8-6. Specifying Parameter Types

```
def test(s: Set[AnyRef]) {}
```

```
scala> def test(s: Set[AnyRef]) {}
test: (s: Set[AnyRef])Unit
```

For example, trait Set in Listing 8-6 defines a generic set where the specific sets are Set[Int] and Set[String], and so forth. Thus, Set is a trait, and Set[String] is a type. The Set is a generic trait.

■ **Note** In Scala, List, Set, and so on could also be referred as a type constructors, because they are used to create specific types. You could construct a type by specifying a type parameter. For example, List is the type constructor for List[String] and List[String] is a type. While Java allows raw types, Scala requires that you specify type parameters and does not allow you to use just a List in the place of a type, as it's expecting a real type–not a type constructor.

In the light of inheritance, type parameters raise an important question regarding whether Set[String] be considered a subtype of Set[AnyRef]. That is, if S is a subtype of type T, then should Set[S] be considered a subtype of Set[T]? Next you will learn a generic type concept that defines the inheritance relation and answers the aforementioned question.

Variance

Variance defines inheritance relationships of parameterized types, which brings to light whether a Set[String], for example, is a subtype of Set[AnyRef]. A declaration like class Set[+A] means that Set is parameterized by a type A. The + is called a variance annotation.

Variance is an important and challenging concept. It defines the rules by which parameterized types can be passed as parameters. In the beginning of the chapter, we showed how passing a String[] (Java notation) to a method expecting an Object[] can cause problems. Java allows you to pass an array of something to a method expecting an array of something's superclass. This is called covariance. On the surface, this makes a lot of sense. If you can pass a String to a method expecting an Object, why can't you pass an Array[String] (Scala notation) to a method expecting an Array[Object]? Because Array is mutable; it can be written to in addition to being read from, so a method that takes an Array[Object] may modify the Array by inserting something that cannot be inserted into an Array[String].

Defining the type variance for type parameters allows you to control how parameterized types can be passed to methods. Variance comes in three flavors: invariant, covariant, and contravariant. Type parameters can be individually marked as covariant or contravariant and are by default invariant. Variance in Scala is defined by using + and - signs in front of type parameters.

Covariant Parameter Types

Covariant parameter types are designated with a + before the type parameter. A covariant type is useful for read-only containers. Scala's List is defined as List[+T], which means that it's covariant on type T. List is covariant because if you pass a List[String] to a method that expects a List[Any], then every element of the List satisfies the requirement that is an Any and we cannot change the contents of the List. Figure 8-2 gives a very clear picture of Covariance, i.e. if S extends T then Class[S] extends Class[T].

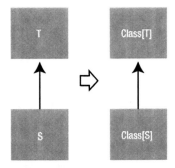

Figure 8-2. *Covariance in Scala*

■ **Tip**   Covariance: If S extends T then Class[S] extends Class[T].

Let's define an immutable class, Getable (see Listing 8-7). Once an instance of Getable is created, it cannot change, so we can mark its type, T, as covariant.

Listing 8-7. Immutable Class Getable

```
class Getable[+T](val data: T)
```

```
scala> class Getable[+T](val data: T)
defined class Getable
```

Let's define a method that takes a Getable[Any] (see Listing 8-8).

Listing 8-8. Defining a Method That Takes a Getable

```
def get(in: Getable[Any]) {println("It's "+in.data)}
```

```
scala> def get(in: Getable[Any]) {println("It's "+in.data)}
get: (Getable[Any])Unit
```

We define an instance of Getable[String] in Listing 8-9.

Listing 8-9. Instance of Getable

```
val gs = new Getable("String")
```

```
scala> val gs = new Getable("String")
gs: Getable[java.lang.String] = Getable@10a69f0
```

We can call get with gs:

```
scala> get(gs)
It's String
```

Let's try the same example but passing a Getable[java.lang.Double] into something that expects a Getable[Number] (see Listing 8-10).

Listing 8-10. Passing Double

```
def getNum(in: Getable[Number]) = in.data.intValue
def gd = new Getable(new java.lang.Double(33.3))
getNum(gd)
```

```
scala> def getNum(in: Getable[Number]) = in.data.intValue
getNum: (Getable[java.lang.Number])Int
scala> def gd = new Getable(new java.lang.Double(33.3))
gd: Getable[java.lang.Double]
scala> getNum(gd)
res7: Int = 33
```

Yes, the covariance works the way we expect it to. We can make read-only classes covariant. That means that contravariance is good for write-only classes.

Contravariant Parameter Types

So, if covariance allows us to pass List[String] to a method that expects List[Any], what good is contravariance? Contravariance indicates if S extends T, then Class[T] extends Class[S] as illustrated in Figure 8-3.

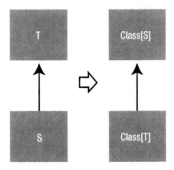

Figure 8-3. *Contravariance in Scala*

■ **Tip**   Contravariance: If S extends T then `Class[T]` extends `Class[S]`.

Let's first look at a write-only class, `Putable` (see Listing 8-11).

Listing 8-11. Putable Class

```
scala> class Putable[-T] {
def put(in: T) {println("Putting "+in)}
}
```

Next, let's define a method that takes a `Putable[String]`:

```
scala> def writeOnly(in: Putable[String]) {in.put("Hello")}
writeOnly: (Putable[String])Unit
```

And let's declare an instance of `Putable[AnyRef]`:

```
scala> val p = new Putable[AnyRef]
p: Putable[AnyRef] = Putable@75303f
```

And what happens if we try to call `writeOnly`?

```
scala> writeOnly(p)
Putting Hello
```

Okay, so we can call a method that expects a `Putable[String]` with a `Putable[AnyRef]` because we are guaranteed to call the put method with a String, which is a subclass of `AnyRef`. Standing alone, this is not particularly valuable, but if we have a class that does something with input that results in output, the value of contravariance becomes obvious.

The inputs to a transformation are contravariant. Calling something that expects at leastany AnyRef with a String is legal and valid. But the return value can be covariant because we expect to get back a Number, so if we get an Integer, a subclass of Number, we're okay. Let's see how it works. We'll define DS with a contravariant In type and a covariant Out type:

```scala
scala> trait DS[-In, +Out]{def apply(i: In): Out}
defined trait DS
```

Let's create an instance that will convert Any into an Int:

```scala
scala> val t1 = new DS[Any, Int]{def apply(i: Any) = i.toString.toInt}
t1: java.lang.Object with DS[Any,Int] = $anon$1@14dcfad
```

We define check, a method that takes a DS[String, Any]:

```scala
scala> def check(in: DS[String, Any]) = in("333")
check: (DS[String,Any])Any
```

And we call check with t1:

```scala
scala> check(t1)
res14: Any = 333
```

Invariant Parameter Types

In Scala, Array[T] is invariant. This means that you can only pass an Array[String] to foo(a: Array[String]) and that you can only pass an Array[Object] to bar(a: Array[Object]). Figure 8-4 gives a clear picture of Invariant parameter types.

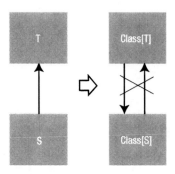

Figure 8-4. *Invariance in Scala*

This ensures that what is read from or written to the array is something of the correct type. So, for anything that's mutable, the type parameter should be invariant. You do this by doing nothing with the type parameter. So, let's define an invariant class (see Listing 8-12).

Listing 8-12. Defining an Invariant Class

```
class Holder[T](var data: T)
```

The class holds data of type T. Let's write a method (see Listing 8-13).

Listing 8-13. add Method

```
def add(in: Holder[Int]) {in.data = in.data + 1}
```

```
scala> def add(in: Holder[Int]) {in.data = in.data + 1}
add: (Holder[Int])Unit
scala> val h = new Holder(0)
h: Holder[Int] = Holder@bc0eba
scala> add(h)
scala> h.data
res2: Int = 1
```

Because the add method expects an Int to come out of Holder and puts an Int back into the Holder, the type of the Holder must be invariant. That does not mean that invariant containers lose their ability to hold subclasses of their declared type. A Holder[Number] can contain a Double, and an Array[Object] can contain String, Integer, and so on. Let's put a Double into a Holder[Number]:

```
scala> val nh = new Holder[Number](33.3d)
nh: Holder[java.lang.Number] = Holder@340c9c
```

And we define a method that rounds the number:

```
scala> def round(in: Holder[Number]) {in.data = in.data.intValue}
round: (Holder[java.lang.Number])Unit
```

We call the round method, and let's see what we get out the other side:

```
scala> round(nh)
scala> nh.data
res16: java.lang.Number = 33
```

We put in a Number and got back a Number. What's the underlying class for the Number?

```
scala> nh.data.getClass
res17: java.lang.Class[_] = class java.lang.Integer
```

Great. Integer is a subclass of Number, so we can put an Integer or a Double into the Holder[Number]. We preserve the ability to use class hierarchies with invariant type parameters. Let's finally see what happens when we try to pass a Holder[Double] into round.

```
scala> val dh = new Holder(33.3d)
dh: Holder[Double] = Holder@1801e5f
scala> round(dh)
<console>:8: error: type mismatch;
found : Holder[Double]
required: Holder[java.lang.Number]
```

So, invariant type parameters protect us when we have mutable data structures such as arrays.

Rules of Variance

So, we've successfully defined and used an invariant type. The invariant type was mutable, so it both returned and was called with a particular type. We created a covariant type that was an immutable holder of a value. Finally, we created a transformer that had contravariant input and covariant output. Wait, that sounds like a function. That's right, Scala's FunctionN traits have contravariant parameters and covariant results. This leads us to the simple rules of variance:

- Mutable containers should be invariant.

- Immutable containers should be covariant.

- Inputs to transformations should be contravariant, and outputs from transformations should be covariant.

Type Bounds

When defining a parametrized type, bounds allow you to place restrictions on type parameters. Thus a bounded type is restricted to a specific type or its derived type.

Upper Type Bounds

An upper bound type is restricted to a specific type or one of its derived types Scala provides the upper bound relation operator (<:), which you can use to specify an upper bound for a type.

The type parameter A <: AnyRef means any type A that is a subtype of AnyRef. So the <: operator signifies that the type to the left of the <: operator must be a subtype of the type to the right of the <: operator. Moreover the type the left of the <: operator could be the same type of the right of the <: operator.

The type parameter A <: AnyRef means that the type to the left of the <: operator must be derived from the type to the right of the <: operator or the type to the left of the <: operator could be the same type of the right of the <: operator. In other words, the upper type bounds (and as we will explain in the next section, lower type bounds) restrict the allowed types that can be used for a type parameter when instantiating a type from a parameterized type as illustrated in the following Listing 8-15:

Listing 8-15. Defining an Upper Type Bound

```
def test[A <: AnyRef]
```

In Listing 8-15, the upper type bound says that any type used for parameter A must be a subtype of AnyRef.

The upper type bound is different from type variance in that type variance determines how actual types of the type are related, for example how the actual types List[AnyRef] and List[String] of the type List are related. Let's explore this with an example illustrated in Listing 8-16.

Listing 8-16. Defining an Employee Class Hierarchy

```
class Employee (val name: String)
class Internal (name: String) extends Employee(name)
class FreeLancer(name: String) extends Employee(name)
class Customer (name: String)
```

```
scala> class Employee (val name: String)
defined class Employee
scala> class Internal (name: String) extends Employee(name)
defined class Internal
scala> class FreeLancer(name: String) extends Employee(name)
defined class FreeLancer
scala> class Customer (name: String)
defined class Customer
```

Now define a function that takes a parameter with an upper bound as illustrated in Listing 8-17.

Listing 8-17. Defining a Function that Takes a Parameter with an Upper Bound

```
def employeeName [A <: Employee](emp: A) { println(emp.name) }
```

```
scala> def employeeName [A <: Employee](emp: A) { println(emp.name) }
employeeName: [A <: Employee](emp: A)Unit
```

Now test the employeeName as shown:

```
employeeName (new Internal ("Paul"))
```

```
scala> employeeName (new Internal ("Paul"))
Paul
```

Now test with FreeLancer as shown:

```
employeeName (new FreeLancer ("John"))
```

```
scala> employeeName (new FreeLancer ("John"))
John
```

Now test with the `Customer` class as shown in Listing 8-18.

Listing 8-18. The Customer Class Is Not a subtype of Employee

```
employeeName (new Customer ("Peter"))
```

```
scala> employeeName (new Customer ("Peter"))
<console>:35: error: inferred type arguments [Customer] do not conform to method
 employeeName's type parameter bounds [A <: Employee]
              employeeName (new Customer ("Peter"))
              ^
<console>:35: error: type mismatch;
 found    : Customer
 required: A
              employeeName (new Customer ("Peter"))
```

As you can see, because of the upper bound restriction, Listing 8-18 does not compile, as the `Customer` class is not a subtype of `Employee`.

Lower Type Bounds

A lower bound type is restricted to a specific type or its supertype. The type selected must be equal to or a supertype of the lower bound restriction. Listing 8-19 defines a lower type bound.

Listing 8-19. Defining Lower Type Bound

```
class A {
type B >: List[Int]
def someMethod(a : B) = a
}
```

As you can see, we define `type B` inside `class A` to have a lower bound of `List[Int]`. We instantiate a variable `st` as a subtype of `A` as shown in Listing 8-20.

Listing 8-20. Instantiate the Subtype

```
scala> val st = new A { type B = Traversable[Int] }
```

We can call the `some Method` with a `Set` class. This is because `Set`, even if not a supertype of the `List` class, is a subtype of `Traversable`.

Implicit Class

Using types, especially when type inferencing makes them invisible, is simple and doesn't take a lot of thought away from the task at hand. Well-defined types and type interactions will stay out of the library consumer's way but guard against program errors.

We've seen a little bit of stuff so far that looks like magic. The String class seems to have grown methods:

```scala
scala> "Hello".toList
res0: List[Char] = List(H, e, l, l, o)
```

You may be wondering how a Java class that is final could have additional methods on it. Well, Scala has a feature called implicit conversion. If you have an instance of a particular type, and you need another type, and there's an implicit conversion in scope, Scala will call the implicit method to perform the conversion. For example, some date-related methods take Long, and some take java.util.Date. It's useful to have conversions between the two. We create a method that calculates the number of days based on a Long containing a millisecond count:

```scala
scala> def millisToDays(in: Long): Int = (in / (1000L * 3600L * 24L)).toInt
```

We can calculate the number of days by passing a Long to the method:

```scala
scala> millisToDays(5949440999L)
res3: Int = 68
```

Let's try to pass a Date into the method:

```scala
scala> import java.util.Date
import java.util.Date
scala> millisToDays(new Date)
res31: Int = 16429
```

But sometimes it's valuable to convert between one type and another. We are used to the conversion in some contexts: Int ➤ Long, Int ➤ Double, and so on. We can define a method that will automatically be called when we need the conversion:

```scala
scala> implicit def dateToLong(d: Date) = d.getTime
dateToLong: (java.util.Date)Long
```

And this allows us to call millisToDays with a Date instance:

```scala
scala> millisToDays(new Date)
res5: Int = 14286
```

You may think that implicit conversions are dangerous and reduce type safety. In some cases that's true. You should be very careful with them, and their use should be an explicit design choice. However, we see that sometimes implicit conversions (e.g., Int ➤ Long) are very valuable, for example, when we have a method that takes a parameter that must be a Long:

```
scala> def m2[T <: Long](in: T): Int = (in / (1000L * 3600L * 24L)).toInt
m2: [T <: Long](T)Int
scala> m2(33)
<console>:8: error: inferred type arguments [Int] do not conform to method m2's
type parameter bounds [T <: Long]
m2(33)
^
```

So having to type the following could get very old:

```
scala> m2(33.toLong)
res8: Int = 0
```

What is the scope of implicits? The Scala compiler considers an implicit in the current scope if:

- The implicit is defined in the current class or in a superclass.

- The implicit is defined in a trait or supertrait, or is mixed into the current class or a superclass.

- The implicit is defined on the companion object of the current target class.

- The implicit is available on an object that has been imported into the current scope.

When designing libraries, be careful about defining implicits, and make sure they are in as narrow a scope as is reasonable. When consuming libraries, make sure the implicits defined in the objects are narrow enough and are not going to cause problems such as getting stuff from every Option.

Implicit conversions are powerful tools and potentially very dangerous. We mean wicked dangerous. Back in the day, we put the implicit in Listing 8-21 into a library.

Listing 8-21. Implicit Conversion

```
implicit def oToT[T](in: Option[T]): T = in.get
```

This was convenient, very convenient. We no longer had to test Options. We just passed them around, and they were converted from an Option to their underlying type. And when we removed the implicit, we had 150 code changes to make. That was 150 latent defects. Using implicits to convert to a class that has a particular method is a good reason. There's very little likelihood of damage.

```
scala> implicit def oToT[T](in: Option[T]): T = in.get
warning: there were 1 feature warning(s); re-run with -feature for details
oToT: [T](in: Option[T])T
```

Until Scala 2.10, implicit conversion was handled by implicit def methods that took the original instance and returned a new instance of the desired type. Implicit methods have been supplanted by implicit classes, which provide a safer and more limited scope for converting existing instances.

Scala 2.10 introduced a new feature called implicit classes. An implicit class is a class marked with the implicit keyword. This keyword makes the class's primary constructor available for implicit conversions when the class is in scope.

To create an implicit class, simply place the implicit keyword in front of an appropriate class. Here's an example:

Listing 8-22. Implicit Class

```
object Helper {
        implicit class Greeting(val x: Int) {
          def greet= "Hello " * x
        }
      }
```

```
scala> object Helper {
     |           implicit class Greeting(val x: Int) {
     |             def greet= "Hello " * x
     |           }
     |         }
defined object Helper
```

To use this class, just import it into scope and call the greet method:

```
scala> import Helper._
import Helper._
scala> println(3.greet)
Hello Hello Hello
```

For an implicit class to work, its name must be in scope and unambiguous, like any other implicit value or conversion.

Implicit classes have the following restrictions:

- They must be defined inside of another trait/class/object.

    ```
    object Helpers {
    implicit class RichInt(x: Int) // OK!
    }
    implicit class RichDouble(x: Double) // BAD!
    ```

- They may only take one non-implicit argument in their constructor.

    ```
    implicit class RichDate(date: java.util.Date) // OK!
    implicit class Indexer[T](collecton: Seq[T], index: Int) // BAD!
    implicit class Indexer[T](collecton: Seq[T])(implicit index: Index) // OK!
    ```

While it's possible to create an implicit class with more than one non-implicit argument, such classes aren't used during implicit lookup.

- There may not be any method, member or object in scope with the same name as the implicit class. This means an implicit class cannot be a case class.

```
object Bar
implicit class Bar(x: Int) // BAD!
val x = 5
implicit class x(y: Int) // BAD!
implicit case class Baz(x: Int) // BAD!
```

Abstract Types

The abstract type allows you to define generic classes, but instead of using the conventional syntax, you name them inside the class as shown in Listing 8-23.

Listing 8-23. Abstract Type

```
trait Container {
  type A
  def value: A
}
```

```
scala> trait Container {
     |    type A
     |    def value: A
     | }
defined trait Container
```

In Listing 8-23, type A is an abstract type member. Now we can implement the value method which returns an Int.

Listing 8-24. Implementing the Method

```
object OnlyInt extends Container {
  type A = Int

  def value = 2
}
```

You can also apply constraints to an abstract type member so that the container can only store anything that is of a Number instance. Such constraint can be annotated on a type member right where we defined it first as illustrated in Listing 8-25.

Listing 8-25. Applying Constraint

```
trait AnyNumber{
  type A <: Number
}
```

Let's now mix in the trait AnyNumber as shown in Listing 8-26.

Listing 8-26. Mix in the Trait

```
trait Container{
  type A <: Number
  def value: A
}

object AnyNumber extends Container {
  def value = 2
}
```

Higher-Kinded Types

Higher-kinded types use other types to construct a new type. This is similar to higher-order functions that take other functions as parameters. A higher-kinded type can have one or more other types as parameters. In Scala, you can do this using the type keyword.

We will use the :kind command. It allows you to check whether a type is higher kind. Let's check it out on a simple type constructor, such as List[+A]:

```
:kind List
```

```
scala> :kind List
scala.collection.immutable.List's kind is F[+A]
```

:kind -v List

```
scala> :kind -v List
scala.collection.immutable.List's kind is F[+A]
* -(+)-> *
This is a type constructor: a 1st-order-kinded type.
```

Here we see that scalac can tell us that List, in fact, is a type constructor. Let's investigate the syntax right above this information:

```
*  -(+)->  *
```

This says "takes one type, returns another type."
Something that takes two parameters, say Map[_, _] has the kind:

```
*  ->  *  -(+)->  *
```

```
scala> :kind -v Map[_, _]
scala.collection.immutable.Map's kind is F[A1,+A2]
*  ->  *  -(+)->  *
This is a type constructor: a 1st-order-kinded type.
```

You can have kinds that are themselves parameterized by higher-kinded types. So, something could not only take a type, but take something that itself takes type parameters.

Summary

In this chapter you learned Scala's rules about variance, Type bounds, and implicit classes and also a brief overview on Abstract types and higher-kinded types in Scala.

CHAPTER 9

Scala and Java Interoperability

One of the main design goals of Scala is running on a JVM and providing interoperability with Java. The need for Scala and Java interoperability arises when you want to use existing Java libraries or frameworks. Scala code is often used in tandem with large Java programs and frameworks. Even though integration with Java is easy for the most part, we encourage you to use pure Scala as much as possible. When you are working with the Java library or framework, first try to find something equivalent in Scala, and use Java if there's no equivalent Scala library available.

Scala is compiled to Java bytecodes, and you can use tools like Java class file disassembler javap to disassemble bytecodes generated by the Scala compiler. By running on a JVM you can take advantage of all the frameworks and tools built into other JVM languages. In most cases, Scala features are translated into Java features so that Scala can easily integrate with Java. However, some Scala features don't directly map to Java, and in such case you have to learn how to handle features that are available in Java but not in Scala. The features that are available in Java but not in Scala are static members and checked exceptions, and some of the Scala features that are not available in Java is traits. If you are using Java from Scala, you have to deal with mutability, exceptions, and nulls that are interdicted in the Scalaworld. Because Scala works seamlessly with Java, most of the time you can combine the languages without worrying too much.

This chapter describes how Scala is translated to Java and the use of Java annotations in Scala framework. The goal of this chapter is to show you how easily you can integrate Scala with Java. You'll also learn how Scala annotations help in integration—for example, generating JavaBean-style getters and setters.

Translating Java Classes to Scala Classes

The interoperability between Scala and Java classes makes it straightforward to replace or extend an existing Java class with a Scala class. Listing 9-1 shows a Class declaration in Java.

Listing 9-1. A Class Declaration in Java

```
public class Book {}
```

Contrast Listing 9-1 with Listing 9-2.

Listing 9-2. Scala Equivalent of a Class Declaration

```
class Book
```

As you learned in the Chapter 3, you don't need braces when there's no content and everything is public in Scala by default.

Now define a Java class with constructor that binds instance variables with accessors as illustrated in Listing 9-3.

Listing 9-3. A Java Class with a Constructor

```java
public class Book {
  private final int isbn;
  private final String title;

  public Book(int isbn, String title) {
    this.isbn = isbn;
    this.title = title;
  }

  public int getIsbn() {
    return isbn;
  }

  public String y() {
    return y;
  }
}
```

As you can see in Listing 9-3, the constructor binds the instance variables isbn and title with accessors getIsbn and getTitle. Let's see the Scala equivalent as shown in Listing 9-4.

Listing 9-4. Scala Equivalent of Listing 9-3

```scala
class Book(val isbn: Int, val title: String)
```

As you can see in Listing 9-4, adding val makes the constructor arg bind to a field of the same name. Listing 9-5 shows the Java class NonFiction with a constructor that calls the superclass.

Listing 9-5. Constructor Calling Superclass in Java

```java
public class NonFiction extends Book {
  public NonFiction(String title) {
    super(title)
  }
}
```

Listing 9-6 shows the Scala equivalent of Listing 9-5.

Listing 9-6. Scala Equivalent of Listing 9-5

```scala
class NonFiction (title: String) extends Book(title)
```

You can see in Listing 9-6 that the primary constructor goes in the declaration. What about the multiple constructors? You will see that in the section that follows. Let's compare the mutable and immutable instance variables in Java and Scala. Listing 9-7 illustrates the mutable instance variable in Java.

Listing 9-7. Mutable Instance Variable in Java

```java
public class Book {
  private String title = "Beginning Scala";

  public String getTitle() {
    return title;
  }

  public void setTitle(String t) {
title = t;
  }
}
```

Listing 9-8 illustrates the Scala equivalent of Listing 9-7.

Listing 9-8. Scala Equivalent of Listing 9-7

```scala
class Book {
  var  title = "Beginning Scala"
}
```

As you can see in Listing 9-8, just writing var in the class body defines a mutable field. Now let's see the immutable instance variables in Java and Scala. Listing 9-9 illustrates an immutable instance variable in Java.

Listing 9-9. Immutable Instance Variable in Java

```java
public class Book {
  private final intisbn = 999;

  public int getIsbn() {
    return isbn;
  }
}
```

Listing 9-10 illustrates the Scala equivalent of Listing 9-9.

Listing 9-10. Scala Equivalent of Listing 9-9

```scala
class Book {
  val isbn = 999
}
```

As you may have noticed in Listing 9-9, isbn is also the name of an accessor method.

TRANSLATING JAVA IMPORTS TO SCALA IMPORTS

```
// import in Java
importcom.modA.ClassA;
import com.modB.ClassB1;
import com.modB.ClassB2;
importcom.modC.*;

// import in Scala
importcom.modA.ClassA;
importcom.modB.{ClassB1, ClassB2} // You can stack multiple imports from the same
package in braces.
importcom.modC._ // Underscore in Scala imports is equivalent of * in Java imports.
```

Fortified with these reflections, let's now see how to translate multiple constructors while refactoring a Java class to a Scala class. For instance, let's take the Book Java class shown in Listing 9-11:

Listing 9-11. Java class with Multiple Constructors

```
public class Book {
private Integer isbn;
private String title;
public Book(Integer isbn) {
this.isbn = isbn;
}
public Book(Integer isbn, String title) {
this.isbn = isbn;
this.title = title;
}
public Integer getIsbn() {
return isbn;
}
public void setIsbn(Integer isbn) {
this.isbn = isbn;
}
public String getTitle() {
return title;
}
public void setTitle(String title) {
this.title = title;
}
}
```

As you can see in the Listing 9-11, the Book Java class has two constructors, one that takes isbn as the parameter and the other that takes isbn and title as the parameters. The Book Java class also has getters and setters for title and isbn. Now let's refactor the Book Java class into a Scala class with class parameters and create an instance as shown in Listing 9-12.

Listing 9-12. Refactoring Listing 9-11

```
class Book ( var isbn: Int, var title: String)
```

You can try Listing 9-12 on the REPL:

```
scala> class Book ( var isbn: Int, var title: String)
defined class Book
scala> val book = new Book(999, "Beginning Scala")
book: Book = Book@10ddb0e
```

However, a constructor that takes only a single parameter title does not exist in the Listing 9-12 definition. For example if you create the Book instance with a constructor that takes a single title parameter, you will get an error, as following on the REPL:

```
<console>:8: error: not enough arguments for constructor Book: (isbn: Int, title: String)
Book.
Unspecified value parameter title.
        val book2 = new Book("Beginning Java")
                    ^
```

To complete our refactoring of the Java class, we need an extra constructor as shown in Listing 9-13:

Listing 9-13. Scala Equivalent of Listing 9-11

```
class Book ( var isbn: Int, var title: String) {
def this( title: String) = this(0,title)
}
```

Is Listing 9-13 comprehensible to you? You learned about auxiliary constructors in Chapter 3. As you may recall, any auxiliary constructor must immediately call another this(...) constructor and call the primary constructor to make sure all the parameters are initialized.

Now you can try Listing 9-13 on the REPL as shown:

```
scala> class Book ( var isbn: Int, var title: String) {
     | def this( title: String) = this(0,title)
     | }
defined class Book
scala> val book1 = new Book(999, "Beginning Scala")
book1: Book = Book@132c5fd
scala> val book2 = new Book("Beginning Java")
book2: Book = Book@3e4e8a
```

This time, we created an instance with the auxiliary constructor.

Now access title and isbn on REPL as shown:

```
scala> book1.title
res38: String = Beginning Scala
scala> book2.title
res39: String = Beginning Java
scala> book1.isbn
res40: Int = 9999
```

You can also set title as following:

```
scala> book2.title = "Beginning Groovy"
book2.title: String = Beginning Groovy
scala> book2.title
res42: String = Beginning Groovy
```

So we can get and set title and isbn. But if you compare Listing 9-13 with Listing 9-11, you will see that we did not add the getters and setters to Listing 9-13 corresponding to Listing 9-11. But you can still get and set isbn and title because of the generated getters and setters that follow the Scala convention. When you compile Listing 9-13 with scalac and then disassemble it with javap, you'll see that no getter or setter methods corresponding to Listing 9-11 are generated and the only getters and setters that are generated are the ones that follow the Scala convention as shown in Listing 9-14:

```
>scalac Book.scala
>javap Book
```

Listing 9-14. Compiled from "Book.scala" in Listing 9-11

```
public class Book {
  public int isbn();
  public void isbn_$eq(int);
  public java.lang.String title();
  public void title_$eq(java.lang.String);
  public Book(int, java.lang.String);
  public Book(java.lang.String);
}
```

So the class definition in Listing 9-13 generates getter and setters that follow scala convention but not that follow Java convention as shown in the Listing 9-11. Generating getters and setters that follow Java convention becomes important when you need to interact with a Java class or a library that accepts only classes that conform to the JavaBean specification. We will see this in the next section.

JavaBeans Specification Compliant Scala Classes

To ensure compatibility with Java frameworks, you may need Java-style getters and setters on the fields of your class to interact with a Java class or library that accepts only classes that conform to the JavaBean specification. To have Java-style getters and setters is to annotate the field with `scala.beans.BeanProperty` as shown in the following lines of command in Listing 9-15:

Listing 9-15. Annotating Constructor Parameter with @BeanProperty

```
import scala.beans.BeanProperty
class Book(@BeanProperty var isbn:Int, @BeanProperty var title:String)
```

You can run the Listing 9-15 in REPL as following:

```
scala> import scala.beans.BeanProperty
import scala.beans.BeanProperty
scala> class Book(@BeanProperty var isbn:Int, @BeanProperty var title:String)
defined class Book
```

You can see how the @BeanProperty annotation works by compiling the Book class and then disassembling it. First, save these contents to a file named `Book.scala`:
Then compile the class:

```
$ scalac Book.scala
```

After it's compiled, disassemble it with the javap command:

```
$ javap Book
```

Listing 9-16 shows the compiled Book class from `Book.scala`.

Listing 9-16. Compiled from "Book.scala" in Listing 9-15

```
public class Book {
  public int isbn();
  public void isbn_$eq(int);
  public void setIsbn(int);
  public java.lang.String title();
  public void title_$eq(java.lang.String);
  public void setTitle(java.lang.String);
  public int getIsbn();
  public java.lang.String getTitle();
  public Book(int, java.lang.String);
}
```

As you can see from the disassembled code, the methods getTitle, setTitle, getIsbn, and setIsbn have all been generated because of the @BeanProperty annotation. Note that without these methods, your class will not follow the JavaBean specification.

■ **Note**   Use the @BeanProperty annotation on your fields, also making sure you declare each field as a var. if you declare your fields as type val, the setter methods (setTitle, setIsbn) won't be generated.

You saw how to use the @BeanProperty annotation on class constructor parameters. In the same manner, you can also use the @BeanProperty annotation on the fields in a Scala class.

Next you will learn to use a Scala feature not available in Java, such as traits.

Java Interfaces and Scala Traits

A Java class can't extend a Scala trait that has implemented methods. To understand the problem let's first look at a regular Java interface as shown in Listing 9-17.

Listing 9-17. A Regular Java Interface Declaration

```java
public interface Book {
  public abstract boolean isBestSeller();
}
```

The Scala equivalent of Listing 9-17 is shown as following:

Listing 9-18. Scala Equivalent of Listing 9-17

```scala
trait Book {
  def isBestSeller: Boolean
}
```

As you can see in the Listing 9-17, isBestSeller is an abstract method. In Scala, methods are denoted with a def keyword. But isBestSeller in Listing 9-17 is an abstract method. How do we represent abstract method in Scala? In Scala, if there is no = assignment, then the methods denoted with a def keyword or the functions denoted with a val keyword are abstract. For example, let's look at the Java method that returns some value in Listing 9-19.

Listing 9-19. A Concrete Java Method

```java
public String someMethod(int arg1, boolean arg2) {
  return "voila";
}
```

The Scala equivalent of Listing 9-19 is shown in Listing 9-20.

Listing 9-20. Scala Equivalent of Listing 9-19

```scala
def someMethod(arg1: Int, arg2: Boolean): String = "voila"
```

As you can see in Listing 9-20, =denotes the implementation.

Now let's look at an abstract Java method as illustrated in Listing 9-21.

Listing 9-21. An Abstract Java Method

```
abstract int doTheMath(int i);
```

The Scala equivalent of an abstract Java method doStuff is shown in Listing 9-22.

Listing 9-22. Scala Equivalent of Listing 9-21

```
def doTheMath(i: Int): Int
```

■ **Note**   If there's no definition provided with =, then it's automatically abstract.

Now let's go back to the original problem. A Java class can't extend a Scala trait that has implemented methods. So if you are trying to use Scala a trait (that has implemented methods in it) from Java you will run into problems. To demonstrate the problem, first create a trait with a simple implemented method named add (see Listing 9-23).

Listing 9-23. A Scala Trait

```
trait Computation {
def add(a: Int, b: Int) = a + b
}
```

You've written a Scala trait with implemented methods and need to be able to use an add method from a Java application (see Listing 9-24).

Listing 9-24. A Java Application

```
public class DoTheMath{
public static void main(String[] args) {
DoTheMath d = new DoTheMath();
// do the math here
}
}
```

The type Computation cannot be the superclass of Java class DoTheMath simply because a superclass in Java must be a class; that is, Java class DoTheMath cannot use the extend keyword to extend Computation. Moreover, the Java class DoTheMath cannot implement the trait Computation because in Java you implement interfaces, and the trait Computation has an implemented behavior, so Computation is not a like a regular Java interface. To be able to use the implemented method add of a Scala trait Computation from Java class DoTheMath, you must wrap the trait Computation in a Scala class. Listing 9-25 shows a Scala class that wraps the trait Computation.

Listing 9-25. Scala Class that Wraps the Trait Computation

```
class JavaInteroperableComputation extends Computation
```

Now the Java class DoTheMath can extend the Scala Java Interoperable Computation class, and access the add method as shown in the Listing 9-26.

Listing 9-26. Accessing the add Method of the Scala Trait from Java Class

```
public class DoTheMath extends JavaInteroperableComputation{
public static void main(String[] args) {
DoTheMath d = new DoTheMath();
d.add(3,1);
}
}
```

■ **Note** Wrap your Scala traits with implemented behavior in the Scala class for its Java callers.

Java Static Members and Scala Objects

Java code often refers to the static keyword to implement a singleton object as shown in Listing 9-27.

Listing 9-27. A Singleton in Scala

```
public class Book{
    private static Book book;
    private Book() {}
    public static synchronized Book getInstance() {
        if (book == null) {
book = new Book();
        }
        return book;
    }
}
```

There is no such thing as static in Scala. In Java, the static does not belong to an object, can't be inherited, and doesn't participate in polymorphism, thus statics aren't object-oriented. Scala, on the other hand, is purely object-oriented. Scala does not support the static, but instead provides the notion of an object in place of the class declaration. If you need to refactor Java code in Listing 9-27 into Scala, simply use the object declaration instead of class as shown in Listing 9-28.

Listing 9-28. Scala Equivalent of Listing 9-27

```
object Book{
}
```

Scala objects give you extra advantage in that Scala objects can also extend interfaces and traits. So Scala provides a special syntax that gives you a singleton for free, without all the syntax involved in declaring (see in Listing 9-27). But what if you want to mix static and instance members? In Java, you can do this as shown in Listing 9-29.

Listing 9-29. Java class with Instance and Static Methods

```java
public class Book {
    public String getCategory() {
        return "Non-Fiction";
    }

    public static Book createBook() {
        return new Book();
    }
}
```

In addition to the notion of object, Scala provides the notion of companion object, which consists of an object that cohabits with a class of the same name in the same package and file. The companion object enables storing of static methods and from this, you have full access to the classes' members, including private ones. Scala allows you to declare both an object and a class of the same name, placing the static members in the object and the instance members in the class. The Scala equivalent of Listing 9-29 is shown in Listing 9-30.

Listing 9-30. Scala Equivalent of Listing 9-29

```scala
class Book {
  defgetCategory() = " Non-Fiction"
}
object Book {
  def createBook() = new Book()
}
```

Handling Exceptions

You can define the Scala method as shown in Listing 9-31, without declaring that it throws an exception.

Listing 9-31. A Scala Method that Throws an Exception

```scala
class SomeClass {
def aScalaMethod {
throw new Exception("Exception")
}
}
```

This method can then be called from Java as shown in Listing 9-32.

Listing 9-32. Calling a Scala Method from a Java Class

```java
public static void main(String[] args) {
SomeClass s = new SomeClass();
s.aScalaMethod();
}
```

However, when the Java developer calls scalaMethod, the uncaught exception causes the Java method to fail:

```
[error] (run-main) java.lang.Exception: Exception!
java.lang.Exception: Exception!
at SomeClass.aScalaMethod
```

If you don't mark the aScalaMethod method with the @throws annotation, a Java developer can call it without using a try/catch block in her method, or declaring that her method throws an exception.

For the Java callers of your Scala methods, add the @throws annotation to your Scala methods so they will know which methods can throw exceptions and what exceptions they throw. For example, Listing 9-33 shows how to add an @throws annotation to let callers know that the aScalaMethod method can throw an Exception.

Listing 9-33. Annotating Scala method with @throws

```
class SomeClass {
@throws(classOf[Exception])
def aScalaMethod {
throw new Exception("Exception")
}
}
```

Your annotated Scala method works just like a Java method that throws an exception. If you attempt to call aScalaMethod from a Java class without wrapping it in a try/catch block, or declaring that your Java method throws an exception, the compiler (or your IDE) will throw an error.

In your Java code, you'll write a try/catch block as usual to handle the exception See Listing 9-34).

Listing 9-34. Calling Annotated ScalaMethod from Java

```
SomeClasss = new SomeClass();
try {
s.aScalaMethod();
} catch (Exception e) {
System.err.println("Caught the exception.");
e.printStackTrace();
}
```

Summary

This chapter showed how Scala is translated to Java, which is especially important if you call Scala code from Java. You learned that in most cases, Scala features are translated to Java features so that Scala can easily integrate with Java. You learned how to handle features that are available in Java but not in Scala, such as static members and checked exceptions, and how to use Scala features such as traits in Java code. You also learned how Scala annotations help in integration—for example, generating JavaBean-style get and set. Scala code is often used in tandem with large Java programs and frameworks. In the next chapter you will learn about some best-practice Scala idioms.

CHAPTER 10

■ ■ ■

DSL and Parser Combinator

The dichotomy of generic and specific manifests itself in the programming sphere. Domain-specific languages (DSLs) are one of the forms of the manifestations of this dichotomy. Domain-specific languages are just what they are called: domain specific. All programming languages are domain-specific languages when they come into existence, but that changes as they evolve. Domain-specific languages are created to solve problems in a certain area (or more precisely, in a certain domain) but as they gradually evolve to solve problems in several domains, the line that distinguishes them as specific blurs. Thus, such a language transgresses from the specific to the generic. A DSL is a special purpose language, the other extreme of which is a general purpose language, such as Scala and Java. Unfortunately, these general purpose languages have drawbacks, for example, if you want to execute a task on a database, then it is necessary to write a computer program for executing this task using a general purpose language. However, a DSL could be used to perform a number of such tasks on a database. And this is why some experts regard SQL, the structured query language, as a DSL.

In other words, a DSL is a special purpose programming language designed to express solutions to problems that belong to a particular problem domain. DSLs are focused on the domain or problem and can be of an external or internal type. An external DSL defines a new language with its own custom grammar and parser combinator. An internal DSL defines a new language as well, but within the syntactical boundaries of another language. No custom parser is necessary for internal DSLs. Instead, they are parsed just like any other code written in the language. Interest in DSLs has surged recently, driven in part by the Ruby [1] and Groovy [2] community, because they are very easy to implement in these languages. Ant [3], which uses XML, is an example of an external DSL. Gant [4], on the other hand, uses Groovy to solve the same problem and is an example of an internal DSL. Groovy with its metaprogramming [5] capabilities and flexible syntax is better suited to designing and implementing internal DSLs. As an illustration, using Groovy's optional parameters and MOP [6], you can turn this into code that only a programmer can love:

```
println this.class.getResourceAsStream('readme.txt').getText()
```

into:

```
write 'readme.txt'.contents()
```

---

[1] https://www.ruby-lang.org/en/
[2] http://groovy.codehaus.org/
[3] http://ant.apache.org/
[4] http://gant.codehaus.org/
[5] http://en.wikipedia.org/wiki/Metaprogramming
[6] http://c2.com/cgi/wiki?MetaObjectProtocol

You do not have to be a Groovy programmer to notice that with the second option, even a non-programmer has a chance of understanding the intent of the code. As we'll see, Scala provides excellent support for the creation of internal and external DSLs.

This chapter explains what a DSL is and how to write an internal DSL in Scala. This chapter then takes you through the building blocks of a parser called parser combinator in Scala, which is used to an write external DSL.

Domain Specific Language (DSL)

Domain specific language (DSL) is usually useful to simplify the interaction with a system by application to a small particular domain. DSL can be targeted to programmers by providing a simplified API to communicate with a system; or they may concern business users who might understand a domain well enough to create some scripts, but are not programmers and could have difficulty dealing with a general-purpose programming language.

There are two types of DSLs: internal and external DSLs.

Some well-known-examples of DSLs include ErlangOTP[7], HTML, SQL, Verilog[8], Mathematica[9], YACC[10]. Xpath[11], CSS[12], YAML[13], MATLAB[14], and ANT.

Internal DSLs

Internal DSLs are most often embedded in a host language with the addition of syntactic sugar through tricks and special constructs of the language. Many of these languages support a meta-object protocol that you can use to implement dynamic behaviors onto your DSL. Most of these languages are dynamically typed, such as Ruby and Groovy. Groovy was used as a host language for DSL in the example at beginning of the chapter. Statically typed languages, such as Scala, offer abstraction capabilities to model your DSL.

Some of the features of Scala that make it a host language for an internal DSL are

- Implicit conversions

- Scala's advanced type system

- Currying

- Infix and postfix operator notation of Scala

- Syntactic sugar

For example, you can omit the parentheses and dot for any method that takes a single parameter as shown:

```
map.get("key") is equivalent to map get "key"
```

[7]http://www.erlang.org/faq/introduction.html
[8]http://www.verilog.com/
[9]http://www.wolfram.com/mathematica/
[10]http://dinosaur.compilertools.net/yacc/
[11]http://www.w3.org/TR/xpath/
[12]http://www.w3.org/Style/CSS/Overview.en.html
[13]http://en.wikipedia.org/wiki/YAML
[14]http://nl.mathworks.com/products/matlab/

In this section you learn to build an internal DSL using Scala as a host language. Implicit conversion (see Chapter 8) gets you halfway to adding methods to a final class. The second half of the journey is that the Scala compiler looks to a possible implicit conversion from the type you have to a type with the method that you're invoking. The Scala compiler inserts code to call the implicit conversion and then calls the method on the resulting instance. The ability to add new methods to existing classes has a lot of value for making code more readable and expressive. More importantly, implicit conversions make it possible to define DSLs in Scala. As a library producer, we can create syntactically pleasing ways to express concepts in a type-safe way. Wouldn't it be nice to express a time span as 3 days or 15 seconds? That would make code a lot more readable than (3L * 24L * 3600L * 1000L). Wouldn't it be great to set a timeout or a trigger with 2 hours later? Let's define a library using implicit conversions (see Listing 10-1) and then break it down.

Listing 10-1. Timespan DSL

```
import java.util.Date
object TimeHelpers {
case class TimeSpanBuilder(val len: Long) {
def seconds = TimeSpan(TimeHelpers.seconds(len))
def second = seconds
def minutes = TimeSpan(TimeHelpers.minutes(len))
def minute = minutes
def hours = TimeSpan(TimeHelpers.hours(len))
def hour = hours
def days = TimeSpan(TimeHelpers.days(len))
def day = days
def weeks = TimeSpan(TimeHelpers.weeks(len))
def week = weeks
}
def seconds(in: Long): Long = in * 1000L
def minutes(in: Long): Long = seconds(in) * 60L
def hours(in: Long): Long = minutes(in) * 60L
def days(in: Long): Long = hours(in) * 24L
def weeks(in: Long): Long = days(in) * 7L
implicit def longToTimeSpanBuilder(in: Long): TimeSpanBuilder =
TimeSpanBuilder(in)
implicit def intToTimeSpanBuilder(in: Int): TimeSpanBuilder =
TimeSpanBuilder(in)
def millis = System.currentTimeMillis
case class TimeSpan(millis: Long) extends Ordered[TimeSpan] {
def later = new Date(millis + TimeHelpers.millis)
def ago = new Date(TimeHelpers.millis - millis)
def +(in: TimeSpan) = TimeSpan(this.millis + in.millis)
def -(in: TimeSpan) = TimeSpan(this.millis - in.millis)
def compare(other: TimeSpan) = millis compare other.millis
}
object TimeSpan {
implicit def tsToMillis(in: TimeSpan): Long = in.millis
}
class DateMath(d: Date) {
def +(ts: TimeSpan) = new Date(d.getTime + ts.millis)
def -(ts: TimeSpan) = new Date(d.getTime - ts.millis)
}
implicit def dateToDM(d: Date) = new DateMath(d)
}
```

We imported java.util.Date because we're going to make use of it.

```
import java.util.Date
object TimeHelpers {
```

We then defined a class that takes a Long as a parameter and has a series of methods that convert the Long into a TimeSpanBuilder represented by the length.

```
case class TimeSpanBuilder(len: Long) {
def seconds = TimeSpan(TimeHelpers.seconds(len))
def second = seconds
def minutes = TimeSpan(TimeHelpers.minutes(len))
def minute = minutes
def hours = TimeSpan(TimeHelpers.hours(len))
def hour = hours
def days = TimeSpan(TimeHelpers.days(len))
def day = days
def weeks = TimeSpan(TimeHelpers.weeks(len))
def week = weeks
}
```

Then we defined a bunch of helper methods (called from TimeSpanBuilder) that convert to the correct number of milliseconds.

```
def seconds(in: Long): Long = in * 1000L
def minutes(in: Long): Long = seconds(in) * 60L
def hours(in: Long): Long = minutes(in) * 60L
def days(in: Long): Long = hours(in) * 24L
def weeks(in: Long): Long = days(in) * 7L
```

Next, we defined a bunch of implicit methods that convert from Int or Long into a TimeSpanBuilder. This allows the methods such as minutes or days on TimeSpanBuilder to appear to be part of Int and Long.

```
implicit def longToTimeSpanBuilder(in: Long): TimeSpanBuilder =TimeSpanBuilder(in)
implicit def intToTimeSpanBuilder(in: Int): TimeSpanBuilder = TimeSpanBuilder(in)
```

Then we defined a helper method that gets the current time in milliseconds:

```
def millis = System.currentTimeMillis
```

We defined the TimeSpan class that represents a span of time. We can do math with other Timespans or convert this TimeSpan into a Date by calling the later or ago methods. TimeSpan extends the Ordered trait so that we can compare and sort TimeSpans:

```
case class TimeSpan(millis: Long) extends Ordered[TimeSpan] {
def later = new Date(millis + TimeHelpers.millis)
def ago = new Date(TimeHelpers.millis - millis)
def +(in: TimeSpan) = TimeSpan(this.millis + in.millis)
def -(in: TimeSpan) = TimeSpan(this.millis - in.millis)
```

Next we compared this TimeSpan to another to satisfy the requirements of the Ordered trait:

```
def compare(other: TimeSpan) = millis compare other.millis
}
```

Then we defined a companion object that has an implicit method that will convert a Timespan into a Long. If there is an object with the same name as a class, that object is considered a companion object. If there are any implicit conversions defined in the companion object, they will be consulted if an instance of the class needs to be converted. We defined an implicit conversion from TimeSpan to Long in the companion object. This results in TimeSpan instances being automatically converted to Long if the TimeSpan is assigned to a Long variable or passed as a parameter that requires a Long.

```
object TimeSpan {
implicit def tsToMillis(in: TimeSpan): Long = in.millis
}
```

We can define TimeSpan instances with simple syntax, such as 3 days. Time Spans can be converted to Dates with the later and ago methods. But it would be helpful to add addition and subtraction of TimeSpans to Date instances. That's pretty simple using implicit conversions. First, we defined a DateMath class that has + and - methods that take a TimeSpan as a parameter.

```
class DateMath(d: Date) {
def +(ts: TimeSpan) = new Date(d.getTime + ts.millis)
def -(ts: TimeSpan) = new Date(d.getTime - ts.millis)
}
```

Next we defined the implicit conversion:

```
implicit def dateToDM(d: Date) = new DateMath(d)
```

With all the 50 or so lines of code written, let's see how it works.

```
scala> import TimeHelpers._
```

```
import TimeHelpers._
```

```
scala> 1.days
```

```
res0: TimeHelpers.TimeSpan = TimeSpan(86400000)
```

```
scala> 5.days + 2.hours
```

```
res1: TimeHelpers.TimeSpan = TimeSpan(439200000)
```

```
scala> (5.days + 2.hours).later
```

```
res2: java.util.Date = Mon Feb 16 19:11:29 PST 2009
```

```
scala> import java.util.Date
```

```
import java.util.Date
```

```
scala> val d = new Date("January 2, 2005")
```

```
d: java.util.Date = Sun Jan 02 00:00:00 PST 2005
```

```
scala> val lng: Long = 7.days + 2.hours + 4.minutes
```

```
lng: Long = 612240000
```

So, we've defined a nice DSL for time spans, and it converts itself to Long when necessary. We saw how Scala's implicit conversions lead to very simple and concise DSLs. Choosing implicit conversions and designing domain-specific languages (DSLs) takes time, thought, and deliberation. Next, a brief introduction to external DSLs.

External DSLs

External DSLs build their own language-processing infrastructure: the parsers, the lexers, and the processing logic. You need to define a grammar (such as Backus–Naur Form[15] (BNF)), that is, define all the rules that apply to parse a meaning or script successfully. The internal DSLs get this infrastructure free from the underlying host language, but you need to build them from scratch for external DSLs. In Scala, parser combinators are a notion close to the definition of BNF grammars and can provide very concise and elegant code when writing external DSLs. An external DSL has separate infrastructure for lexical analysis, parsing, interpretation, compilation, and code generation. When you write a parser for an external DSL, you can use a parser generator tool such as Antlr[16]. However, Scala includes a powerful parser combinator library that can be used for parsing most external DSLs that have a context-free grammar. Scala comes with a parser combinator library so you don't have to implement your own language infrastructure. We discuss Scala parser combinator in the next section.

Parser Combinator

Parser combinators are one of the most important applications of functional programming. Parser combinators offer an internal DSL to use for designing external DSLs so you don't have to implement your own language infrastructure as discussed earlier. Parser combinators are building blocks for parsers. Parsers that handle specific kinds of input can be combined to form other parser combinators for larger expressions. Scala comes with a parser combinator library that makes writing parsers simple. Furthermore, because your parser is written in Scala, there's a single compilation step, and you get all the benefits of Scala's type safety. In this section, we're going to explore combinators and Scala's parser combinatory library.

---

[15]http://en.wikipedia.org/wiki/Backus%E2%80%93Naur_Form
[16]http://www.antlr.org/

Higher-Order Functions and Combinators

Scala's parser combinator library gives us a view of a powerful DSL, and it has its roots in a lot of computer science and mathematics. Let's look at higher-order functions (functions that take functions as parameters), then at how higher-order functions can be combined to yield powerful functionality.

Higher-Order Functions

We've been using higher-order functions throughout this book. These are functions, or methods, which take functions as parameters. List.map is a higher-order function:

```
scala> List(1, 2, 3).map(_ + 1)
```

```
res0: List[Int] = List(2, 3, 4)
```

We've also seen how to compose functions:

```
scala> def plus1(in: Int) = in + 1
```

```
plus1: (Int)Int
```

```
scala> def twice(in: Int) = in * 2
```

```
twice: (Int)Int
```

```
scala> val addDouble = plus1 _ andThen twice
```

```
addDouble: (Int) => Int = <function>
```

```
scala> List(1,2,3).map(addDouble)
```

```
res2: List[Int] = List(4, 6, 8)
```

In this example, we've composed a function, addDouble, out of two other functions, plus1 and twice. We can compose complex functions. We can even compose functions dynamically based on user input. We saw an example of this in the "Building New Functions" section in Chapter 4.

Combinators

You might be asking, what is a parser combinator? A combinator is a function that takes only other functions as parameters and returns only functions. Combinators allow you to combine small functions into big functions. In the case of the parser combinator library, you can combine small functions that match individual characters or small groups of characters into bigger functions that can parse complex documents. So, you have input a Seq[Char] (sequence of characters), and you want to parse the stream, which will either contain t, r, u, e or f, a, l, s, e—true or false. So, you would express such a program as

```
def parse = (elem('t') ~ elem('r') ~ elem('u') ~ elem('e')) |
(elem('f') ~ elem('a') ~ elem('l') ~ elem('s') ~ elem('e'))
```

where the elem method returns a subclass of Function[Seq[Char], ParseResult[Char]] that also has ~ and | methods. The first call to elem returns a function that will attempt to match the first character in an input stream to the letter "t." If the first letter of the input stream matches, then the function returns Parsers.Success; otherwise it returns a Parsers.NoSuccess. The ~ method is called "and then," so we can read the first part as t, then r , then u, and then e. So, elem('t') ~ elem('r') returns another one of these special Function[Seq[Char], ParseResult[List[Char]]] things. So we combine the functions with the ~ method into one bigger function. We keep doing this with each successive ~ method invocation. The following code:

```
elem('t') ~ elem('r') ~ elem('u') ~ elem('e')
```

builds a single function that consults the characters t, r, u, e and returns a Parsers.Success[List[Char]] or a Parsers.NoSuccess if the input does not contain t, r, u, e. The | operator also takes two of these combinated function thingies and combines them into a single function thingy that tests the first clause, true, and if that succeeds, its value is returned, but if it does not succeed, then the second clause, false, is tried. Let's call that function thingy a Parser. So, we can combine these Parser instances with each other into other Parser instances using operators such as "and then," "or else," and so on. We can combine little Parsers into big Parsers using logic and thus construct complex grammars out of little building blocks. Let's use a little bit of Scala's implicit functionality to make the definition of our grammar easier. Scala's parser combinator library has implicit conversions from Char into Parser[Char], so we can write

```
def p2 = ('t' ~ 'r' ~ 'u' ~ 'e') |
('f' ~ 'a' ~ 'l' ~ 's' ~ 'e')
```

Yes, that definitely looks better. But, there's still a question of what these Parsers return when we pass a Seq[Char] into them. Or put another way, we want to get a Boolean true or false when we pass our input into them. So, let's define the return type of our expression:

```
def p3: Parser[Boolean] = ('t' ~ 'r' ~ 'u' ~ 'e') |
('f' ~ 'a' ~ 'l' ~ 's' ~ 'e')
```

That's what we want, but the compiler complains that it doesn't know how to convert the combined Parser into a Boolean. So, let's add a little bit of code to tell the Parser how to convert its result into a Boolean.

```
def p3: Parser[Boolean] = ('t' ~ 'r' ~ 'u' ~ 'e' ^^^ true) |
('f' ~ 'a' ~ 'l' ~ 's' ~ 'e' ^^^ false)
```

That works. The ^^^ method on Parser says, "If we match the input, return this constant." We've built a function that will match true or false and return the appropriate Boolean value if either pattern of characters is matched. But we can also use the characters that are part of the pattern to create the value returned when the input is applied to the function using the ^^ method. We'll define positiveDigit and digit Parsers:2

```
def positiveDigit = elem('1') | '2' | '3' | '4' | '5' | '6' | '7' | '8' | '9'
def digit = positiveDigit | '0'
```

In positiveDigit, we needed to specify elem('1') as the first part of the expression because '1' | '2' is a legal expression, so the implicit conversion of '1' to elem('1')does not take place. Note that we combined the positiveDigit Parser with elem('0') into a Parser that accepts all digits. Let's make this into a Parser that converts the digits into a Long:

```
def long1: Parser[Long] = positiveDigit ~ rep(digit) ^^ {
case (first: Char) ~ (rest: List[Char]) => (first :: rest).mkString.toLong
}
```

We create a Parser that matches a positiveDigit and then zero or more digits using rep(digit). If application of the predicate (positiveDigit ~ rep(digit)) succeeds, then we convert to a Long by applying the conversion function:

```
case (first: Char) ~ (rest:List[Char]) => (first :: rest).mkString.toLong.
```

The ^^ method on Parser causes the conversion function to be applied if the predicate succeeds. In this example, I was explicit about the types, but the type inferencer will get it right. Let's tighten up the example a little by only accepting rest if it's fewer than 18 digits so we don't overflow the Long:

```
lazy val long2: Parser[Long] = positiveDigit ~ rep(digit) ^? {
case first ~ rest if rest.length < 18 => (first :: rest).mkString.toLong
}
```

In this case, we've used the ^? method to connect the predicate to the conversion. In order for the Parser to succeed, we need to satisfy the predicate, and the partial function passed to ^? must be defined for the result of the predicate. In this case, the partial function will be satisfied if the length of rest is fewer than 18 characters. We've also changed from a method to a lazy val. This is because the method does not do the parsing; rather, the method combines smaller Parsers into a single Parser. This building of the Parser need only happen once, and the resulting Parser can be used over and over, even simultaneously on multiple threads. With the basics under our belt, let's put our parser mojo to use.

The Calculator Parser

In this section, we're going to use the parser combinator to build a four-function calculator. Yes, it's time to swat flies with a Buick. You'll see how easy it is to describe what we want to build, create a Parser for it, and then make sure the Parser returns the correct things. But first, let's define a utility trait that will allow us to more easily run the Parsers from the Scala REPL. The RunParser trait can be mixed into any Parser and adds a run method.

```
import scala.util.parsing.combinator._
trait RunParser {
this: RegexParsers =>
type RootType
def root: Parser[RootType]
def run(in: String): ParseResult[RootType] = parseAll(root, in)
}
```

The RunParser trait can be mixed into a class that extends RegexParsers. By mixing RunParser into your Parser, you can type MyParser.run("Thing to test") and see the result. It's a convenience trait. We'll define the skeleton of our four-function calculator. Let's first describe how our calculator works. A sum expression is a product expression followed by zero or more + or –symbols followed by a product expression. A product expression is a factor followed by zero or more * or / symbols followed by another factor. This means that the precedence of production expressions is higher than the precedence of sum expressions. Finally, we define a factor as a number or parentheses around a sum expression. In BNF, we'd write

```
<sumExpr> ::= <prodExpr> [("+" <prodExpr>) | ("-" <prodExpr>)]
<prodExpr> ::= <factor> [("*" <factor>) | ("/" <factor>)]
<factor> ::= <float> | ("(" <sumExpr> ")")
```

We've described our parsing rules in English and BNF. Now let's see how that translates to Scala.

```
object CalcSkel extends JavaTokenParsers with RunParser {
lazy val sumExpr = multExpr ~ rep("+" ~ multExpr | "-" ~ multExpr)
lazy val multExpr = factor ~ rep("*" ~ factor | "/" ~ factor)
lazy val factor: Parser[Any] = floatingPointNumber | "(" ~ sumExpr ~ ")"
type RootType = Any
def root = sumExpr
}
```

We've extended JavaTokenParsers, which gives us access to a bunch of stuff that will parse tokens as defined by the Java Language Specification. We're taking advantage of floatingPointNumber and automatic white space consumption between elements. Cool. Let's see how this works in the REPL.

```
scala> CalcSkel.run("1")
```

```
res0: [1.2] parsed: ((1~List())~List())
```

```
scala> CalcSkel.run("1 + 1")
```

```
res1: [1.6] parsed: ((1~List())~List((+~(1~List()))))
```

```
scala> CalcSkel.run("1 + 1 / 17")
```

```
res2: [1.11] parsed: ((1~List())~List((+~(1~List((/~17))))))
```

```
scala> CalcSkel.run("1 + 1 / archer")
```

```
res3: CalcSkel.ParseResult[CalcSkel.RootType] =
[1.9] failure: `(' expected but ` ' found
1 + 1 / archer
        ^
```

This is pretty encouraging. Our English and BNF descriptions of what we wanted to parse correspond very closely to our Scala code. Furthermore, our parse correctly parses valid input and rejects input with errors in it. The results, however, are pretty tough to read. Next, let's turn the results into something that performs the calculations. Our Parser doesn't change, but we add a function to convert the parsed items into a Double. First comes Listing 10-2 and then we'll comb through the code.

Listing 10-2. Calculator parser

```scala
import scala.util.parsing.combinator._
object Calc extends JavaTokenParsers with RunParser {
lazy val sumExpr = prodExpr ~
rep("+" ~> prodExpr ^^ (d => (x: Double) => x + d) |
"-" ~> prodExpr ^^ (d => (x: Double) => x - d)) ^^ {
case seed ~ fs => fs.foldLeft(seed)((a, f) => f(a))
}
lazy val prodExpr = factor ~
rep("*" ~> factor ^^ (d => (x: Double) => x * d) |
"/" ~> factor ^^ (d => (x: Double) => x / d)) ^^ {
case seed ~ fs => fs.foldLeft(seed)((a, f) => f(a))
}
lazy val factor: Parser[Double] =
floatingPointNumber ^^ (_.toDouble) | "(" ~> sumExpr <~ ")"
type RootType = Double
def root = sumExpr
}
```

First we import the appropriate classes and then get down to business:

```scala
import scala.util.parsing.combinator._
object Calc extends JavaTokenParsers with RunParser {
lazy val sumExpr = prodExpr ~
rep("+" ~> prodExpr ^^ (d => (x: Double) => x + d) |
"-" ~> prodExpr ^^ (d => (x: Double) => x - d)) ^^ {
case seed ~ fs => fs.foldLeft(seed)((a, f) => f(a))
}
```

The rep method results in a list of whatever is parsed by the parameter of rep. When we match the
+ ~>prodExpr, we convert this into a function that adds the two numbers. Please note the ~> method.
This method matches both items but only passes the stuff on the right to the converter function. There's a
corresponding <~ operator. Back in the code we've got a prodExpr, which is a Parser[Double] and then a
Parser[List[Double => Double]], and we need to convert this into a Parser[Double]. The line

```
case seed ~ fs => fs.foldLeft(seed)((a, f) => f(a))
```

extracts the seed and the list of functions (add or subtract) and uses foldLeft to perform the calculation. We
do the same for multiplication and division:

```
lazy val prodExpr = factor ~
rep("*" ~> factor ^^ (d => (x: Double) => x * d) |
"/" ~> factor ^^ (d => (x: Double) => x / d)) ^^ {
case seed ~ fs => fs.foldLeft(seed)((a, f) => f(a))
}
```

Next, we define factor, which is either a number or parentheses around a sumExpr. Because sumExpr,
prodExpr, and factor reference each other and, thus, are recursive, we must define the type of at least one of
the three vals so the type inferencer can do its work.

```
lazy val factor: Parser[Double] =
floatingPointNumber ^^ (_.toDouble) | "(" ~> sumExpr <~ ")"
```

We convert floating PointNumber into a Double by passing a function that converts a String to a Double.
Next, we use ~> and <~ to discard the parentheses around sumExpr. Calc mixes in RunParser, so we have to
define the abstract RootType type and the root method.

```
type RootType = Double
def root = sumExpr
}
```

That's it. We've defined the conversions from the Strings and List to Doubles. Let's see how well it works.

```
scala> Calc.run("1")
```

```
res0: Calc.ParseResult[Calc.RootType] = [1.2] parsed: 1.0
```

```
scala> Calc.run("1 + 1")
```

```
res1: Calc.ParseResult[Calc.RootType] = [1.6] parsed: 2.0
```

```
scala> Calc.run("1 + 1 / 17")
```

```
res2: Calc.ParseResult[Calc.RootType] = [1.11] parsed: 1.0588235294117647
```

```
scala> Calc.run("(1 + 1) / 17")
```

```
res3: Calc.ParseResult[Calc.RootType] = [1.13] parsed: 0.11764705882352941
```

In this section, we've converted from a BNF description of the grammar to a running application using Scala's parser combinator library. The simple example was a four-function calculator.

This brief introduction concludes our tour of DSLs and parser combinators. DSL is a broad and rapidly emerging arena and deserves a book of its own. With a good sense of the business domain and the coding conventions, you may design domain-specific languages for use by other team members. DSLs deliver value because they allow the program to more closely match the language that business people use to describe solutions in a given domain. As we've seen with Scala's parser combinator library as well as Specs, Scala makes it easy to create code that corresponds to the language a human would use to describe the answer to a problem. If your business people understand the code, and they should if the DSLs are well crafted, they will be able to give direct feedback as to the program reflecting the business rules.

Summary

Scala's parser combinator library demonstrates the flexibility of Scala's syntax, the usefulness of implicit conversions, and the power of functional composition. The parser combinator is an excellent example of a domain-specific language. The domain is parsing text, and the syntax is nearly one-for-one with BNF. This library also gives you some idea of the kind of domain-specific languages you can create using Scala. There's nothing specific in the Scala compiler for the parser combinator library—it's just that, a library. On a practical level, using a single language—Scala—for defining your Parser rather than using a tool like ANTLR means that you and your team use a single language for describing your system. This means that your brain thinks Scala. This means that you edit code in a single language and take advantage of the type safety of the language. In the next chapter, we'll explore how you can integrate Scala into your projects and take advantage of the power of Scala without losing the infrastructure that you've built around Java.

CHAPTER 11

■ ■ ■

Simple Build Tool - SBT

Software development typically includes activities such as compiling source code into binary code, executing tests, packaging binary code into archives, and deploying archives to production systems. A build is a term that refers to compiled code packaged and deployed on production. A build is a technical term for a deliverable. Deliverable is the set of executable code expected by the stakeholders. The process through which a build has to go to become the deliverable is called a build process. Thus a build process, in general, is comprised of compilation, testing, packaging, and deployment.

Build automation is the act of automating the aforementioned build process by means of a build tool. These build tools require you to define the project configuration and dependencies in an artifact called build definition.

■ **Note** A dependency is the term that refers to interdependencies between software constructs and is measured by the term coupling. Coupling is the degree of interdependencies between software constructs.

Figure 11-1 shows a quick overview of the popular build tools in the timeline. Make[1] is atypical in this list, but it was included because it pioneered the build automation. All the build tools except Make in Figure 11-1 are popular in the JVM landscape.

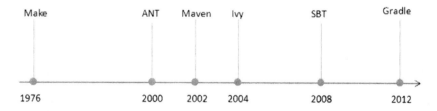

Figure 11-1. Build tools timeline

As mentioned, Make pioneered the build automation and allowed dependency management from the outset. Make remains widely used, especially in Unix.

---

[1]http://www.gnu.org/software/make/.

Apache Ant[2] is similar to Make but is implemented in the Java language and unlike Make, it uses XML to describe the build process and its dependencies. It necessitates the Java platform, and befits building Java projects. Contrary to Ant, Maven[3] allows convention over configuration for the build procedure by providing sensible default behavior for projects.

■ **Note**   Convention over configuration (CoC) refers to, in general, a development approach centered on conventions. It enables developers to specify and configure only the unconventional aspects of the development.

Apache Ivy[4] is a dependency manager. It is a sub-project of the Apache Ant project, and helps to resolve project dependencies.

■ **Note**   Apache Ivy competes to a large extent with Apache Maven, which also manages dependencies. However, Maven is a complete build tool, whereas Ivy focuses purely on managing dependencies.

Gradle[5] builds upon Apache Ant and Apache Maven and but uses a Groovy-based domain-specific language (DSL) to declare the project configuration instead of XML.

Although you can use Ant and Maven to build your Scala projects, SBT[6], is the standard build tool for Scala applications. Like Maven, SBT uses the same directory structure and convention over configuration approach and Apache Ivy for handling dependency management.

In essence, the build automation automates all the steps in the build process with build tools like Ant, Maven, Ivy, Gradle, or SBT and the best practice is to run the build continuously. This process is known as continuous integration. There are several tools that offer continuous integration such as Hudson[7] and Jenkins[8].

Getting Started with SBT

In this section you will see sbt in action using a simple hello world project. First you need to install sbt.

Installing SBT

The installation of sbt, in a nutshell, is akin to launching a JAR `sbt-launch.jar` which can be downloaded from `http://www.scala-sbt.org/0.13/tutorial/Manual-Installation.html`, if you want to install sbt manually. Or you can install using sbtmsi, which you can download from `http://www.scala-sbt.org/download.html`.

SBT provides different installation packages for Mac, Windows, Linux, Typesafe[9] Activator, or manual installation. You can find information on installation at `http://www.scala-sbt.org/0.13.5/docs/Getting-Started/Setup.html#installing-sbt`.

---

[2]`http://ant.apache.org/`.
[3]`http://maven.apache.org/`.
[4]`http://ant.apache.org/ivy/`.
[5]`https://gradle.org/`.
[6]`http://www.scala-sbt.org/`.
[7]`http://hudson-ci.org/`.
[8]`http://jenkins-ci.org/`.
[9]`https://typesafe.com/`.

Typesafe Activator is a custom version of sbt that adds two extra commands, activator ui and activator new. The activator command is a superset of sbt, in short. You can obtain Activator from typesafe.com. Activator offers two downloads; the small "minimal" download contains only the wrapper script and launch jar, while the large "full" download contains a preloaded Ivy cache with jars for Scala, Akka[10], and the Play[11] Framework. You will use both sbt and activator in the next chapter when you build web application in Scala.

Once you have downloaded sbt you can check the version as shown:

```
F:\sbt\helloworld>sbt --version
sbt launcher version 0.13.7
```

Creating Hello World Project

In order to see sbt in action, set up a simple hello world project by creating a project directory helloworld with a hello.scala source file in it as shown in Listing 11-1.

Listing 11-1. hello.scala

```
object Helloworld {
def main(args: Array[String]) = println("Hello world!")
}
```

Now you can run sbt by typing sbt as shown

```
F:\sbt\helloworld>sbt
[info] Set current project to helloworld (in build file:/F:/sbt/helloworld/)
>
```

We will explain the [info] part of the preceding output a little later. When you run sbt in your project directory helloworld with no command-line arguments, sbt starts in an interactive mode. The interactive mode provides a command prompt with features such as tab completion and history.

Interactive mode remembers what you typed previously (history), even if you exit sbt and restart it. Sbt lists all the history commands when you type ! on sbt prompt as shown.

```
> !
History commands:
    !!      Execute the last command again
    !:      Show all previous commands
    !:n     Show the last n commands
    !n      Execute the command with index n, as shown by the !: command
    !-n     Execute the nth command before this one
    !string      Execute the most recent command starting with 'string'
    !?string      Execute the most recent command containing 'string'
>
```

---

[10]http://akka.io/.
[11]https://www.playframework.com/.

Sbt provides a long list of commands. For a more complete list, see Command Line Reference at `http://www.scala-sbt.org/release/docs/Command-Line-Reference.html`.

Here are some of the most common sbt commands.

Command	Description
clean	Deletes all generated files (in the target directory)
compile	Compiles the main sources (in src/main/scala and src/main/java directories)
run	Runs the main class for the project in the same virtual machine as sbt
help <command>	Displays help for the specific command when you type help<command>. Displays brief description of all the commands if you type just help.

You can exit the interactive mode by typing `exit`.

Now you can run the project by typing `run` at the sbt prompt of the interactive mode as shown:

```
> run
[info] Updating {file:/F:/sbt/helloworld/}helloworld...
[info] Resolving org.scala-lang#scala-library;2.10.4 ...
  [info] Resolving org.scala-lang#scala-compiler;2.10.4 ...
  [info] Resolving org.scala-lang#jline;2.10.4 ...
  [info] Resolving org.fusesource.jansi#jansi;1.4 ...
  [info] Resolving org.scala-lang#scala-reflect;2.10.4 ...
[info] Done updating.
[info] Compiling 1 Scala source to F:\sbt\helloworld\target\scala-2.10\classes..
[info] Running Helloworld
Hello world!
[success] Total time: 15 s, completed Jan 27, 2015 8:45:39 PM
>
```

As you can see in the preceding output, sbt runs the helloworld project and displays Hello World!. We will now explain the [info] part of the output.

```
F:\sbt\helloworld>sbt
  [info] Set current project to helloworld (in build file:/F:/sbt/helloworld/)
>
```

Sbt requires you to set the name of the project to helloworld and allows you generate a build definition. We will explain build definition in greater detail later in this chapter. Meanwhile, enter the following on sbt console:

```
set name:= "helloworld"
```

You will get the following output:

```
> set name:= "helloworld"
[info] Defining *:name
[info] The new value will be used by *:description, *:normalizedName and 5 others.
[info] Run `last` for details.
[info] Reapplying settings...
[info] Set current project to helloworld (in build file:/F:/sbt/helloworld/)
```

Now save the session by entering the following:

```
session save
```

Now you will see the following output:

```
> session save
[info] Reapplying settings...
[info] Set current project to helloworld (in build file:/F:/sbt/helloworld/)
```

Now enter exit and this generates build.sbt in the root directory, helloworld. Listing 11-2 shows the generated build.sbt.

Listing 11-2. generatedbuild.sbt

```
name:= "helloworld"
```

You can edit the build.sbt to add the basic information as follows:

Listing 11-3. generatedbuild.sbt

```
name := "helloworld"
version := "1.0"
scalaVersion := "2.11.1"
```

We will go through the code in the Listing 11-3 and related concepts in the next section.

Build Definition

As we mentioned earlier, a build tool requires you to define the project configuration and dependencies in an artifact called build definition.

In Scala, there are three types of build definition:

- .sbt build definition

- .scala build definition

- combination of .scala and .sbt build definition

As you learned earlier, the base directory of your hello world project—helloworld directory—is comprised of the build definition.sbt file. In addition to .sbt file there may also be build definitions as a .scala file located in the project/ subdirectory of the base directory. A sbt build definition consists of a list of settings as shown in Listing 11-4.

Listing 11-4. .sbt Build Definition

```
name := "helloworld"

version := "1.0"

scalaVersion := "2.11.1"
```

In the previous version of sbt, you were required to separate the setting expression by blank lines. You could not write an .sbtfile as shown in Listing 11-5 as it did not compile because of absence of blank lines.

Listing 11-5. .sbt Without Blank Lines (will not compile)

```
name := "helloworld"
version := "1.0"
scalaVersion := "2.10.x"
```

This restriction does not exist any longer from sbt0.13.7. but we mentioned this because you may find yourself into situations where older versions of SBT are still being used with newer versions of scala, and in such cases the build file without the blank lines won't compile.

You learned how to set up a hello world scala project in sbt, but in general, industry strength applications are far more complex than a hello world project. In order to use sbt with industry strength applications efficiently, it is important to understand how the build definition works. We insert the Listing 11-3 to explain the build definition as Listing 11-6.

Listing 11-6. Generated build.sbt (from Listing 11-3)

```
name := "helloworld"
version := "1.0"
scalaVersion := "2.11.1"
```

A build definition is made up of build properties, where each property is a key value pair. From Listing 11-6 one build property is shown as follows:

```
name :=  "helloworld"
```

name is the key and the String "helloworld" is its value type and := is an operator method for transformation. Assignment with := is the simplest of all the transformation that sbt provides. The other transformation methods will be introduced in the later section of this chapter.

In SBT, keys are defined for different purposes. A key can be categorized into one of the following categories:

Key	Description
Setting key	When you define the key as a Setting key, the value of the key is computed on loading the project
Task key	When you define the key as a Task key, the value of the key is recomputed each time it is executed
Input key	When you define the key as an Input key, the value of the key take command-line arguments as input

The Setting keys provide build configuration. The keys such as name, version, and scalaVersion that you saw in Listing 11-3 are Setting keys. We will look at two other useful types of setting keys: libraryDependencies and resolvers keys in the following section.

The Task keys, as the name suggests, are geared toward tasks such as clean, compile, test, and so on.

■ **Note**   Because a Task key is computed on each execution, a Setting key cannot depend on a Task key. Trying to do so will throw an error.

The Input keys are the keys that have command-line arguments. An example of an input key is run key. The run key is used to run a main class with the command-line arguments. If no arguments are provided, a blank string is used. You execute run without any arguments when you run the hello world project.

■ **Note**   Each key can have more than one value, but in different context called scopes. In a given scope, a key has only one value.

In the following section you will learn about the Setting keys called libraryDependencies key and resolvers key.

LibraryDependencies and Resolvers

The libraryDependencies key is used to declare managed dependencies and the resolvers key is used to provide additional resource URIs for automatically managed dependencies. As we mentioned earlier, SBT uses Apache Ivy to implement managed dependencies. You should list your dependencies in the setting libraryDependencies. You can declare the dependency as shown in Listing 11-7.

Listing 11-7. Declaring Dependencies

```
libraryDependencies += groupID % artifactID % revision
```

In Listing 11-7, groupId, artifactId, and revision are strings.
You can also declare the dependencies as shown in Listing 11-8.

Listing 11-8. Declaring Dependencies With Configuration Value

```
libraryDependencies += groupID % artifactID % revision % configuration
```

In Listing 11-8, configuration can be a string or val.
In Listing 11-7 and Listing 11-8, you add a ModuleID created by % method to libraryDependencies. An astute reader might have noticed that we used a different operator method for transformation in Listing 11-7 and Listing 11-8 than the assignment operator method you learned in Listing 11-6.
The operator += appends to the existing value. You can also use another operator ++=, which appends the sequence of values to the existing value as shown in Listing 11-9.

Listing 11-9. Using ++=

```
libraryDependencies ++= Seq(
  groupID % artifactID % revision,
  groupID % otherID % otherRevision
)
```

Listing 11-9 uses++= to add a list of dependencies at the same time.
Listing 11-10 shows using the Apache Derby as the library dependency.

Listing 11-10. Using Apache Derby Dependency

```
libraryDependencies += "org.apache.derby" % "derby" % "10.4.1.3"
```

In Listing 11-10, SBT uses the default repository for downloading Derby. If you want to use the library dependency that is not in one of the default repositories, you need to add a resolver to help Ivy locate it. In order to provide the location of repository you can use the following syntax:

```
resolvers += name at location
```

Here name is the String name of the repository and location is the String location of the repository. Listing 11-11 shows how to add the additional repository.

Listing 11-11. Using Resolvers

```
resolvers += "Sonatype OSS Snapshots" at https://oss.sonatype.org/content/repositories/
snapshots
```

In Listing 11-11 we add the sonatypeoss snapshots repository, which is located at the given URL.

Plugins

A plugin is an artifact that extends the build definition, usually by adding new settings. In order to declare this plugin dependency you need to pass the plugin's Ivy module ID to addSbtPlugin as shown in Listing 11-12. Next we show you how to use an eclipse plugin using the hello world project we created earlier. You can obtain the sbt eclipse plugin's Ivy module ID from https://github.com/typesafehub/sbteclipse.
First create an .sbt file for the plugin in the helloworld project directory as shown in Listing 11-12.

Listing 11-12. plugin.sbt

```
addSbtPlugin("com.typesafe.sbteclipse" % "sbteclipse-plugin" % "3.0.0")
```

Now you can run the eclipse command on the sbt prompt as shown:

```
> eclipse
[info] About to create Eclipse project files for your project(s).
[info] Updating {file:/F:/sbt/helloworld/}helloworld...
[info] Resolving org.scala-lang#scala-library;2.10.4 ...
[info] Resolving org.scala-lang#scala-compiler;2.10.4 ...
  [info] Resolving org.scala-lang#jline;2.10.4 ...
  [info] Resolving org.fusesource.jansi#jansi;1.4 ...
  [info] Resolving org.scala-lang#scala-reflect;2.10.4 ...
[info] Done updating.
[info] Successfully created Eclipse project files for project(s):
[info] helloworld
>
```

This creates the project directory structure for eclipse that adheres to convention over configuration and is same as the Maven directory structure.

Now open Eclipse and navigate File ➤ Import as illustrated in the Figure 11-2.

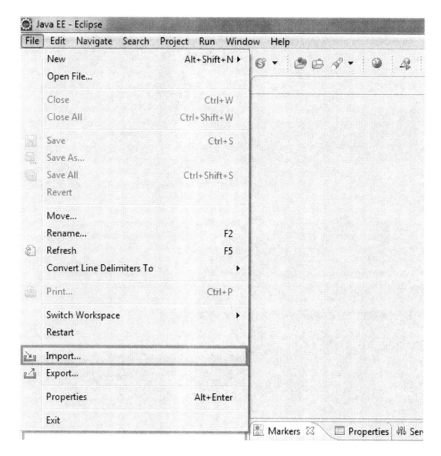

Figure 11-2. *Importing the project*

Once you click Import, you will see the select form as illustrated in Figure 11-3.

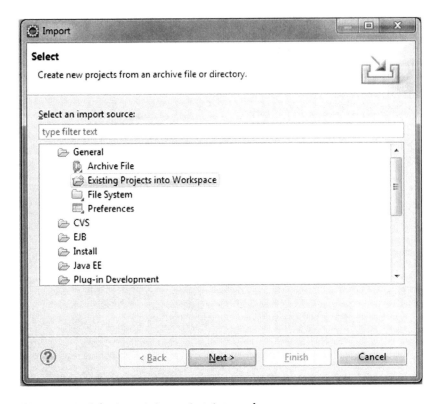

Figure 11-3. Selecting existing projects into workspace

Now navigate to "Existing Projects into Workspace." You will now see the Import dialog as illustrated in Figure 11-4. Click Browse to get to the base directory helloworld as illustrated in Figure 11-4.

Figure 11-4. *Selecting the root directory*

Now click Finish to see the project structure shown in Figure 11-5.

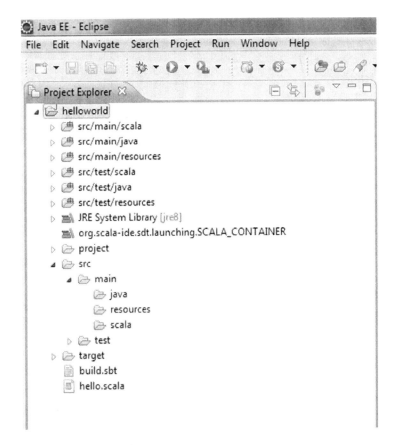

Figure 11-5. *Project directory structure*

SBT also allows you to generate IDEA project configuration. To do this you use an sbt plugin located at `https://github.com/mpeltonen/sbt-idea`. To generate NetBeans configuration you can find the sbt plugin for NetBeans at `https://github.com/dcaoyuan/nbsbt`.

One chapter is not enough to list all the features of SBT and it deserves a book of its own. For a detailed treatment on SBT we recommend you to go through the reference manual of SBT at `http://www.scala-sbt.org/release/docs/`.

This chapter did provide you a brief introduction to SBT, which is sufficient to use it in the next chapter for building a web application.

Summary

In this chapter you learned how to create a simple project with SBT and execute basic operations, such as compile, test, and run. You learned how to configure library dependencies and how to configure a dependency when it is not in a default repository. In the next chapter you will learn how to create web applications in Scala.

CHAPTER 12

■ ■ ■

Scala for Web Application

The web continues to evolve in a sort of benign continuum and has become the central town of all applications with its architecture transcending to real-time, due to the emerging new requirements such as asynchrony, reactivity and responsivity, collaborating with both structured and unstructured datastore and so on. The aforementioned factors have made web development a non-trivial undertaking, which means several web frameworks have emerged to address these issues. In this chapter, we begin our journey of the Scala web landscape through one of the highly popular web frameworks Play 2. We elected Play framework, because it enables web development for the modern era using both Scala and Java. We introduce both Play 2 for Scala and Play 2 for Java, because we believe that most Scala developers are experienced in Java through industrial projects or academia. The remaining Scala developers are the ones who transitioned to Scala from Java and so, we believe, having familiarity with Java will make the transition to Play framework much easier and it allows Play framework to position itself in an already established segment of Java web.

Scala Web Frameworks

The Scala web frameworks are rapidly evolving. In the Scala world, alternatives to web development span from micro-frameworks, such as Scalatra, to feature-rich frameworks such as Play. In many ways, these web frameworks concentrate on, addressing the aforementioned complexity of the web development. In Table 12-1 we list the key players in Scala web development. The list presented, however, is not exhaustive because this list is in a perpetual state of evolution as the technology and the web advance.

Table 12-1. *Scala Web Frameworks and Libraries*

Web Framework/Library	Location
Play 2	https://www.playframework.com/
Lift	http://liftweb.net/
BlueEyes	https://github.com/jdegoes/blueeyes
Hyperscala	https://github.com/darkfrog26/hyperscala
Scalatra	https://github.com/scalatra/scalatra#readme
Vaadin with Scala support	https://vaadin.com/home
Dispatch	http://dispatch.databinder.net/Dispatch.html

Lift

Lift is an expressive and elegant framework for writing web applications. Lift stresses the importance of security, maintainability, scalability, and performance, while allowing for high levels of developer productivity. Lift open source software is licensed under an Apache 2.0 license.

The Lift Web Framework has Comet support. That means that state change on the serverside is immediately pushed to the browser. Lift's Comet support makes chat applications, multiuser games, and other browser-based applications trivial to write. Listing 12-1 has the entire code required to write a multi-user chat application in Lift.

Listing 12-1. Multiuser Chat Application in Lift

```scala
case class Messages(msgs: List[String])
object ChatServer extends Actor with ListenerManager {
private var msgs: List[String] = Nil
protected def createUpdate = Messages(msgs)
override def highPriority = {
case s: String if s.length > 0 =>
msgs ::= s
updateListeners()
}
this.start
}
class Chat extends CometActor with CometListenee {
private var msgs: List[String] = Nil
def render =
<div>
<ul>{msgs.reverse.map(m =><li>{m}</li>)}</ul>
{ajaxText("", s => {ChatServer ! s; Noop})}
</div>
protected def registerWith = ChatServer
override def lowPriority = {
case Messages(m) => msgs = m ; reRender(false)
}
}
```

There's nothing magic about Lift's Comet support, but it would be much harder to do in Java. Lift has Comet Actors, which represent server-side state in a section of browser real estate. The real estate is demarcated by a <span> with a GUID. All Lift pages are rendered using Scala's built-in XML support. After the render phase, but before the page is streamed to the browser, Lift looks through the page to see whether the page contains HTML that points to any Comet Actors. If yes, Lift rewrites the XML and inserts JavaScript to do Comet-style long polling. After the page is loaded, the browser opens an XMLHTTPRequest to the server with the GUIDs of all the Comet components on the page along with the version number of each of the Comet components. The server receives the request and creates an Actor for each GUID, and each Actor registers itself as a listener with the appropriate Comet component. The registration includes the version number of the component as contained by the browser. If the servlet is running in Jetty or a Servlet 3.0 container, Lift automatically invokes the container's "continuation" mechanism so that the pending request is consuming no threads. It is consuming an NIO socket, and it's also consuming one Actor per Comet component on the page.

When the Comet component receives the listener registration, it compares the version number with the current version number. If they differ, the Comet component immediately sends the Actor a message containing the diffs between the version that the Actor/browser has and the current version of the Comet component. If the version number is current, the Comet component does nothing. If the Comet component receives a message and updates itself, it notifies the listener of the diff between the old version and the new version of the component.

During the "no changes" phase, the only system resources being consumed are memory and an NIO connection. No threads or stacks are involved. When the Actor receives an update from the Comet component (or after 120 seconds), the Actor creates a response to the Ajax request. It then invokes the continuation and sends the response to the browser (either JavaScript containing commands to perform the diffs or a Noop). The browser executes the JavaScript, waits 100 milliseconds, and restarts the process. You could implement all this in Java. In fact, there is a Comet library that sits on top of Jetty and Dojo that has the same scaling characteristics. However, the amount of code to implement this scheme in Scala contains roughly the same number of characters as the preceding description.

Play 2

Play 2 provides an asynchronous HTTP API leveraging on the Actor model by means of Akka,[1] to handle highly concurrent systems. Akka is the implementation of Actor model for both Scala and Java.

Play 1 used the Java language and provided support for Scala by means of plugins. Play 2.0 was released in 2012 in concurrence with the Typesafe[2] Stack and was built using Scala as the core language. Table 12-2 lists the key features of Play 2.

Table 12-2. *Key Features of Play 2*

Feature	Description
Asynchronous I/O	Service of long requests asynchronously using JBoss Netty[3] as its web server.
Built-in Web server	JBoss Netty web server out of the box, but Play web applications can also be packaged to be distributed to Java EE application servers.
Dependency management	SBT for dependency management
Hot reloading	In the development mode, the code is verified for updates upon new requests, and modified files are automatically recompiled and in case of error, the error is displayed in the browser directly unlike the classic web applications where the errors are displayed in the console of application server.
In-memory database	Support for embedded database like H2 out of the box.
Native Scala support	Native support for Scala natively at the same time complete interoperability with Java.
ORM	Ebean[4] as the ORM replacement of JPA to access database.
Stateless	Fully RESTful and without the Java EE session per connection
Templating	Use of Scala for the template engine.
Testing framework	Built-in test framework such as JUnit and Selenium[5] for unit and functional testing
WebSocket	Out of the box WebSocket implementation to enable a bi-directional connection between a client and the server

[1]http://akka.io/
[2]https://typesafe.com/
[3]http://netty.io/
[4]http://www.avaje.org/
[5]http://www.seleniumhq.org/

Play 2 exists in two flavors—the classic Play 2 standalone distribution and Typesafe Activator-based distribution. Because classic Play 2 was very popular and you may still find it in legacy applications, we will introduce both classic and Typesafe distribution; however, you can choose to migrate from classic Play 2 to activator-based Play 2. If you want learn about migration to Play 2.3, check the Play 2.3 migration guideat https://www.playframework.com/documentation/2.3.x/Migration23.

Getting Started with the Standalone Distribution

To run the Play framework, you need JDK 6 or later. If you are using Linux, make sure to use either the Sun JDK or OpenJDK (and not gcj, which is the default Java command on many Linux distros). If you are using Windows, just download and install the latest JDK package. If you are using MacOS, Java comes built-in.

- Download the latest Play 2.2 standalone distribution from here: https://www.playframework.com/download#older-versions.

- Extract the archive to a location and add the play script to your PATH, that is, add the framework installation directory to your system PATH.

On Windows you'll need to set the PATH in environment variables. On UNIX systems do the following:

```
export PATH=$PATH:/relativePath/to/play
```

You can enter the following command in the command line tool to check whether Play is correctly installed:

```
> play
```

If Play is correctly installed, you will see the output on the console as illustrated in Figure 12-1.

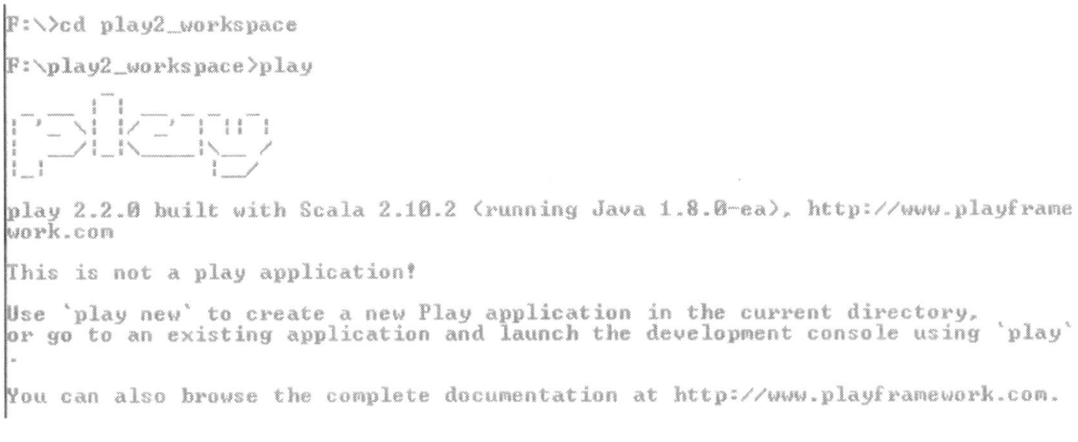

Figure 12-1. *Verifying whether Play 2 is correctly installed*

You can also get help by means of the help command as illustrated in the Figure 12-2.

```
> play help
```

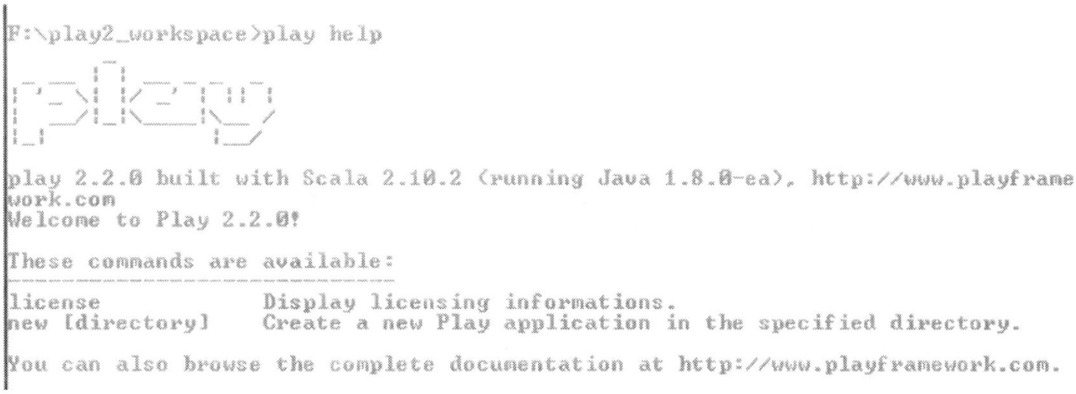

```
F:\play2_workspace>play help

 _ _
| '_ \| |   __ _  _  _
|  __/| |   / _` || || |
|_|   |_|   \__,_| \__, |
                   |___/

play 2.2.0 built with Scala 2.10.2 (running Java 1.8.0-ea), http://www.playframe
work.com
Welcome to Play 2.2.0!

These commands are available:
------------------------------------
license              Display licensing informations.
new [directory]      Create a new Play application in the specified directory.

You can also browse the complete documentation at http://www.playframework.com.
```

Figure 12-2. *Help in Play 2*

Now that Play is correctly installed, you can go on to create your first Scala web application with Play. Let's Play! You can create a helloworld-scala application as illustrated in Figure 12-3. To create a new application, you just have to use the play command-line tool with the parameter new followed by the name of the new application—helloworld as illustrated in Figure 12-3.

```
F:\play2_workspace>play new helloworld

 _ _
| '_ \| |   __ _  _  _
|  __/| |   / _` || || |
|_|   |_|   \__,_| \__, |
                   |___/

play 2.2.0 built with Scala 2.10.2 (running Java 1.8.0-ea), http://www.playframe
work.com

The new application will be created in F:\play2_workspace\helloworld

What is the application name? [helloworld]
>
```

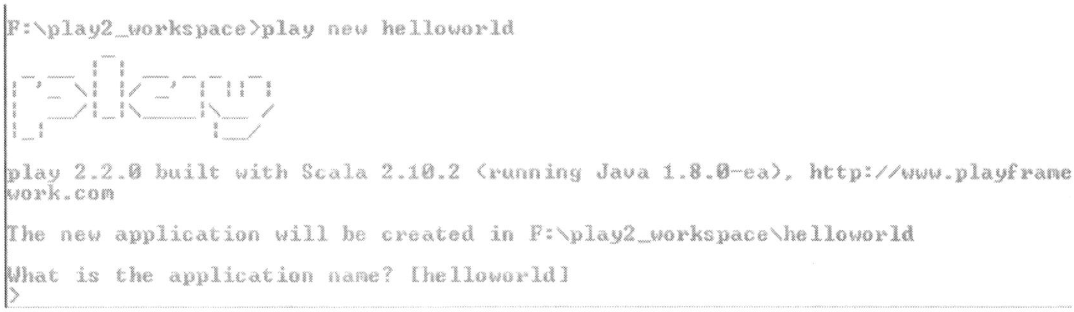

Figure 12-3. *Creating helloworld application*

As mentioned earlier, Play 2 allows you to create both Java- and Scala-based web applications. Play 2 asks you to specify whether your application is a Scala or Java application as illustrated in Figure 12-4.

```
What is the application name? [helloworld]
> helloworld

Which template do you want to use for this new application?

  1              - Create a simple Scala application
  2              - Create a simple Java application

>  ▬
```

Figure 12-4. *Specifying whether the application is a Scala or a Java application*

You have to specify 1 because you want to create a Scala application. Specifying 1 creates the source files and the structure of the application for the Scala as illustrated in Figure 12-5.

```
Which template do you want to use for this new application?

  1              - Create a simple Scala application
  2              - Create a simple Java application

> 1
OK, application helloworld is created.

Have fun!
```

Figure 12-5. *Creation of the helloworld project*

You can run the application using the run command from the helloworld directory. To do this, enter the Play Console as illustrated in the Figure 12-6.

```
> cd helloworld
>play
```

```
F:\play2_workspace>cd helloworld

F:\play2_workspace\helloworld>play
Java HotSpot(TM) Client VM warning: ignoring option MaxPermSize=256M; support wa
s removed in 8.0
[info] Loading project definition from F:\play2_workspace\helloworld\project
[info] Set current project to helloworld (in build file:/F:/play2_workspace/hell
oworld/)

 _            _
| | ___  __ _| |_   _
| '_ \| |/ _` | | | | |
|  __/ | | (_| | | |_| |
|_|   |_|\__,_|_|\__, |
                 |___/

play 2.2.0 built with Scala 2.10.2 (running Java 1.8.0-ea), http://www.playframe
work.com

> Type "help play" or "license" for more information.
> Type "exit" or use Ctrl+D to leave this console.

[helloworld] $
```

Figure 12-6. *Entering the Play console*

Now type run. This starts the server that runs your application.

```
$ run
```

The output on the console is shown here.

```
[helloworld] $ run
[info] Updating {file:/F:/play2_workspace/helloworld/}helloworld...
[info] Resolving org.scala-lang#scala-library;2.10.2 ...
[info] Resolving com.typesafe.play#play-jdbc_2.10;2.2.0 ...
  [info] Resolving com.typesafe.play#play_2.10;2.2.0 ...
  [info] Resolving com.typesafe.play#sbt-link;2.2.0 ...
  [info] Resolving org.javassist#javassist;3.18.0-GA ...
  [info] Resolving com.typesafe.play#play-exceptions;2.2.0 ...
.................
.................
[info] Resolving org.scala-lang#scala-compiler;2.10.2 ...
  [info] Resolving org.scala-lang#jline;2.10.2 ...
  [info] Resolving org.fusesource.jansi#jansi;1.4 ...
[info] Done updating.
--- (Running the application from SBT, auto-reloading is enabled) ---
[info] play - Listening for HTTP on /0:0:0:0:0:0:0:0:9000
(Server started, use Ctrl+D to stop and go back to the console...)
```

As you can see, the console says that it has started the application and an HTTP server is listening for HTTP request on the port 9000. You can now send the request to this server by going to the URL http://localhost:9000/. Upon requesting the server, a welcome screen is displayed as illustrated in the Figure 12-7.

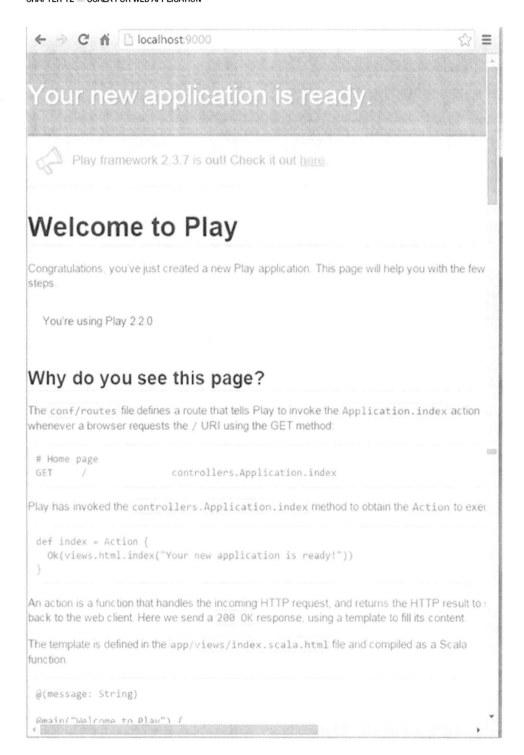

Figure 12-7. Default Welcome page of Play 2 framework

Tip The default welcome page of the application provides impressive practical information and it is recommended you read the welcome page.

Anatomy of Play Application

The run command creates the structure of the application inside the helloworld directory. The structure is illustrated in Figure 12-8.

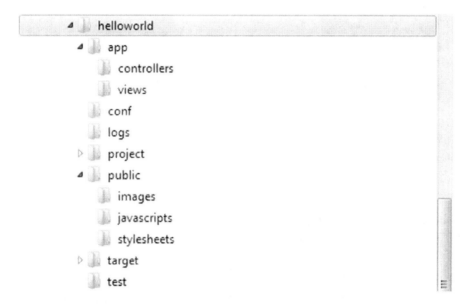

Figure 12-8. *The directory structure of the helloworld application*

Here are the contents of each folder in Figure 12-8:

- app: This is the root of all the server-side source files such as Java and Scala source code, templates, and compiled assets' sources. Only two subfolders, controllers and views, for Controller and View component of the MVC architectural pattern are created. You can add the directory app/models for the Model component of the MVC. There is also an optional directory called app/assets for compiled assets such as LESS[6] sources and CoffeeScript[7] sources.

- conf: The conf directory contains the application's configuration files. These configuration files are meant to, as the name suggests, configure the application, external services, and so on. There are two main configuration files:

- application.conf: The main configuration file for the application, that comprises standard configuration parameters

- routes: The routes definition file.

---

[6]http://lesscss.org/
[7]http://jashkenas.github.io/coffee-script/

- project: The project folder comprises all the necessary files to configure the Scala built tool SBT.

- public: This directory comprises three standard sub-directories for images, CSS stylesheets, and JavaScript files.

■ **Note** Resources stored in the public directory are static assets that are served directly by the web server.

- target: The target directory comprises artifacts generated by the build system such as:

- classes: All compiled classes (from both Java and Scala sources).

- classes_managed: Only the classes that are managed by the framework (such as the classes generated by the router or the template system).

- resource_managed: Generated resources, typically compiled assets such as LESS CSS and CoffeeScript compilation results.

- src_managed: Generated sources, such as the Scala sources generated by the template system.

- test: Comprises all test files along with some samples provided by the framework.

MVC in Play 2

A Play 2 application follows the MVC architecture pattern. In a Play 2 application these MVC layers are defined in the app directory, each one in a separate package as shown in Figure 12-9.

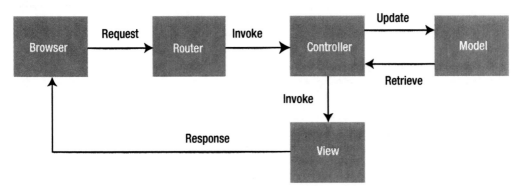

Figure 12-9. *MVC in Play 2*

The request flow in the MVC architecture illustrated in Figure 12-9 constitutes following:

- The Router intermediates the HTTP request.

- The Router determines the action defined in the controller to process this request.

- The Controller listens for HTTP requests, extracts appropriate data from the requests, and applies changes to the model.

- Controller renders a template file to generate the view.

- The result of the action method is finally sent as an HTTP response.

Router

The router constitutes the main entry point of the web application through the conf/routes file, which defines the routes required by the application. Each route comprises an HTTP method and a URI pattern. A call to an action method is associated with the URI. Conf/routes is the configuration file used by the built-in component called Router that translates each incoming HTTP request to an action call.

Note The HTTP method can be any of the valid methods supported by HTTP (GET, POST, PUT, DELETE, HEAD).

The router is responsible for mediating and translating an incoming HTTP request to an Action. The MVC framework sees the HTTP request as an event comprising the request path, including the query string and the HTTP method (e.g., GET, POST, ...). Routes are defined in the conf/routes file. This file is compiled and if there are any errors, you see them in your browser directly without recompiling your code or restarting the server. When the route file is modified, it is automatically reloaded. This feature is called hot reloading. We will now test this feature by introducing an error in form or unclosed string literal as illustrated in Listing 12-2.

Listing 12-2. Testing Hot Reload

```
def index = Action {
  Ok("Hello world)
}
```

When you reload the home page in your browser, the compilation error is displayed (see Figure 12-10).

Figure 12-10. *Installing the Eclipse plug-in for Scala-IDE*

As you see errors are directly displayed in your browser and you do not have to go to the console to check the error. But if you want to check the error on the console, it is also available on the console as shown.

```
[error] F:\play2_workspace\helloworld\app\controllers\Application.scala:9: unclo
sed string literal
[error]    Ok("Hello world)
[error]        ^
[error] F:\play2_workspace\helloworld\app\controllers\Application.scala:10: ')'
expected but '}' found.
[error] }
[error] ^
[error] two errors found
[error] (compile:compile) Compilation failed
[error] application -! @6kmmbl6fg - Internal server error, for (GET) [/] ->play.PlayExceptions$
CompilationException: Compilation error[unclosed string literal]
at play.PlayReloader$$anon$1$$anonfun$reload$2$$anonfun$apply$14$$anonfun$apply$16.
apply(PlayReloader.scala:304) ~[na:na]
at play.PlayReloader$$anon$1$$anonfun$reload$2$$anonfun$apply$14$$anonfun$apply$16.
apply(PlayReloader.scala:304) ~[na:na]
at scala.Option.map(Option.scala:145) ~[scala-library.jar:na]at play.PlayReloader$$anon$1$$a
nonfun$reload$2$$anonfun$apply$14.apply(PlayReloader.scala:304) ~[na:na]
at play.PlayReloader$$anon$1$$anonfun$reload$2$$anonfun$apply$14.apply(PlayReloader.
scala:298) ~[na:na]
at scala.Option.map(Option.scala:145) ~[scala-library.jar:na]
```

Controller

The Controller responds to requests, processes them, and invokes changes on the model. A Controller in Play 2 is an object in Scala that extends the Controller type. This Controller type is provided in the play.api.mvc package. A Controller in Play 2 comprises a function called an action to process the request parameters, and produce a result to be sent to the client. Controllers are, by default, defined in the controllers package under the source root—the app folder. A Controller in Java is a class and comprises public, static method called an action

---

▪ **Note** A controller is a type that extends a Controller provided in the play.api.mvc package.

Model

The Model is the domain-specific representation of the information (in the form of data structures and operations) on which the application operates. The most commonly used object for such representation is the JavaBean. However the JavaBean leads to plenty of boilerplate code. Play 2 reduces this boilerplate code by generating the getters and setters for you by means of byte-code enhancement. The model objects might contain persistence artifacts, such as JPA annotations if they need to be saved into persistent storage.

View

In a Java EE–based web application the view is usually developed using JSP. That is, the view in JavaEE–based web applications consists of JSP elements and template text. As Play is not Java EE–centric, the view comprises the template that contains a mix of HTML and Scala code. In Play 1 the templates were based on Groovy but starting with Play 2, templates are Scala based. Using Play 2 you can develop both Java- and Scala-based web applications and the templates are exactly the same in both Java- and Scala-based web applications.

■ **Note**   In Play 1 the templates were based on Groovy but starting from Play 2, templates are Scala based.

Now let's look at the controller generated by Play 2 for helloworld-scala. You can find the controller in helloworld-scala\app\controllers (see Listing 12-3).

Listing 12-3. Application Controller in Scala

```
package controllers

import play.api._
import play.api.mvc._

object Application extends Controller {

def index = Action {
 Ok(views.html.index("Your new application is ready."))
        }

}
```

In Scala, the controller is an object and an action is a function. Now that you have seen the controller in Scala, it is time to see the template in helloworld-scala, which you can find in helloworld-scala\app\views (see Listing 12-4).

Listing 12-4. Template in helloworld-scala

```
@(message: String)

@main("Welcome to Play") {

@play20.welcome(message)

}
```

The action in Listing 12-3 returns a 200 OK response filled with HTML content. The HTML content is provided by a template in Listing 12-4. The Scala templates in Play 2 are compiled to Scala functions. A template is like a function, and thus it needs parameters, which are declared at the top of the template file. The Scala statement starts with the special @ character. The first line defines the function signature, which takes a single String parameter. Then the template content mixes HTML (or any text-based language) with Scala statements. The Scala statements start with the special @ character. A function named `main` with one string argument is invoked. The `welcome`, provided by Play 2 to render the default welcome HTML page. This page is located in the file named `main.scala.html` in apps/views folder. Now let's modify the application by modifying the response as shown in Listing 12-5.

Listing 12-5. Modifying the Response

```
def index = Action {
  Ok("Hello world")
}
```

Now the index action responds with a text/plain Hello world response because of the modification. Refresh the home page in your browser to test this modification (see Figure 12-11).

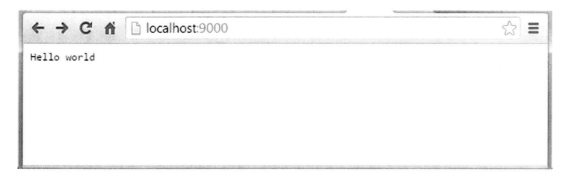

Figure 12-11. *Changed content of the response*

Configuring Eclipse for Scala

The Scala IDE is an Eclipse plug-in and you can install this plug-in from Help ➤ Install New Software. In the Work with field, enter the path for the plug-in (http://scala-ide.org/download/current.html) as shown in the Figure 12-12. You can find detailed instructions for configuring Eclipse for Scala at http://scala-ide.org/documentation.html.

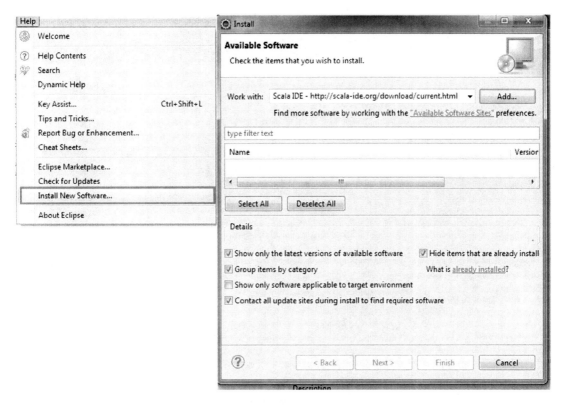

Figure 12-12. *Installing the Eclipse plug-in for Scala-IDE*

You can use the Eclipse IDE with Play 2. To do this you need to ask Play 2 to generate the Eclipse project configuration. You can do this by invoking Eclipse in the play console as illustrated in Figure 12-13.

```
[helloworld] $ eclipse
[info] About to create Eclipse project files for your project(s).
[info] Compiling 4 Scala sources and 2 Java sources to E:\ModernJava\play2-works
pace\helloworld\target\scala-2.10\classes...
[info] Successfully created Eclipse project files for project(s):
[info] helloworld
[helloworld] $
```

Figure 12-13. *Generating the project for Eclipse*

To import the project, go to File ➤ Import, then select General ➤ Existing Projects into Workspace and click Next as illustrated in the Figure 12-14.

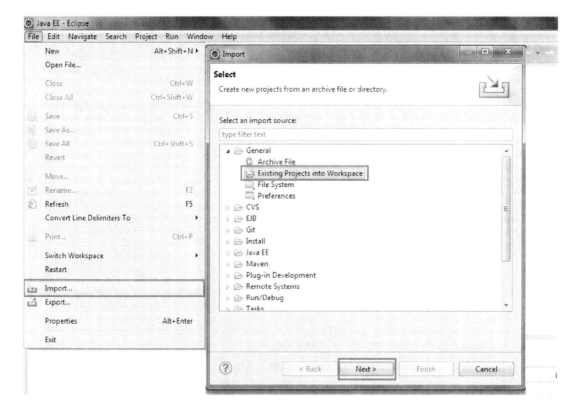

Figure 12-14. *Importing the project*

Now browse your file system, select the project folder helloworld, click OK, and then click Finish. All the files necessary to configure an Eclipse project are generated.

HelloWorld Java Application with Play

Now let's create a Java application with Play 2. You can follow the same steps as when you created the Scala application as illustrated in Figure 12-15.

```
E:\ModernJava\play2-workspace>play new helloworld

        _            _
  _ __ | | __ _ _  _| |
 | '_ \| |/ _` | || |_|
 | .__/|_|\__,_|\_, (_)
 |_|            |__/

play 2.2.0 built with Scala 2.10.2 (running Java 1.8.0-ea), http://www.playframe
work.com

The new application will be created in E:\ModernJava\play2-workspace\helloworld

What is the application name? [helloworld]
>
```

Figure 12-15. *Creating the helloworld application*

Play 2 asks you to specify whether your application is a Scala or Java application as illustrated in Figure 12-16.

```
Which template do you want to use for this new application?

    1              - Create a simple Scala application
    2              - Create a simple Java application

>
```

Figure 12-16. *Specifying whether the application is a Scala or a Java application*

To create a Java application, you have to specify 2 as illustrated in Figure 12-17 and the source files and the structure of the application for the Java will be created.

```
E:\ModernJava\play2-workspace>play new helloworld

       _            _
 _ __ | | __ _ _  _|
| '_ \| |/ _` | || |
|  __/|_|\__,_|\_, |
|_|            |__/

play 2.2.0 built with Scala 2.10.2 (running Java 1.8.0-ea), http://www.playframe
work.com

The new application will be created in E:\ModernJava\play2-workspace\helloworld

What is the application name? [helloworld]
> helloworld

Which template do you want to use for this new application?

    1              - Create a simple Scala application
    2              - Create a simple Java application

> 2
OK, application helloworld is created.

Have fun!

E:\ModernJava\play2-workspace>_
```

Figure 12-17. *Creation of the helloworld project*

Run the application using the run command from the helloworld directory. To do this, enter the Play Console as illustrated in the Figure 12-18.

```
> cd helloworld
>play
```

```
E:\ModernJava\play2-workspace\helloworld>play
[info] Loading project definition from E:\ModernJava\play2-workspace\helloworld\
project
[info] Set current project to helloworld (in build file:/E:/ModernJava/play2-wor
kspace/helloworld/)

 _            _
| |_   ____  | |   ____   _   _ /
| '_ \ / ___\ | |  / _  \ | | | | /
| |_) ) ___ | | | __ | |_| | /
| .__/ \____/ |_| \____| \__  | /
|_|                         |_/

play 2.2.0 built with Scala 2.10.2 (running Java 1.8.0-ea), http://www.playframe
work.com

> Type "help play" or "license" for more information.
> Type "exit" or use Ctrl+D to leave this console.

[helloworld] $
```

Figure 12-18. *Entering the Play console*

Now type run to start the server to run your application.

$ run

The output on the console is shown here.

```
[helloworld] $ run
[info] Updating {file:/E:/ModernJava/play2-workspace/helloworld/}helloworld...
[info] Resolving org.scala-lang#scala-library;2.10.2 ...
[info] Resolving com.typesafe.play#play-java-jdbc_2.10;2.2.0 ...
  [info] Resolving com.typesafe.play#play-jdbc_2.10;2.2.0 ...
  [info] Resolving com.typesafe.play#play_2.10;2.2.0 ...
..............................................
  [info] Resolving org.fusesource.jansi#jansi;1.4 ...
[info] Done updating.
--- (Running the application from SBT, auto-reloading is enabled) ---
[info] play - Listening for HTTP on /0:0:0:0:0:0:0:0:9000
(Server started, use Ctrl+D to stop and go back to the console...)
```

As you can see, the console says that it has started the application and an HTTP server is listening for HTTP request on the port 9000. You can now send request to this server by going to the URL http://localhost:9000/. Figure 12-19 illustrates the default Play 2 welcome page.

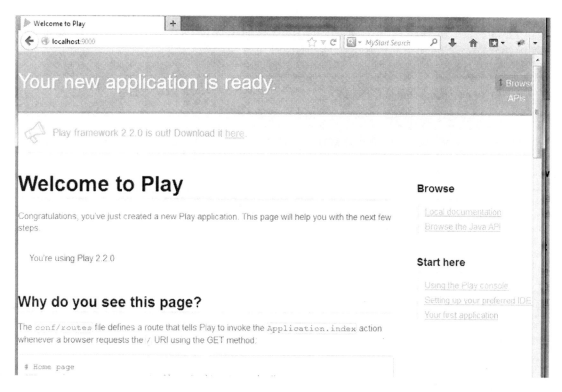

Figure 12-19. *Default welcome page of Play 2 framework*

Now you will see what the Java controllers.Application.index method looks like in comparison to the Scala controller. Open the app/controllers/Application.java source file. This file is illustrated in the Listing 12-6.

Listing 12-6. Application Controller

```
package controllers;

import play.*;
import play.mvc.*;

import views.html.*;

public class Application extends Controller {

public static Result index() {
return ok(index.render("Your new application is ready."));
}

}
```

The Java Application controller class extends play.mvc.Controller. The public static index() action returns a Result. The Result represents the HTTP response to be sent back to the browser. Here, the action returns a 200 OK response with an HTML response body.

■ **Note** All action methods return a Result.

The HTML content is provided by a template. An action always returns an HTTP response, which is represented in Play 2 by the Result type. The Result type must be a valid HTTP response, so it must include a valid HTTP status code. OK sets it to 200. The render() references a template file in Play 2.

You can now configure Eclipse for Java in the same way you learned when configuring Eclipse for Scala. To import the project, you can repeat the steps that you performed earlier in generating the project configuration for Eclipse in the helloworld Java application.

You saw how to create a project and import it to your development environment. Now you will modify the application. In Application.java change the content of the response in the index action as illustrated in Listing 12-7.

Listing 12-7. Modifying the index Action

```
public static Result index() {
    return ok("Hello world");
}
```

The index action now responds with Hello world (as illustrated in Figure 12-20) when accessed using http://localhost:9000/.

Figure 12-20. *Running Hello world application*

Play 2 provides several sample applications in the samples folder in play-2.2.0\samples\java\. You can run the helloworld application as illustrated in the Figure 12-21.

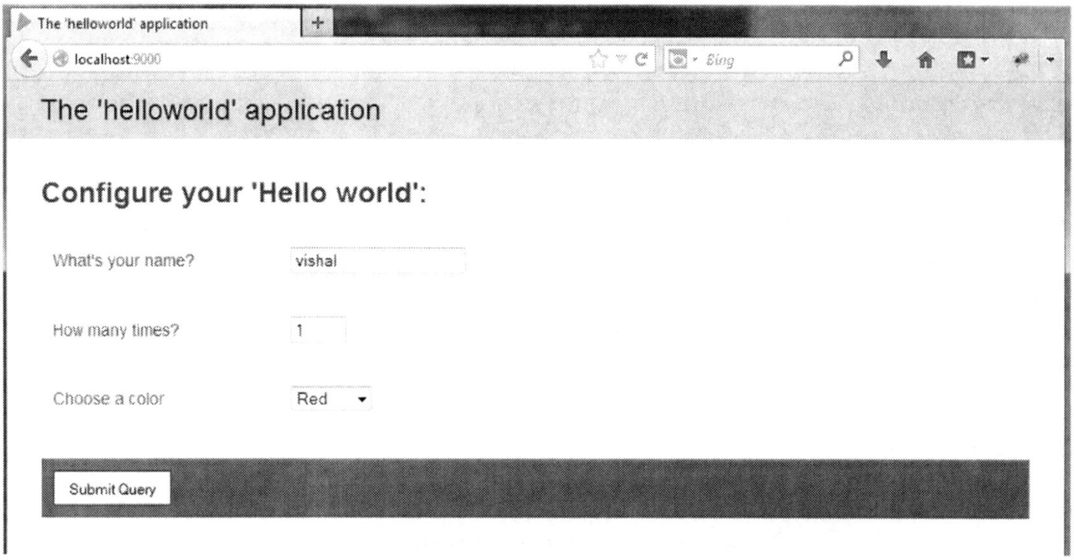

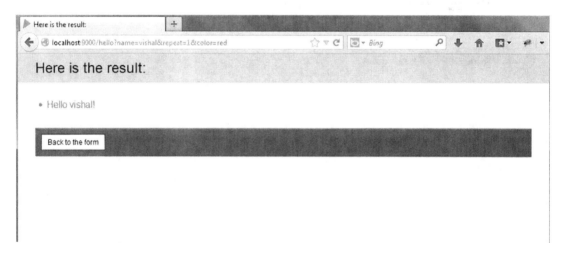

Figure 12-21. *The sample Helloworld application provided by Play 2*

When you click Submit Query the user's name is displayed based on the selection (as illustrated in the Figure 12-22).

Figure 12-22. *Running the sample Helloworld application*

You can go through the code to improve the application on your own.

Getting Started with the Activator Distribution

In this section you will create a Scala web application using the Typesafe Activator. The Typesafe Activator is a web and command-line tool that aids developers when working on the Typesafe platform. From Play 2.3 onward, Play is distributed as an activator distribution that comprises all the dependencies of the Play framework. Play 2.3 is the latest activator distribution and in this distribution the `play` command from the classic distribution has now become the `activator` command. Activator comes with a rich library of project templates. You can extend the templates or add new templates. Activator provides a rich web UI for creating web applications.

▧ **Note** The `play` command features of the classic distributions are still available with the `activator` command. Because the `activator` command and the `play` command are both wrappers around SBT, if you prefer, you can directly use the SBT commands.

To get started with activator distribution, perform the following steps:

- Access the Typesafe page URL at `http://www.typesafe.com/platform/getstarted`.

- Download the Typesafe Activator. If you prefer, you can also download a minimal (1MB) version of Activator from the Activator site. The minimal version of Activator downloads dependencies only when they're needed.

- Extract the downloaded zip archive to your system in a directory of your choice.

- Locate the activator script within the extracted archive.

- Right-click on it and select Open if you are running Windows or just go to the Typesafe Activator installation directory and enter the following command:

  ```
  > ./activator ui
  ```

This launches the activator in a browser window, similar to Figure 12-23.

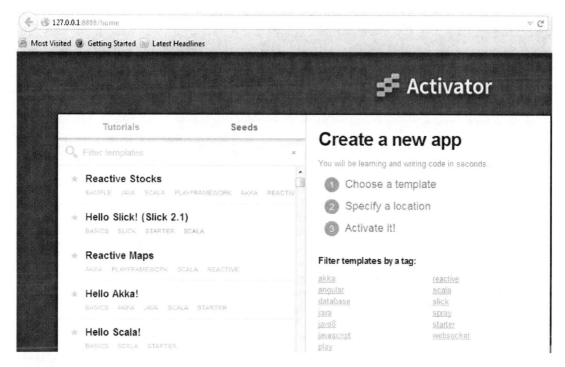

Figure 12-23. *Launching the Activator in the browser*

■ **Note** The minimal version of Activator downloads dependencies only when they're needed.

The basic starter Scala project is found in the *hello-scala* template.

1. Select the template.

2. Note the default location that indicates where the project will be created.

3. Click Create, which takes you to the screen shown in Figure 12-24.

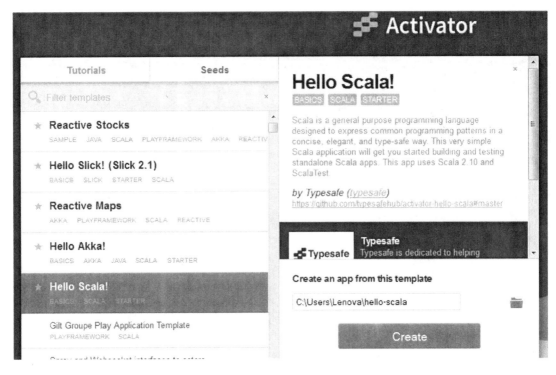

Figure 12-24. *Creating the new app*

■ **Note** The default location where the project will be created before clicking on Create.

Now run the project by entering the following command on the command prompt:

```
> ./activator run
```

Open the `http://localhost:9000/` URL in a browser. It may take a few seconds for the application to open as shown in the Figure 12-25.

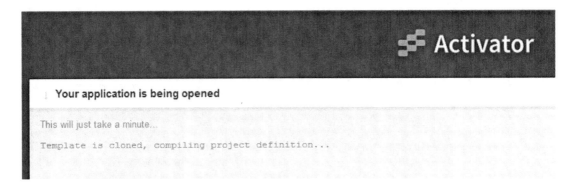

Figure 12-25. *Compiling the project definition*

Figure 12-26 illustrates the running *hello-scala* application.

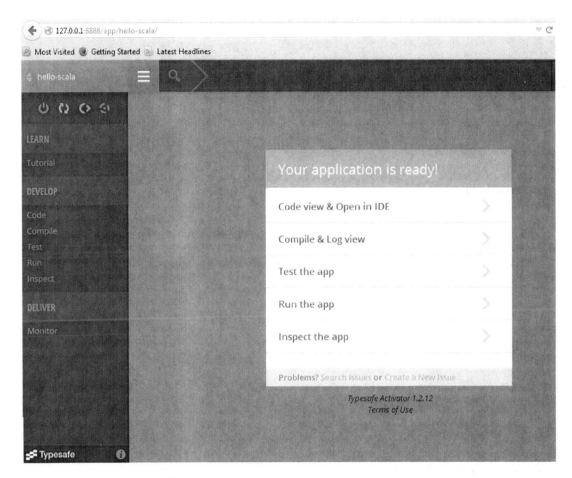

Figure 12-26. *Running the helloscala application*

Actions, Controllers, and Results

Earlier when you created the helloworld project, you saw the controller in `helloworld-scala\app\controllers`. Here is the controller code (see Listing 12-8) again for quick reference.

Listing 12-8. Application Controller

```
package controllers
import play.api._
import play.api.mvc._

object Application extends Controller {
```

```
def index = Action {
  Ok(views.html.index("Your new application is ready."))
}

}
```

You see that `controllers.Application.index` returns an `Action`. A controller is something that generates an action. A controller is a singleton object as illustrated in Listing 12-8. The action handles the requests received by a Play application and generates a Result, which is then sent to the client. An action in Play is a function that returns a `play.api.mvc.Result` value as illustrated in the Listing 12-9.

Listing 12-9. index.scala.html

```
def index = Action {
  Ok("Hello world!")
}
```

An action must always return a result. The result value embodies the HTTP response. In Listing 12-9, Ok constructs a 200 OK response to be sent to the client.

The `Action` is a companion object that provides helper methods to construct an action. Listing 12-10 shows a simple way to construct an action.

Listing 12-10. index.scala.html

```
Action {
  Ok("Hello world")
}
```

In Listing 12-10, the reference to the request is not available. More often you need the access to request. When you need the reference to the request you can construct the action as illustrated in Listing 12-11.

Listing 12-11. index.scala.html

```
Action { req =>
  Ok("request access [" + req + "]")
}
```

The actions can return several types of results. Table 12-3 shows some of the common results. A complete list of results can be found at `https://www.playframework.com/documentation/2.3.x/api/scala/index.html#play.api.mvc.Results`.

Table 12-3. *Commonly Used Results*

Results	Description
BadRequest	Generates a '400 BAD_REQUEST' result
InternalServerError	Generates a '500 INTERNAL_SERVER_ERROR' result
NotFound	Generates a '404 NOT_FOUND' result.
Ok	Generates a '200 OK' result.
Redirect	Generates a redirect simple result.
Status	Generates a simple result.

We present the ways in which results can be used in Listing 12-12 through Listing 12-17.

Listing 12-12. Using BadRequest

```
val badReq= BadRequest(views.html.form(formWithErrors))
```

Listing 12-13. Using InternalServerError

```
val error = InternalServerError("some error")
```

Listing 12-14. Using NotFound

```
val notFound = NotFound
```

Listing 12-15. Using OK

```
val ok = Ok("Hello world!")
```

Listing 12-16. Using Status

```
val  status = Status(488)("response")
```

Listing 12-17. Using Redirect

```
defredirect = Action {
Redirect("/adminPage")
}
```

One chapter is not enough to cover all the features of the Play 2 framework (or any framework for that matter). The best way to learn any framework is to play with it. We recommend you spending some time playing with Play 2.

Summary

This chapter took a high-level look at the Play 2 framework, covering the basics that are common to all the Play 2–based web applications. This chapter provided a brief introduction to both the classic and Typesafe Activator distribution. You developed a Hello World web application for both Scala and Java. You learned to write controllers and actions, and examined the differences between Scala and Java controllers.

CHAPTER 13

■ ■ ■

Scala Best Practices

Thanks for hanging in and reading all this way. We've covered a lot of ground so far. We've discussed the Scala language and developed a collection of idioms for building applications using Scala. We've explored how Scala can be used by different team members in different ways. We've seen how Scala allows you to compose fine-grained pieces of code together into complex systems that work well together.

But no technology is an island. No matter how good Scala is in the abstract, it's only valuable if it can help your organization produce better and more maintainable code, faster. The good news is that Scala compiles down to JVM bytecode and works great with existing Java libraries. If you're working at a Java shop, the cost of using Scala on some projects is minimal. You can test Scala with your existing Java test tools. You store compiled Scala code in JAR and WAR files, so it looks and feels to the rest of your organization like what they're used to—Java bytecode. The operational characteristic of Scala code on web servers is indistinguishable from the operational characteristics of Java code.

In this chapter, we're going to explore some Scala idioms and Scala design patterns. Scala is not just a programming language; it is a new way of thinking and reasoning about programming. It will take you time to design code that fits into Scala paradigms and to discover and devise paradigms of your own. So, write that Java-style code in Scala and then apply the idioms and see how your code changes and how your thought patterns emerge. The first step is to recognize the functional style and the immediately obvious differences between imperative and functional styles.

Recognizing the Functional Style

Scala supports both functional and imperative style of programming. If you come from an imperative background, that is, if you are a Java programmer, Scala also allows you to program in an imperative style, but it encourages functional approach. The functional style of programming enables you to write concise and less error-prone code. However, programming in functional style proves to be a daunting task for a Java programmer. This section, gives few pointers to figure out how to program in the functional style. The first and foremost step is to recognize the difference between the imperative and functional styles in code.

A quick way to distinguish between functional and imperative style is that vars signify an imperative style and using vals is more akin to a functional approach. Therefore, transitioning from imperative to functional style means your program should be free of vars.

Listing 13-1 shows a simple string array that stores names.

Listing 13-1. A String Array

```
val strArray = Array("Vishal Layka", "David Pollak")
```

If you want to print the contents of the array shown in Listing 13-1, and if you were a Java programmer before you moved to Scala, you might write the while loop akin to the while loop show in Listing 13-2.

Listing 13-2. Print in an Imperative Style

```
def print(strArray: Array[String]): Unit = {
var i = 0
while (i <strArray.length) {
println(strArray (i))
i += 1
}
}
```

Listing 13-2 uses a var and is therefore in the imperative style. When you run Listing 13-2 in REPL, you see the following output:

```
scala> val strArray = Array("Vishal Layka", "David Pollak")
strArray: Array[String] = Array(Vishal Layka, David Pollak) scala> def print(strArray:
Array[String]): Unit = {
     | var i = 0
     | while (i < strArray.length) {
     | println(strArray (i))
     | i += 1
     | }
     | }
print: (strArray: Array[String])Unit
scala> print(strArray)
Vishal Layka
David Pollak
```

As you can see Listing 13-2 uses var and therefore is of an imperative style. You can transform this bit of code into a more functional style by first getting rid of the var, as shown in Listing 13-3.

Listing 13-3. Moving Toward Functional Style

```
def print(strArray: Array[String]): Unit = {
strArray.foreach(println)
}
```

```
scala> def print(strArray: Array[String]): Unit = {
     | strArray.foreach(println)
     | }
print: (strArray: Array[String])Unit
scala> print(strArray)
Vishal Layka
David Pollak
```

As you can see in Listing 13-3, the refactored functional code is much clearer, more concise, and less error-prone than the original imperative code in Listing 13-2. Listing 13-3 is more functional but not purely functional. We will transform Listing 13-3 to purely functional in the next section.

Writing Pure Functions

We refactored print method in the Listing 13-2 which was in imperative style to Listing 13-3. Listing 13-3 is functional but not purely functional, because it causes side effects. The side effect caused by Listing 13-3 is that it prints the output to the output stream. The functional equivalent will be a more defining method that manipulates the passed args for printing. For example, it formats it, but does not print it and returns the formatted string for printing, as shown in Listing 13-4.

Listing 13-4. Function with No Side Effect

```
def formatArgs(strArray: Array[String]) = strArray.mkString(":")
```

⬛ **Note** If a function's result type is Unit, the function has side effects.

Now the function in Listing 13-4 is purely functional, that is, it causes no side effect affected by var. The mkString method is defined on collections that is meant to return a string that results from calling toString on each element. You can call mkString on any iterable collection.

The overridden toString method is used to return the string representation of an object, as shown in Listing 13-5.

Listing 13-5. Using mkSting

```
val x = List("x", "y", "z")
println(x.mkString(" : "))
```

You get the following output:

```
scala> val x = List("x", "y", "z")
x: List[String] = List(x, y, z)
scala> println(x.mkString(" : "))
x : y : z
```

The function in Listing 13-4 doesn't print anything like the print method in Listing 13-3 did. You can pass the result of formatArgs to println to print the output shown in Listing 13-6.

Listing 13-6. Using formatArgs

```
println(formatArgs(strArray))
```

You can run this in REPL as shown:

```
scala> val strArray = Array("Vishal Layka", "David Pollak")
strArray: Array[String] = Array(Vishal Layka, David Pollak)
scala> def formatArgs(strArray: Array[String]) = strArray.mkString(":")
formatArgs: (strArray: Array[String])String
scala> println(formatArgs(strArray))
Vishal Layka:David Pollak
```

That said, the essential useful feature of a program is to cause side effects; otherwise it purports no real application. Creating methods that do not cause side effects encourages you to minimize the code that would cause side effects, thus leading you to design robust programs.

Leverage Type Inferencing

Scala is a statically typed language. In a statically typed language the values and the variables have types. And also, Scala, is a type-inferred language, which means you do not have to write the boilerplate code because this boilerplate code is inferred by Scala. This type inference is the feature of a dynamic type language. In this manner, Scala brings best of the two worlds.

■ **Note**   In a dynamic type system, unlike static typing, only values have types, variables do not have types.

We now create an array of maps (as shown in Listing 13-7) to illustrate how type inferencing works.

Listing 13-7. How Type Inferencing Works

```
val books = Array(
Map("title" -> "Beginning Scala", "publisher" -> "Apress"),
Map("title" -> "Beginning Java", "publisher" -> "Apress")
)
```

If you run this Scala code in the Scala REPL, you'll see the following output:

```
scala> val books = Array(
     | Map("title" -> "Beginning Scala", "publisher" -> "Apress"),
     | Map("title" -> "Beginning Java", "publisher" -> "Apress")
     | )
books: Array[scala.collection.immutable.Map[String,String]] = Array(Map(title -> Beginning
Scala, publisher -> Apress), Map(title -> Beginning Java, publisher -> Apress))
```

As you might notice, only the array and maps were specified in Listing 13-7, not their types. As you can see in the output in REPL, the Scala compiler inferred the types of the array and the map. In this way you could let the type inferencer determine the type for you, which can help you trim down a lot of ceremonious code thus keep the code clean and lean and central to the business logic.

■ **Tip**   Let the type inferencer determine the type to trim down the ceremonious code.

Think Expressions

As you learned in Chapter 4, expressions evaluate to a value, so there's no need of a return statement. While in Java, a return statement is common-place as illustrated Listing 13-8.

Listing 13-8. Return Statement in Java

```
def phoneBanking(key: Int) : String = {
var result : String = _
errorCode match {
case 1 =>
result = "Banking service"
case 2 =>
result = "Credit cards"
case _ =>
result = "Speak to the customer executive"
}
return result;
}
```

As you can see, the final result is stored in a `result` variable. The code, while flowing through a pattern match, assigns strings to the `result` variable. To improvise on this code you need to follow an expression-oriented approach, which is explained in detail in Chapter 4. This can be done in the following way.

- As mentioned earlier, the first and foremost way to adopt a functional style is to use `val` instead of `var`. We first change the `result` variable to a `val`.

- Instead of assigning through the case statements, use the last expression of the case statement for assigning the result, t.

Listing 13-9 shows the code refactored for an expression-oriented pattern match.

Listing 13-9. Listing 13-8 in an Expression-Oriented Style

```
def phoneBanking (key: Int) : String = {
val result = key match {
case 1 => "Banking service"
case 2 => "Credit cards"
case 3 => "Speak to the customer executive"
}
return result
}
```

Listing 13-9 looks a lot more concise, but it can still be improved further. We can remove the intermediate `result` variable altogether from the `phoneBanking` method. Listing 13-10 shows the purely expression-oriented style.

Listing 13-10. Purely Expression-Oriented Listing 13-8

```
def phoneBanking (key: Int) : String = keymatch{
case 1 => "Banking service"
case 2 => "Credit cards"
case 3 => "Speak to the customer executive"
}
```

Listing 13-10 follows the expression-oriented approach. You can run the code in the REPL as shown:

```
scala> def phoneBanking(key: Int) : String = key match{
    | case 1 => "Banking service"
    | case 2 => "Credit cards"
    | case 3 => "Speak to the customer executive"
    | }
phoneBanking: (key: Int)String
scala>phoneBanking (3)
res8: String = Speak to the customer executive
```

▓ **Note**   The key to using expressions is realizing that there's no need for a return statement.

Focus on Immutability

In Java, mutability is the default. Variables are mutable unless they're marked final. JavaBeans have getters and setters. Data structures in Java are instantiated, set, and passed along to other methods. Try changing the paradigm in your Scala code.

The first thing to do is use immutable collections classes by default. If you choose to use a mutable collections class, make a comment in your code as to why you chose mutability. There are times when mutable collections make sense. For example, in a method where you are building a List, using ListBuffer is more efficient, but don't return the ListBuffer, return the List. This is like using a StringBuilder in Java but ultimately returning a String. So, use immutable collections by default, and use mutable data structures with a justification.

Use vals by default, and only use vars if there is a good reason that is justified by a comment. In your method, use val unless there's going to be a significant performance hit. Using val in methods often leads to thinking recursively. Listing 13-11 shows a mutable implementation of a method that consumes all the lines from a BufferedReader:

Listing 13-11. A Mutable Implementation of read

```
def read1(in: java.io.BufferedReader): List[String] = {
varret: List[String] = Nil
varline = in.readLine
while(line!=null) {
ret ::= line
line = in.readLine
}
ret.reverse
}
```

The code in Listing 13-11 is readable but uses a couple of vars. Let's rewrite the code without vars and see how we can use tail recursion to give us a while loop (see Listing 13-12):

Listing 13-12. Immutable Implementation of read

```
def read2(in: java.io.BufferedReader): List[String] = {
defdoRead(acc: List[String]):List[String] = in.readLinematch{
case null=> acc

case s => doRead(s :: acc)
}
doRead(Nil).reverse
}
```

Look ma, no vars. We defined the doRead method, which reads a line of input. If the line is null, we return the accumulated List. If the line is non-null, we call doRead with the accumulated List. Because doRead is in the scope of read2, it has access to all of read2's variables. doRead calls itself on the last line, which is a tail call. The Scala compiler optimizes the tail call into a while loop, and there will only be one stack frame created no matter how many lines are read. The last line of read2 calls doRead with Nil as the seed value for the accumulator.

Using vals in your code makes you think about alternative, immutable, functional code. This small example demonstrates that removing vars leads to refactoring. The refactoring leads to new coding patterns. The new coding patterns lead to a shift in your approach to coding. This shift in approach yields transformative code that has fewer defects and is easier to maintain.

Keep Methods Short

Keep methods short. See whether you can code methods in a single line. If not a single line, see whether you can code them in a single statement. If you keep methods short, then the logic in each method is more obvious when you or someone else looks at the code. Let's see how the previous code can be made into single statements as illustrated in Listing 13-13.

Listing 13-13. A Shorter Implementation of read

```
privatedef readLines(in:java.io.BufferedReader,
acc:List[String]): List[String] =
in.readLinematch {
case null => acc
case s => readLines(in,s :: acc)
}
defread3(in: java.io.BufferedReader): List[String] =
readLines(in,Nil).reverse
```

When you code Scala, try not to have a curly brace around the method body. If you can't write your code this way, you have to justify to yourself why your method should exceed a single statement. Keeping methods short allows you to encapsulate a single piece of logic in a method and have methods that build upon each other. It also allows you to easily understand the logic in the method.

Use Options Instead of Null Testing

The first thing to do is ban null from any of your code. You should never return null from a method—ever, ever, ever. If you are calling Java libraries that may return null or throw an exception because of input problems, convert these to Options. We did this for parsing Strings to Ints. The pattern is basic: no nulls.

When you write code, ban null from your code. In the case of uninitialized instance variables, either assign a default value that is not null or, if there's a code path where the variable could be used prior to initialization, use Option, and the default value becomes None. If there's no logical value that can be returned from a method given legal input, the return type should be Option. The get method should never be called on an Option. Instead, Options should be unpacked using map/flatMap, the for comprehension, or pattern matching.

The first benefit using Option is the obvious avoidance of null pointer exceptions. The second benefit is a little more subtle. The use of Option and the transformative nature of mapping Options leads to a different style of approaching your code. The style is more transformative, more functional. The impact of repeatedly using immutable data structures will move your brain toward the functional side. You should familiar with null pointer exception in Java. For example, consider the Java method in Listing 13-14.

Listing 13-14. Java Method that Returns an Int

```
publicIntcomputeArea() { ... }
```

This computeArea method returns, as you might expect, the area of type Int, but it might return null, and you cannot tell just by looking at the method that it might return null. Because of this, the caller of the Java method is obliged to put null checks in his code and, if the caller is lucky and the method never actually returns null, the null checks merely clutter the caller's code. Scala solves this problem by getting rid of null altogether and providing a new type for optional values, that is, values that may or may not be present by means of the Option class. Now we will show you how you can write computeArea method in Scala that may or may not return a value as shown in Listing 13-15.

Listing 13-15. ScalaMethod that May or May Not Returnan Int

```
defcomputeArea: Option[Int] = { ... }
```

The return type of the computeArea method is Option[Int] and merely by looking at this return type, the caller of computeArea method will know that it may not always return an Int. And to complete the picture, the computeArea method uses Some and None types to determine what to return as illustrated in Listing 13-16, for example, in one implementation fragment example of computeArea method.

Listing 13-16. Using Some and None

```
computeArea match {
  case Some(area) => ...
  case None => ...
}
```

Option, Some, and None used in this way is one of the several unique features of Scala that's how that Scala is a state-of-the-art language. This also means that when a Scala function always returns a value, its return type is not an Option type but the type of the object that the method returns. If the Scala function never returns null, why is there a Null type in Scala? We take a brief pause here to let you envisage the answer. Good, that's correct. Scala supports Null type for compatibility with Java.None is the counterpart to Some, used when you're using Scala's Option class to help avoid null references.

Refactor Mercilessly

In the beginning, you can write your Scala code as you would your Java code. It's a great place to start. Then, start applying the idioms you learned in the previous sections in this chapter. In Listing 13-17 we start with the imperative code.

Listing 13-17. Imperative Code

```
def validByAge(in: List[Person]): List[String] = {
varvalid:List[Person] = Nil
for(p<- in){
if (p.valid) valid = p :: valid
}
deflocalSortFunction(a: Person,b:Person) = a.age < b.age
val people = valid.sort(localSortFunction _)
varret: List[String] = Nil

for(p<- people){
ret = ret ::: List(p.first)
}

returnret
}
```

Turn your vars into vals as illustrated in Listing 13-18.

Listing 13-18. Transforming vars to vals

```
def validByAge(in: List[Person]): List[String] = {
val valid:ListBuffer[Person] = newListBuffer // displacedmutability
for(p<- in){
if (p.valid) valid += p
}
deflocalSortFunction(a: Person,b:Person) = a.age < b.age
val people = valid.toList.sort(localSortFunction _)
val ret:ListBuffer[String] = newListBuffer
for(p<- people){
ret += p.first
}
ret.toList
}
```

Turn your mutable data structures into immutable data structures as illustrated in Listing 13-19.

Listing 13-19. Transforming Mutable Data Structures into Immutable Data Structures

```
def validByAge(in: List[Person]): List[String] = {
val valid = for (p<- in if p.valid) yieldp
deflocalSortFunction(a: Person,b:Person) = a.age < b.age
val people = valid.sort(localSortFunction _)
for(p<- people)yield p.first
}
```

Make your method into a single statement as illustrated in Listing 13-20.

Listing 13-20. Making a Method into a Single Statement

```
def validByAge(in: List[Person]): List[String] =
in.filter(_.valid).
sort(_.age < _.age).
map(_.first)
```

While you can argue that this is too terse, we can refactor another way as seen in Listing 13-21.

Listing 13-21. Refactoring in Another Way

```
def filterValid(in: List[Person]) = in.filter(p=> p.valid)
def sortPeopleByAge(in: List[Person]) = in.sort(_.age < _.age)
def validByAge(in: List[Person]): List[String] =
(filterValid_ andThen sortPeopleByAge_)(in).map(_.name)
```

Either of the refactoring choices you make, the business logic of your code is a lot more visible. The refactoring also moves you toward thinking about the transformations in your code rather than the looping constructs in your code.

Compose Functions and Compose Classes

In the previous example, we composed filter Valid and sortPeopleByAge into a single function. This function is the same as shown in Listing 13-22.

Listing 13-22. Function Composition

```
(in: List[Person]) =>sortPeopleByAge(filterValid(in))
```

However, the composition of the two functions results in code that reads like what it does. We started by turning our methods into single statements. This makes testing easier and makes the code more readable. Next we compose a new function by chaining together the two functions. Functional composition is a later stage Scala-ism, but it results naturally from making methods into single statements.

In Chapter 7, we explored how Scala's traits can be composed into powerful, flexible classes that are more type-safe than Java classes. As you evolve your Scala coding skills and begin to refactor classes rather than methods, start looking for common methods across your interfaces and traits. Move methods from concrete classes into traits. Soon, you'll likely find that many of your classes have little in them other than the logic that is specific to that class and the vals that are needed to evaluate that logic. Once you reach this level in your coding, you will likely find that your traits are polymorphic, that your traits represent logic that can be applied to a contained type, and then you can feel secure that your mind has completely warped into thinking Scala.

Once you're thinking Scala or thinking that you're thinking Scala, you might want to take the next advanced steps toward the goals of best practices. The next section provides some constructs for design patterns in Scala.

Scala Design Patterns

The design pattern is regarded as a reusable solution to a commonly occurring design problem in object-oriented paradigm, traditionally popularized in Java world. Design patterns, however, are not programming language agnostic, that is to say, a design pattern in one programming language could be a language primitive in another programming language. The programming language influences and determines the need of using design patterns and even has a native support for the concept embodied in a pattern. One classic example of this is the way the Singleton design pattern is implemented in Java and the way in which the Singleton design pattern is a native feature of Scala.

Singleton

The Singleton pattern ensures that a class has only one instance, and provides a global point of access to it. Listing 13-23 shows, a typical Java implementation that involves a private static field, a private constructor, and a factory method.

Listing 13-23. A Singleton in Java

```
public class JavaSingleton{
private staticJavaSingleton  instance  = null ;
private JavaSingleton() { }
public staticgetInstance ( ) {
if( instance == null) {
instance = new JavaSingleton();
}
return instance ;
}
}
```

In Listing 13-23, instead of constructing the object with a new expression, the method getInstance is invoked. Listing 13-24 shows how a language construct in Scala provides direct support for the concept of a Singleton pattern.

Listing 13-24. A Singleton in Scala

```
object ScalaSingleton{}
```

In Scala, an object is basically a singleton object. There is only instance of this object in any given program and it can be passed around.

Factory Method

The Factory Method pattern is used to encapsulate the required functionality for selection and instantiation of the implementation class, into a method called Factory Method. A Factory Method pattern removes the tight coupling between the client class and the service provider implementation classes by instantiating a needed class and returning its super type.

Listing 13-25. A Factory Method Pattern in Java

```
public interface Vehicle {}

private class Car implements Vehicle {}

private class Bike implements Vehicle {}

public class VehcileFactory {
    public static Vehicle createVehicle(String type) {
        if ("bike".equals(type)) return new Bike();
        if ("car".equals(type)) return new Car();
        throw new IllegalArgumentException();
    }
}

VehicleFactory.createVehicle("car");
```

Listing 13-26 illustrates the Factory Method Pattern in Scala.

Listing 13-26. A Factory Method Pattern in Scala

```
trait Vehcile
private class Car extends Vehcile
private class Bike extends Vehicle

object Vehicle
  def apply(type: String) = kind match {
    case "car" => new Car()
    case "bike" => new Bike()
  }
}
Vehicle("car")
```

The Factory Method shown in Listing 13-26 is defined in the companion object—a singleton object with the same name, defined in the same source file.

Strategy

The Strategy pattern allows an algorithm to be selected at runtime. The Strategy pattern defines a family of encapsulated algorithms and allows the algorithm to vary loosely coupled from clients that use the algorithm. In Java, the Strategy pattern is implemented by creating a hierarchy of classes that inherit from a base interface as shown in the Listing 13-27.

Listing 13-27. Strategy Pattern in Java

```
public interface Strategy {
    int operation(int a, int b);
}

public class Add implements Strategy {
    public int operation(int a, int b) { return a + b; }
}

public class Multiply implements Strategy {
    public int operation(int a, int b) { return a * b; }
}

public class Context  {
    private final Strategy strategy;

    public Context(Strategy strategy) { this.strategy = strategy; }

    public void execute(int a, int b) { strategy.operation(a, b); }
}

new Context(new Multiply()).execute(5, 5);
```

Listing 13-28 illustrates Strategy pattern in Scala.

Listing 13-28. Strategy Pattern in Scala

```
type Strategy = (Int, Int) => Int

class Context(operation: Strategy) {
  def execute(a: Int, b: Int) { operation(a, b) }
}

val add: Strategy = _ + _
val multiply: Strategy = _ * _

new Context(multiply).execute(5, 5)
```

As you can see in Listing 13-28, we use first-class functions in Scala to design the strategy pattern.

Template Method

The Template Method pattern consists of an abstract class that defines some process in terms of abstract sub-methods. Listing 13-29 illustrates a Template Method pattern in Java.

Listing 13-29. Template Method Pattern in Java

```
public abstract class Template{
public void process(){
subMethodA();
subMethodB();
}
protected abstract void subMethodA();
protected abstract void subMethodB();
}
```

To use it, extend the Template and implement the abstract subMethods.
Listing 13-30 illustrates the Template Method pattern in Scala.

Listing 13-30. Template Method Pattern in Scala

```
def process( operation
subMethodA: () => Unit,
subMethodB: () => Unit) =() => {
subMethodA()
subMethodB ()
}
```

As you can see, the Listing 13-30 passes the subMethods into a Function Builder. To use the Template
Method pattern in Scala, we no longer need to define subMethods and subclasses. Instead of defining
subMethods we use higher order functions; and instead of defining subclasses, we use
function composition.

Adapter

The Adapter pattern allows the classes with incompatible interfaces to work together by converting
the interface of a class into an expected interface. The Adapter pattern does this by defining a wrapper
class around the object with the incompatible interface. Listing 13-31 illustrates the Adapter pattern
using Java.

Listing 13-31. Adapter Pattern Using Java

```
public interface ServiceProviderInterface {
    void service(String property);
}
public final class ServiceProviderImplementation{
    void service(Stringtype, String property) { /* ... */ }
}

public class Adapter implements ServiceProviderInterface {
    private final ServiceProviderImplementation impl;

    public Adapter (ServiceProviderImplementation impl) { this.impl = impl; }

    public void service(String property) {
impl.service(TYPEA, property);
    }
}
ServiceProviderInterface service = new Adapter(new ServiceProviderImplementation ());
```

Scala provides a built-in concept of interface adapters, expressed as implicit classes. Listing 13-32 shows the Adapter pattern using Scala.

Listing 13-32. Adapter Pattern Using Scala

```scala
trait ServiceProviderInterface {
  def service(message: String)
}

final class ServiceProviderImplementation {
  def service(type: String, property: String) { /* ... */ }
}

implicit class Adapter(impl: ServiceProviderImplementation) extends ServiceProviderInterface
{
  def service(property: String) { impl.service(TYPEA, property) }
}

val service: ServiceProviderInterface = new ServiceProviderImplementation ()
```

When the expected type of expression is ServiceProviderInterface, but a ServiceProviderImplementation instance is used, Scala compiler automatically wraps the ServiceProviderImplementation instance in the adapter class.

Summary

Designing and building complex computer software is a serious business. Our livelihoods, and increasingly our whole society, depend on the stability and flexibility of our interconnected computer systems. Our cars and our banks and our grocery stores and our hospitals and our police departments all work better because they are interconnected by computer systems. Those systems run on the software that we write.

We hope that you have enjoyed the journey and are already thinking about new ways to reason about designing software and writing code. We want to end this journey by talking a bit about architecture.

Architecture is very important in overall system performance and team performance. Scala has a lot of the tools that allow for much better architectural decisions. It's kind of a *Zen and the Art of Motorcycle Maintenance* thing—you use the patterns that your language and its libraries make easiest. Scala makes it easier than Java or Ruby for coders to implement architecturally solid designs.

Index

Get the eBook for only $10!

Now you can take the weightless companion with you anywhere, anytime. Your purchase of this book entitles you to 3 electronic versions for only $10.

This Apress title will prove so indispensible that you'll want to carry it with you everywhere, which is why we are offering the eBook in 3 formats for only $10 if you have already purchased the print book.

Convenient and fully searchable, the PDF version enables you to easily find and copy code—or perform examples by quickly toggling between instructions and   applications. The MOBI format is ideal for your Kindle, while the ePUB can be utilized on a variety of mobile devices.

Go to www.apress.com/promo/tendollars to purchase your companion eBook.